Shaping the Future

Shaping
the
Future

**The Ethics of
Dietrich Bonhoeffer**

JAMES H. BURTNESS

FORTRESS PRESS Philadelphia

Library of Congress Cataloging in Publication Data

Burtness, James H.
    Shaping the future.

    Bibliography: p.
    Includes index.
    1. Bonhoeffer, Dietrich, 1906-1945 — Contributions
in Christian ethics.   2. Christian ethics — History —
20th century.   I. Title.
BX4827.B57B86   1985   241'.092'4   85-47723
ISBN 0-8006-1869-6

1728085   Printed in the United States of America   1-1869

For Dolores
sine qua non

Contents

Acknowledgments

Excerpt from Kelley, REVELATION AND THE SECULAR IN THE THEOLOGY OF DIETRICH BONHOEFFER, copyright © 1980 by James Patrick Kelley. Reprinted by permission.

Excerpt from Gerhard Jacobi in I KNEW DIETRICH BONHOEFFER, edited by Wolf Dieter Zimmerman and Ronald Gregor Smith, copyright © 1966 by Collins Publishers, London. Reprinted by permission.

Excerpt from Benjamin Reist, THE PROMISE OF BONHOEFFER, copyright © 1969 by Benjamin A. Reist. Reprinted by permission of Harper and Row, Publishers, Inc.

Excerpt from Dietrich Bonhoeffer, ETHICS, reprinted with permission of Macmillan Publishing Company. Copyright © 1955 by SCM Press Ltd.

The poem, "The Powers of God" from Dietrich Bonhoeffer, LETTERS AND PAPERS FROM PRISON, reprinted by permission of Macmillan Publishing Company. Copyright © 1953, 1967, 1971 by SCM Press Ltd.

Excerpts from Burtness, "For the Sake of the Future" first appeared in 1982 in THE LUTHERAN STANDARD. Reprinted by permission.

Excerpts from Burtness, "Reading Bonhoeffer: A Map to the Literature," Volume 2, No. 3, Summer 1982, WORD & WORLD. Reprinted by permission.

Excerpts from Paul Lehmann, ETHICS IN A CHRISTIAN CONTEXT, copyright © 1963 by SCM Press Ltd. Reprinted by permission.

Excerpts from Dietrich Bonhoeffer, NO RUSTY SWORDS: LETTERS, LECTURES AND NOTES, 1928–1936, copyright © 1947 by Chr. Kaiser Verlag, from GESAMMELTE SCHRIFTEN, English translation copyright © 1965 by William Collins Sons & Co. Ltd. and Harper and Row, Publishers, Inc. Used by permission.

Preface

I bought my first Bonhoeffer volume, *The Cost of Discipleship*, on 27 September 1950. It was the first edition of his first book to appear in English. I had heard his name and the phrase "costly grace," but only that. When I read his words, however — "We Lutherans have gathered like eagles round the carcass of cheap grace, and there we have drunk of the poison which has killed the life of following Christ" — I knew I had been laid hold of in such a way that I would not easily break loose. Today his grasp on me is firmer still, and I continue to struggle with him about the things that touch me most closely and exercise me most deeply. I have found no conversation partner who presses me so relentlessly, who keeps me moving every time I think I have something figured out. Passages that I have read a hundred times continue to sound fresh and new to me. Ideas with which I am well acquainted continue to energize me.

This book is the result of an attempt to converse with Bonhoeffer about ethics. It is not the conversation itself, but the result of a conversation. The conversation continues and finds expression in various ways in everything I do. For this book, however, it is enough to try to present as clearly as possible what I take to be the task he set for himself in thinking about Christian ethics and the lines along which he sought to address that task. The book is not about his position on various ethical issues. It is not a trajectory, asking what he would have thought and said and done had he lived to address our times and our troubles. It is rather an extended expository essay that seeks to get at a style, if not a method, for structuring continuity and responsibility into ethical choices made in a context marked by the demise of metaphysical and moral absolutes. Bonhoeffer welcomed this demise and looked upon it as a result of the penetration of cultural forms by the word about Jesus Christ. Not in spite of but because of this demise, he felt enabled to move toward the future with a boldness, even an optimism, which is born of hope. He was convinced that by "taking hold of the real" those who know and follow Jesus Christ can, as his deputies, participate responsibly in the shaping of the future in line with God's own will. The suggestion sounds presumptuous, even frightening. The risks are high. But against the backdrop of the Nazi nightmare and the inadequate and perverse ways in which many Christians responded to the phenomenon of Adolf Hitler, the struggles of Bonhoeffer to explore new ways of thinking about Christian behavior, sealed as they are with his death at the hands of the Nazis, deserve a hearing.

Some basic knowledge about Bonhoeffer on the part of the reader is assumed, although it is not necessary for engagement with this study. Those wishing to become better acquainted with the literature will find some suggestions in the appendix. It is hoped, however, that there is here sufficient biographical and historical data so that readers wishing to move directly to this statement about Bonhoeffer's ethics will have no difficulty following the argument.

I have decided that the reader who meets Bonhoeffer in his own words will be more likely to pursue the literature independently than will be the reader who encounters him only through an interpreter. I have therefore often allowed him to speak for himself, at times in extended quotations. When quoting from existing translations and also from published secondary materials, I have allowed the generic use of "man" and of male pronouns to remain as printed, assuming that readers will recognize in my own use of inclusive language a sensitivity to its importance. If this book brings readers into serious conversation with Bonhoeffer, and if some are aware of the power of his life and thought for the first time, this book will have more than served its purpose.

A sabbatical study leave during the academic year 1981–82 provided the opportunity to do basic research and write the first draft. The excellent sabbatical program of Luther Northwestern Theological Seminary is strongly supported by its president, Dr. Lloyd Svendsbye, and by its Board of Directors. Their gracious support has not been taken for granted. The award to me of the Fredrik A. Schiotz Post-Doctoral Fellowship from Aid Association for Lutherans was both significant encouragement and welcome financial assistance during the sabbatical year. Eberhard and Renate Bethge turned over their home in Villiprott, Federal Republic of Germany, to us while they were in the United States from August 1981 to January 1982. For these happy and productive days among the great treasures of the Bethge home and library we shall always be grateful. After each day of reading and writing and talking and editing, new ideas emerged and old ideas fell into place during the evening run at dusk through the Kottenforst in Villiprott. After five months in the Bethge house, the work was well on its way.

It is often said among members of the English Language Section of the International Bonhoeffer Society that our kinship is much deeper than mutual academic interest. One realizes how very true it is on the occasion of a project such as this. My colleagues in the society have been overwhelmingly supportive and specifically helpful in countless ways, not least in reading drafts of the manuscript and offering responses. Not one would have written the book as I have written it, but each one asked has engaged me in helpful conversation which has often led to minor changes and sometimes to major alterations. My thanks also go to other friends and colleagues who read and commented on one draft or another. They will know where their suggestions have been specifically helpful. Students at Luther Northwestern and other places where I have been privileged to present Bonhoeffer have sharpened my reading and reflection by persistently pressing me on points where left to my own devices I could have become careless. Splendid people of great skill in the faculty secretarial staff have throughout the project not only done exemplary work, but have done it with uncommon grace. Margaret McLean devoted extraordinary energy to checking footnotes, reading galley proofs, and getting the index underway.

In a category of her own is Dolores. She makes even hard work a joy. Without her this book would not have happened. To her it is gratefully dedicated.

Luther Northwestern Theological Seminary JAMES H. BURTNESS
St. Paul, Minnesota

| PROLOGUE | # For the Sake of the Future |

At Christmastime in 1942, a few months before his arrest by the Nazis, Dietrich Bonhoeffer wrote to his friends, "We will not and must not reach to the events of history with barren criticism or barren opportunism, but must take our share of responsibility for the moulding of history. . . . The ultimate question for a responsible person to ask is . . . how the coming generation is to live."

It was not a surprise to those who knew Bonhoeffer that he would focus his energies on the future, even at such a time. In 1933, when Hitler began to exclude Jews from civil service within weeks of his coming to power, Bonhoeffer gave up his teaching responsibilities at the University of Berlin to serve two German-speaking congregations in London. But he returned to Germany in 1935 to prepare pastors for the Confessing Church that was formed specifically to oppose the "German Christians," as they called themselves, who distorted the Christian faith beyond recognition by combining it with Nazi racism. Bonhoeffer arrived in New York City in 1939, just in time to escape the outbreak of war. But he returned to Germany a few weeks later, this time to work for the defeat of his country. He wrote to Reinhold Niebuhr, explaining his action, "I will have no right to participate in the reconstruction of Christian life in Germany after the war if I do not share the trials of this time with my people."

Niebuhr wrote later that this action was "remarkably symbolic of the spirit of Bonhoeffer's life." Bonhoeffer was executed for his attempts to preserve his German heritage for future generations. He did it in the name of Jesus Christ, who led him into free and responsible action for the sake of the future of God's world.

Bonhoeffer became known to Americans soon after World War II through *The Cost of Discipleship*, his exposition of the Sermon on the Mount that employed the now famous notions of "cheap grace" and "costly

grace." Other writings soon followed in translation as details of Bonhoeffer's life became better known. When his prison letters were published
by his friend Eberhard Bethge, they caused a minor sensation with their
talk of "nonreligious Christianity." Bonhoeffer had used the phrase to indicate the sharp distinction between religious experience and Christian faith,
but it was misunderstood by some at that time to signal an abandonment
of God for a purely ethical Christianity.

Today Bonhoeffer's writings are available in many languages, including
Japanese and Korean. International Bonhoeffer Conferences are now held
about every four years, to which people from around the world — and from
countries with radically differing political orientations — gather to investigate his significance for the church in the modern world.

Whatever interpretation we place on Bonhoeffer's work, there can be no
question but that he was a witness for Jesus Christ throughout his life. That
witness meant concrete confession in specific times and specific places. He
said, "What following Jesus means, that's what I want to know." He asked,
"Who is Jesus Christ for us today?" He asked not because he did not know
but because he knew that knowing requires continued asking. So throughout his life he kept asking about Jesus Christ and pointing to him.

Much was not clear to him. His response to complex issues was neither
automatic nor naive. Yet even in the midst of massive uncertainties, he was
able to live calmly and in good humor, delighting in simple pleasures and
making effective use of each day. The arrogant posturing of the moralist
and the angry shouting of the self-righteous were foreign to his nature and
to his faith.

He was by nature a man of profound openness and genuine civility.
More important, his faith included a robust recognition of sin that kept
him from equating his own intuitions with the will of God. He often
quoted 2 Chron. 20:12 — "We do not know what to do, but our eyes are upon
you."

What he was supremely clear about was the name of the incarnate, crucified, and risen Christ, who was located *not* in the private conscience or
the immortal soul or the spiritual experience or the religious yearnings of
the individual, but rather in the center of history and therefore in the
center of the life of this world. The earth for Bonhoeffer was always the
place "in which the cross of Jesus Christ is planted," and the church was
always "a piece of the world for which Christ died."

It was precisely because Bonhoeffer was clear about Jesus Christ that he
was able to venture into the political arena without inner turmoil. He was
able to make bold moves, as he did with amazing frequency, because he

trusted not in the rightness of his own actions but in the right-making activity of the living God who takes even our inadequate deeds and misguided judgments and uses them for good.

Being clear about Jesus Christ gave Bonhoeffer freedom for responsible action that moralists — on the left as well as on the right of the political spectrum — seldom begin to understand.

Throughout his short life of thirty-nine years, Bonhoeffer received the gift of each new day, fresh every morning, like manna. He knew that cynicism was unbecoming to a Christian, and despair entirely inappropriate. In prison he wrote to his fiancée, "Our marriage shall be a yes to God's earth." And at Christmas in 1942, he wrote to friends:

> There are persons who think it inane, and Christians who think it impious, to hope for a better earthly future and to prepare for it. They believe in chaos, disorder, catastrophe, as the meaning of present events, and in resignation or in flight from the world they give up all responsibility for further life, for new constructions, for the coming generation. It may be that the world will end tomorrow. If so, we will gladly lay down our work for a better future, but not until then.

In these perhaps not worst but surely not best of times, Dietrich Bonhoeffer reminds us to focus clearly on the incarnate, crucified, and risen Jesus Christ who leads his church into free and responsible action for the sake of the future of God's world.

Abbreviations

Books by Bonhoeffer

AB *Act and Being.* Translated by Bernard Noble. New York: Harper & Row, 1962.

CC *Christ the Center.* New translation by Edwin H. Robertson. New York: Harper & Row, 1978.

CD *The Cost of Discipleship.* Translated by R. H. Fuller, revised by Irmgard Booth. New York: Macmillan Co., 1963.

CF/T *Creation and Fall/Temptation.* Translated by John C. Fletcher and Kathleen Downham. New York: Macmillan Co., 1959.

CS *The Communion of Saints.* Translated by Ronald G. Smith et al. New York: Harper & Row, 1963.

E *Ethics.* Translated by Neville Horton Smith from the 6th German edition. New York: Macmillan Co., 1978.

FFP *Fiction from Prison.* Edited by Renate Bethge and Eberhard Bethge with Clifford Green, translated by Ursula Hoffman. Philadelphia: Fortress Press, 1981.

GS *Gesammelte Schriften*, I–VI. Munich: Chr. Kaiser, 1958–74.

LPP *Letters and Papers from Prison.* Enlarged edition, translated by R. H. Fuller, Frank Clarke, John Bowden et al. New York: Macmillan Co., 1971.

LT *Life Together.* Translated by John W. Doberstein. New York: Harper & Row, 1954.

NRS *No Rusty Swords: Letters, Lectures and Notes, 1928–1936.* Edited by Edwin H. Robertson, translated by Edwin H. Robertson and John Bowden. New York: Harper & Row, 1965.

P *Psalms: The Prayerbook of the Bible.* Translated by James H. Burtness. Minneapolis: Augsburg Pub. House, 1970.

PFP   *Prayers from Prison.* Interpreted by Johann Christoph Hampe. Philadelphia: Fortress Press, 1979.

TP   *True Patriotism: Letters, Lectures and Notes 1939–1945.* Edited by Edwin H. Robertson, translated by Edwin H. Robertson and John Bowden. New York: Harper & Row, 1973.

WF   *The Way to Freedom: Letters, Lectures and Notes, 1935–1939.* Edited by Edwin H. Robertson, translated by Edwin H. Robertson and John Bowden. New York: Harper & Row, 1966.

Secondary Literature

DB   Bethge, Eberhard. *Dietrich Bonhoeffer: Man of Vision, Man of Courage.* Translated by Eric Mosbacher, Peter Ross, Betty Ross, Frank Clarke, and William Glen-Doepel, under the editorship of Edwin Robertson. New York: Harper & Row, 1970.

Locating and Interpreting Ethics in the Bonhoeffer Legacy

The Selection of Sources

The Book Entitled Ethics

If one wants to understand the ethics of Dietrich Bonhoeffer, the most obvious place to go is to his book that bears the title *Ethics*. He wrote a number of books whose titles indicate the content in a very straightforward way. His published dissertation on the church has the title *The Communion of Saints*. His book on the Psalms is entitled *Psalms: The Prayerbook of the Bible*. The university lectures on Genesis 1−3 are appropriately entitled *Creation and Fall*. His book entitled *Ethics* seems to be the obvious place to locate a study of Bonhoeffer's ethics.

It is clear that ethics was not a peripheral concern for him, nor was the writing of a book on ethics a casual interest. It began to develop very early. In 1928 his doctoral advisor, Reinhold Seeberg, in response to Bonhoeffer's inquiry about a teaching post at the University of Berlin, suggested to him that he write a history of ethics and ethical dogma.[1] When Bonhoeffer was in Barcelona as a student vicar, he prepared lectures on Christian ethics for the congregation.[2] When he stopped to visit Karl Barth on his way back from the United States in July 1931, Bonhoeffer wrote to his friend Erwin Sutz that he and Barth "very soon came to the problem of ethics."[3] He taught a university seminar (summer semester 1932) on the subject "Is There a Christian Ethic?"[4] He had a persistent interest in ethics, fed by a significant academic and intellectual fascination with the topic. He also lived his entire adult life in times of social unrest and political upheaval, times that gave him no respite from struggle with ethical questions, nor leisure to work through those questions in as thorough a way as he would have liked. He had a book in mind long before he began to write it. When the seminary at Finkenwalde was shut down by the Gestapo in September

1937 and they were preparing for departure, Bonhoeffer remarked that at least now he could get down to the writing of his ethics.[5] Yet years later the book was still in process. From Tegel prison Bonhoeffer wrote to Eberhard Bethge that he felt as though his life was now pretty much over, and that there remained only the task of finishing his ethics.[6] But the book was never finished.

The situation is still more complicated. The book as we have it is an attempt on the part of Bethge to put together a number of documents that Bonhoeffer wrote while working toward an ethics book. Because of Bonhoeffer's stated goal to write a book on ethics, and because of Bethge's closeness to the whole process, it seemed appropriate after the war to publish these documents as an attempt to get into print some approximation of the ethics that Bonhoeffer would have written had he had the chance to do so. Bonhoeffer had even written to Bethge from prison that if the book did not get finished, Bethge was well aware of the directions in which he was moving. So encouraged by another of Bonhoeffer's friends, Bishop George Bell, Bethge took up the task. When the first German edition came out in 1949, there was surprisingly little response to it. Bethge comments that the universities were in the postwar period of reorganization and had little time for serious discussion of scientific theology.[7] It is probably also the case that in 1949 Bonhoeffer was so little known that a book by him bearing the title *Ethics* caused no excitement.

Bonhoeffer had left a tentative outline for his ethics book, which Bethge used as a guide to attempt to arrange the documents in somewhat logical order. The assumption behind that ordering was that the various documents were drafts of various sections of the book that Bonhoeffer had planned. Bethge explained this in his preface to the first edition.[8]

The publication of a book on Bonhoeffer by the East Berlin theologian Hanfried A. Müller raised new questions about the ordering of the documents.[9] Müller attempted to show, in this first major attempt (1961) to look at Bonhoeffer's theological contribution as a whole, that a distinct development takes place, and that this development can be characterized as a movement from the church to the world. Whatever judgments were made about Müller's specific conclusions, it became clear that chronology and biography could not be avoided in the task of editing these ethics materials. Following new investigation and reflection, Bethge rearranged the documents in the sixth edition (1963) in what he considered to be proper chronological order. The first English edition (1955) followed the ordering of the first five German editions. Since 1965 the English editions have followed the ordering of the sixth German edition. In the most recent

German edition (1981), there is an afterword by Bethge in which he again raises the question of the ordering of the documents, specifically Section V, on the basis of new work done by Clifford Green.[10] Not only was the ethics book never finished; there still remain questions about how best to arrange the extant documents.

There are also questions about the nature of the documents. Tiemo Peters, for instance, speaks about four "revisions" of the ethics.[11] This suggests that Bonhoeffer began with an initial document, which he "revised" a number of times. In this case, the last revision would seem to be the one that should be considered most "authoritative." Or the documents are referred to as "drafts." Is each document then a new draft, or a new section, or a new draft of the same section? Some interpreters talk about four "starts." That word seems to indicate that each time Bonhoeffer abandoned the way he had begun and then started again. In that case, also, the last start would seem to be the most important.

In addition to these problems concerning the documents that make up the major section of the *Ethics*, there is the matter of the materials in Part Two of the book. There are documents that Bethge considered to have a direct relationship to Bonhoeffer's work in ethics, but they were not written by Bonhoeffer specifically for inclusion in the projected book. The major piece on the "Primus Usus Legis," for instance, is a paper written as a report for the Reich Brotherhood Council. The piece entitled "What Is Meant by 'Telling the Truth'?" was sketched out in Tegel prison at the time of Bonhoeffer's interrogation. (There are also other extant documents, over one hundred small notes written by Bonhoeffer in connection with the ethics project, some of which have been printed, others not.)

The manuscripts themselves offer their own peculiar problems. There are many pages where there are things written in the margin or items crossed out. There are thus textual-critical decisions that have been made. Deciphering Bonhoeffer's German script is itself a major task. When a critical edition of the *Ethics* is published, together with marginal notes and variant readings, the extent of these problems will be clear even to the casual reader.

All of this indicates that there are numerous questions to be addressed and problems with which to struggle even if one locates Bonhoeffer's ethics strictly in the book that carries that title. The point is that if the book *Ethics* were the only thing we had from Bonhoeffer on this subject or if it were a complete statement, formally published by him as his final constructive effort in the field of Christian ethics, a case could be made for limiting one's research to this one volume. It is not, however, a complete statement, and it is not the only thing we have from Bonhoeffer on Christian ethics.

Additional Sources

There are, fortunately, significant sources in addition to the book entitled *Ethics*. Already mentioned are the Barcelona lectures on Christian ethics and the university lectures on the question "Is There a Christian Ethic?" There is also the interpretation of the Sermon on the Mount, published under the title *The Cost of Discipleship*. The Sermon on the Mount was an important part of the curriculum at Finkenwalde and of obviously more than academic interest to Bonhoeffer. Included in that volume are essays on "costly grace" and on the ethics of Paul. It is difficult to imagine how anyone could justify omitting this volume from a serious study of Bonhoeffer's ethics. Also, one does not have to read very far in *Life Together* before realizing that important ethical statements are being formulated there. There are obvious and specific statements about ethics in the early dissertations, *The Communion of Saints* and *Act and Being*. The handling of texts in sermons by Bonhoeffer often has startling ethical content, particularly when one considers the specific historical and political context in which his sermons were preached. The handling of "the law" in his extensive treatment of Psalm 119[12] is obviously important for an understanding of his ethics, as are the remarkable statements about the Christian life (e.g. "non-religious Christianity") in the prison letters.

As one works in the Bonhoeffer literature, it soon becomes apparent that material important for understanding his ethics is embedded in the entire corpus of his writing. Even seemingly casual letters often contain significant clues about where his reflections are taking him. Everything he wrote is potentially important as a source for getting at his ethics. Nothing can be automatically ruled out. Indeed, a case will be made later that all of Bonhoeffer's theological work can best be grasped under the rubric of "ethical theology."

There are Bonhoeffer interpreters, however, who consider his life more important than his writings. The major source, in that case, for understanding his ethics would be his biography. What he did, it could be said, is a more accurate measure of the man's contribution than what he said. It has already been noted that Hellmut Traub, who helped Bethge and Bonhoeffer pack up the books and nail up the windows when the seminary at Finkenwalde was closed, says that when they parted Bonhoeffer remarked that he would at last get down to writing his ethics. Traub then adds, "He did not. He has been granted to live and die it."[13] The implication seems to be that Bonhoeffer's life and death constitute a more important source for his ethics than do his writings. In the first paragraphs of an article on Bonhoeffer, Ruth Zerner quotes Visser t' Hooft and says that he has "perceptively proposed that 'hunger and thirst for reality, for becoming incarnate, for *living* the Christian life and not merely *talking* about it' provide 'the real key to Bonhoeffer's message.' "[14] This leads one to think that the real source for the ethics of Bonhoeffer should be his life *rather than* his writings. The last line of Zerner's article says it clearly: "But the most eloquent and startling comments on political power, freedom, and the state lie in Dietrich Bonhoeffer's life, not his writings."[15] David Hopper emphasizes the traditional and ordinary character of Bonhoeffer's faith and piety and states in the final paragraph of his book on Bonhoeffer the opinion that his life may be more important for future generations of Christians than his writings.[16] This is not to say that these interpreters are uninterested in Bonhoeffer's writings. It is simply to indicate that they find themselves finally of the opinion that his life supplies most of what there is of value to learn. It is a way of locating ethics in the Bonhoeffer legacy, of selecting the sources for the study of his ethics, not so much in the corpus of his writings as in the life of his discipleship.

A variant of this point of view is to concentrate on the ethical decisions he made and the way in which he went about making them. The source for Bonhoeffer's ethics would be his own procedures for ethical decision making rather than his exemplary moral life. Getting at Bonhoeffer's ethics in this way would not be easy, though, for he shared his internal struggles with very few people. He was not inclined toward extensive self-examination and considered careless exposing of one's inner life to be the mark of people without culture. Some even found him distant and cool in personal relationships. Yet there are interesting little hints with which one could begin such an investigation.

Bonhoeffer seemed at times to have great difficulty coming to decision. He wrote on one occasion, "I can decide nothing in advance."[17] On another occasion he commented that it is "unendingly difficult to know what we should do and what we should not do."[18] One could gather some data with which to argue that he was overly conscientious about arriving at conclusions to ethical questions. On the other hand, Bethge writes: "Before taking decisions about our enterprises, he was long in deliberating, too long; but once the decision was taken, it was neither regretted nor ever questioned."[19] That seems to fit more closely with Bonhoeffer's often-stated rejection of scrupulosity, with his advice to "make up your mind and come out into the tempest of living,"[20] with his frequent statement that to refuse to decide is worse than to make a bad decision. To try to get at Bonhoeffer's ethics by getting at his ethical decision making is not easy, but it is a fascinating and potentially fruitful avenue of investigation. An attempt will be made in chapter 3 of this study to do something of this nature by looking at Bonhoeffer's discussion about truth telling while he was under interrogation at Tegel prison.

One could also go not to the ethical decisions that he made, but to those few places where he spoke specifically, although perhaps offhandedly, about methods of decision making. When, for instance, he was asked by some of his students how to decide whether or not to obtain a "legal" ordination, he responded with what appears to be a specific method for decision making:

> In times of uncertainty the following rules hold for us:
>
> A. I should never make a decision in uncertainty; the *status quo* has precedence over change, unless I recognize the need for change with certainty.
>
> B. I should never act alone, firstly because I need the advice of the brothers, secondly because the brothers need me, and thirdly because there is a church discipline which I must not treat lightly.
>
> C. I should never make a hasty decision or allow it to be forced on me. If one door closes for me today, God will open another one when he wills to.[21]

Another place where there seems to be a by-the-numbers method of ethical decision making is in the essay on truth telling. It reflects Bonhoeffer's own struggles during interrogation at Tegel prison. He asks rhetorically how one can know that one's word is true. He responds:

> a. By perceiving who causes me to speak and what entitles me to speak. b. By perceiving the place at which I stand. c. By relating to this context the object about which I make some assertion.[22]

The problem is that there are very few such passages, and there is no common pattern to them. They are important sources, but no adequate statement of the ethics of Bonhoeffer could possibly be built on these isolated statements.[23]

Almost all interpreters agree that Bonhoeffer's writings and his life must be taken together as sources for his ethics as well as his theology. It is possible to do this, however, in a variety of ways. One can emphasize the situational character of his writing. *Life Together* is a book that comes directly out of the Finkenwalde experiment. It is in some ways almost a documentary record of what went on there. Bonhoeffer in fact warns his readers to remember this.[24] The *Letters and Papers from Prison* are exactly that, slices of his own life at that time. The situational character of *Life Together* and *Letters and Papers from Prison* is obvious. But everything Bonhoeffer wrote was forged in some historical context, and to ignore this is to make of his work an abstract intellectual enterprise which it surely was not. It would be a great mistake, for instance, to read Bonhoeffer's lecture on "the leadership principle"[25] without taking into account the fact that it was delivered over Berlin radio on 1 February 1933, immediately after Hitler came to power. It would make no sense to read Bonhoeffer's sermon on Matt. 16:13-18,[26] Peter's confession, without taking very seriously the fact that it was preached on the day of the church election, 23 July 1933, which would determine the fate of the Confessing Church. One need only page through the biography by Bethge to realize that Bonhoeffer never wrote in the abstract. The unity of life was a lifelong theme for him. He wrote to his friend Helmut Rössler while he was a vicar in Barcelona:

> It is quite a remarkable experience for one to see work and life really coming together—a synthesis which we all look for in our student days, but hardly manage to find; really to live *one* life and not two, or rather half a life. It gives the work value and the worker an objectivity, a recognition of his own limitations, such as can only be gained in real life.[27]

One way to exercise this contextualist approach is to look at the external events that influenced Bonhoeffer's life and writings. A few illustrations have been given in the last paragraphs. The approach can be worked out in great detail. Peters, for instance, reads the political thought of Bonhoeffer almost entirely as specific responses to specific actions by the Nazis.[28] There are no serious interpreters who ignore external events as sources for understanding Bonhoeffer's ethics. Differences exist, however, concerning which details are taken to be most important, which connections are made between Bonhoeffer's actions and writings, and the degree to which concentration on external events dominates the interpretation.

Another way to understand the connection between Bonhoeffer's life and writings is to look not so much at external events as at internal events in Bonhoeffer's personal development. This work has also been done in a number of ways. Most recently there has developed a discrete field of theological investigation known as Theology as Biography, Theology as Autobiography, or Psycho-History. There are already significant papers and articles by Green, Robin Lovin and Jonathan Gosser, and Roger A. Johnson, who use such methodologies.[29] These attempts are usually based on some appreciation of developmental psychology and have to do not simply with the unity of Bonhoeffer's life and writings, but with an attempt to understand this unity in specific stages of development. These stages are often, but not always, brought into congruence with stages of faith or moral development considered to be generally evident in religious people.

Quite independent of these somewhat elaborate procedures is Bethge's more modest but lasting division of Bonhoeffer's life and work into three major parts. It is obvious in the three sections (The Lure of Theology; The Cost of Being a Christian; Sharing Germany's Destiny) of the biography, but was worked out in detail at least as early as Bethge's Alden-Tuthill lectures in 1961.[30] His article on the "two turning points" in Bonhoeffer's life is a further sophistication of this three-part division.[31] It indicates the hinges on which Bonhoeffer's life moves from one phase to another. The divisions seem to indicate a natural and legitimate progression from Bonhoeffer's university life to his work in the Confessing Church to his involvement in the conspiracy. It is obvious, in fact, that Bethge's three-part division has become an almost standard feature of Bonhoeffer scholarship. The question it raises regarding the selection of sources for the study of Bonhoeffer's ethics is how to relate various ethical writings and various decisions for ethical action from the first two periods to the *Ethics*, written in the third period, or whether any attempt to do this should even be made.

A variation on the three-part scheme of development is the attempt to determine a single radical change in Bonhoeffer's life and work. A prime text, although there are others, is the letter to Bethge dated 22 April 1944, in which the following passage occurs.

> I've certainly learnt a great deal, but I don't think I have changed very much. There are people who change, and others who can hardly change at all. I don't think I've ever changed very much, except perhaps at the time of my first impressions abroad and under the first conscious influence of father's personality. It was then that I turned from phraseology to reality. I don't think, in fact, that you yourself have changed much. Self-development is, of course, a different matter. Neither of us has really had a break in our lives. Of course, we have deliberately broken with a good deal, but that again is something quite different. Even our present experiences probably don't represent a break in the passive sense. I sometimes used to long for something of the kind, but today I think differently about it. Continuity with one's own past is a great gift, too.[32]

It is easy to see how this passage could be read from different perspectives. Everything depends on what one underlines. The question of "radical break" (or breaks) or "gradual development" is unavoidable.

Thus the selection of sources for the study of Bonhoeffer's ethics is complicated. There is the book entitled *Ethics*, with all of its own problems.

But there are additional sources, literary and biographical and historical, all of which converge to raise basic questions of interpretation. How one responds to these questions affects how one reads specific passages and how one understands specific events.

The Basic Questions of Interpretation

The Circularity of Interpretive Arguments

All decisions about locating and interpreting ethics in the Bonhoeffer legacy are somewhat circular. Thus issues of interpretation have already been raised in the discussion of the selection of sources. That which biblical scholars call "the hermeneutical circle" comes into play in the investigation of any document, whether the Book of Job or the Constitution of the United States or the legacy of Dietrich Bonhoeffer. The interpreter goes to detailed data to build up an interpretive framework, but that framework in turn influences the selection and interpretation of details.

Only brief mention needs to be made of the fact that interpretation affects translation. One problem in interpreting ethics in the Bonhoeffer legacy is that there is to date no authorized English translation of the material. Different works have come out at different times, translated by different people. Some materials were brought into translation rather hastily. The original translation of the prison letters, for instance, contained not only translation errors, but also a number of unacknowledged omissions. Corrections have been introduced into later editions and, in general, these corrections have been cumulative. Yet one can get some feel for the passion with which Bonhoeffer scholars examine translations by reading Paul Lehmann's review of *No Rusty Swords*. He calls it a "tawdry piece of counterfeit," and continues,

> From start to finish this book is a contrived piece of work in which commentator, translator and publisher have confused misrepresentation with interpretation. One of the youngest of the arts has been linked with the oldest of the professions in an enterprise of seductive solicitation.[33]

Less colorful but no less serious discussions of the problems of reading Bonhoeffer in English translation can be found in works by John D. Godsey, John Deschner, and John Phillips.[34] Some translation problems are more significant than others, and interpreters differ on which translation controversies they consider most important. References to translation problems will occur during the course of this study, but only in those places where such references are thought to be necessary to the argument.

A conclusion drawn by some from the fragmentary character of much of the Bonhoeffer material is that the form in which we have his writings is significant for the interpretation of those writings. At least a good deal was made of this when Americans first began reading Bonhoeffer. Phillips, for instance, stated in a 1967 article that "possibly the most interesting and revolutionary relic Bonhoeffer has left behind him is the *form* in which he chose, finally, to do his theology—the letter to a friend."[35]

> But the prison letters really *are* subversive—they seem to signal the end of the dominance of care, clarity, and system in theology; the triumph of the communique; the notes scribbled for him who must run; disconnected observations on things that matter, written in haste and with passion, to a close friend.[36]

Phillips wanted to affirm the "communications revolution" and the end of the "Gutenberg Era" heralded by Marshall McLuhan. He was enthused about the style of the antinovel, the New Wave movie, Andy Warhol's painting of the Campbell Soup can, and interpreted Bonhoeffer's theology as part of this broad movement away from "linear thinking."[37] Harvey Cox, during these years, even compared Bonhoeffer's writings to Rorschach blots which serve primarily to jog the observer's imagination.[38] While few would now agree that lack of care and clarity characterize Bonhoeffer's writings, it is certainly the case that the form in which Bonhoeffer went about his theological and ethical reflection must be taken into account when interpreting it, and that form and content do interpenetrate one another.

Constructing an interpretive framework for understanding Bonhoeffer's ethics also involves entering into conversation with those who have already worked on the Bonhoeffer materials, particularly with those who have in some way concentrated on his ethics. For a number of years it was common practice among Bonhoeffer interpreters to review the major secondary sources in a systematic way prior to presenting their own position. This was done, for instance, by Heinrich Ott, André Dumas, David Hopper, and Phillips.[39] It was a natural and helpful thing to do. At the present time it is no longer necessary. The summary statements do exist for those who care to use them. But the literature now grows at such a rapid pace that even keeping up with it is a herculean task. There are many authors who deal with Bonhoeffer along the way, incidental to something else, and some of these interpretations may be as significant as are articles or books with Bonhoeffer's name in the title. For instance, an interpretation of Bonhoeffer's ethics worth noting lies embedded in the second chapter of James

Gustafson's book *Christ and the Moral Life*.[40] Another example is Edward LeRoy Long's discussion of "The Relational Motif in Christian Ethics" and his comment on Bonhoeffer under that rubric.[41] It is important to note that interpretations vary because there is always a subjective element at work in the interpretive process. Details are used to build up a perspective, but that perspective in turn affects how one understands the details. The fact is perhaps nowhere as clear as in the basic question of continuity and change in Bonhoeffer's life and work.

The Question of Continuity and Change

It has been stated that Müller made a case for a radical shift in Bonhoeffer from church to world. William Hamilton took essentially the same line, as did Paul van Buren, Cox, and Phillips.[42] All of these saw radical change between the early and the late Bonhoeffer, and concentrated their attention on the last period, which they saw as his most "secular" and also his most important period.

There are also those, however, who have noted distinct changes, but who choose to locate the really important Bonhoeffer in the "middle period," that time of his involvement with the Confessing Church. Barth writes that he would like to incorporate in the *Church Dogmatics* the whole of Bonhoeffer's *The Cost of Discipleship*.[43] He says there is no way to improve on some of the passages. But he writes to Superintendent P. W. Herrenbrück that Bonhoeffer's prison letters are "a particular thorn."[44] Barth is also upset about Bonhoeffer's phrase "revelation positivism," used to describe Barth's theology, and refers to these comments of Bonhoeffer as "enigmatic." Godsey, in his book on the theology of Bonhoeffer, labeled the last period "Theological Fragmentation," thus signaling his own judgment at that time that the middle period is a more reliable guide to Bonhoeffer than is the last period.[45] Green might represent those who have focused on the early period because they see it as absolutely essential and foundational for everything that follows.[46]

There are interpreters who agree on emphasizing change, but who disagree on which period of Bonhoeffer's life and work is most important. There are also those, however, who are more impressed with the continuity in Bonhoeffer's life and work than with the change. None would say that there were no changes. The point is rather that the changes are seen within a life of fundamental continuity. Ernst Feil talks about essential continuity, as does Dumas.[47] Bethge also, in his three-part handling of the biography of Bonhoeffer, is far more on the side of continuity than he is on the side of radical change. He repeatedly points to emphases and themes that emerge later in different form. New things that appear are very often explained in terms of development from an earlier period.

A major commitment of this study is that the continuities in Bonhoeffer's life and work are more impressive than the changes, particularly when one looks at the entire legacy from the viewpoint of ethical issues. It is unnecessary to argue the case at length here. Yet, because the manner in which the Bonhoeffer materials are used in the main body of this study reflects the emphasis on continuity, some brief statement is necessary. The almost embarrassing thing is taken to be not how much Bonhoeffer changes, but rather how repetitive he is; the impressive thing is taken to be not how fragmentary the material is, but rather how the whole is present in almost every part.

There are a number of autobiographical references that indicate Bonhoeffer's awareness of some kind of change or development. Three of these are passages from 1944.

In the letter of 23 February 1944, Bonhoeffer discusses a break between the lifestyle of his parents and that of his own generation. "The longer we are uprooted from our professional activities and our private lives, the more we feel how fragmentary our lives are, compared with those of our parents."[48] Bonhoeffer continues that it is important to discern which fragments of life should be discarded and which are important. Yet "the great counterpoint" is maintained throughout and this makes the special fragmentariness of his time something to be celebrated rather than lamented. In discussing this passage, James Patrick Kelley points to the fact that Bonhoeffer does not talk about some early unity in his own life which was later lost in the church struggle or in World War II. The boundary is rather between his parents' generation and his own.[49]

A second passage from 1944 is dated 22 April.[50] Reference to it has already been made. It has been stated that this letter can be read in different ways, but the position taken here is that Bonhoeffer's feeling of continuity in his life is very strong. If there is an emphasis on a break, or radical change, the reference is to a very early conscious realization of the influence of his father upon him. The further comment in this passage expressing gratitude for "continuity with one's past" seems to confirm this emphasis on his sense of continuity.

A third passage from 1944 is the letter of 21 July.

> I remember a conversation that I had in America thirteen years ago with a young French pastor. We were asking ourselves quite simply what we wanted to do with our lives. He said he would like to become a saint (and I think it's quite likely that he did become one). At the time I was very impressed,

but I disagreed with him, and said, in effect, that I should like to learn to have faith. For a long time I didn't realize the depth of the contrast. I thought I could acquire faith by trying to live a holy life, or something like it. I suppose I wrote *The Cost of Discipleship* as the end of that path. Today I can see the dangers of that book, though I still stand by what I wrote.[51]

There is certainly growth and development indicated in this passage. The impressive comment, however, is Bonhoeffer's insistence that he still wants to "stand by" what he wrote in *The Cost of Discipleship*, even though he sees the dangers there.

There are many other pieces in this fascinating puzzle. One such piece is a letter by Bonhoeffer written from Finkenwalde in January 1936.

Then something happened, something that has changed and transformed my life to the present day. For the first time I discovered the Bible. . . . I had often preached, I had seen a great deal of the church, and talked and preached about it — but I had not yet become a Christian.[52]

A decisive turning point in Bonhoeffer's life is mentioned, but it is clearly a reference to something prior to 1933. The statement is an isolated one, as there are no other such clear references to this "becoming a Christian." In any case, as far as Bonhoeffer's external life and work are concerned, despite the January 1936 reference, it is still possible to be impressed more by continuities than by change.

Kelley states his argument for continuity:

Here, then, is the picture Bonhoeffer himself drew of his developing life. Within a fundamental continuity, in which no radical breaks of the past are noted, at least two basic and identifiable shifts occurred. Like most others, he felt himself decisively changed by the transition from adolescence to adulthood. So he could attribute the most crucial break in his development to first becoming aware of the influence of his father and to his first independent travels abroad as a student in 1924. Within his adult years, however, he saw only two shifts of stress in his developing thought. The first was a movement away from a more exclusively intellectual sort of theology toward an increasing concern to develop the actuality of Christian living within a highly structured and explicitly pious common life, whose norms were regarded as given from the divine source external to it, yet accessible to the empathic student of the Bible. This shift was already under way in 1930–31 in New York, developed significantly at the point of Bonhoeffer's taking up his work in the University and the church in late 1931, and continued to grow until it manifested itself in a mature form in *The Cost of Discipleship* (1937) and *Life Together* (1937) as well as other works from the period 1935–39. The second turn was in some significant respect a disavowal of at least part of that which had predominated in Bonhoeffer's life in the year since that first turn. Any form of piety which publicly separated the Christian from the world at large now came to be avoided at all cost along with the conceptuality which presumes that Christians have access to special sets of ethical principles or special clarity about those available to general ethical reflection. To live as a Christian came now to mean living wholly as a man of the world which was itself now viewed as mature enough in God's own perspective to manage its own affairs without benefit of any direct divine intervention to rescue men from "the ship wrecks" they sometimes create for themselves. Throughout all these shifts the continuous theological question for Bonhoeffer centered in his concern to know in the most concrete terms the present meaning of the actual living of faith in the God revealed in Jesus as the Christ.[53]

Among the questions of interpretation forced on the reader by the Bonhoeffer material, the most fascinating and the one that finally feeds back more than any other into the reading of specific texts and the understanding of specific events is the question of continuity and change in Bonhoeffer's life and work. The position taken here is on the side of continuity, and the argument for that position will develop as the presentation of Bonhoeffer's ethics unfolds.

Responsibility for the Future as Bonhoeffer's Theme

In a brief reminiscence of Bonhoeffer, Gerhard Jacobi writes:

Dietrich Bonhoeffer was a person who reflected on and struggled with the most divergent thoughts, thoughts which often surprised his friends. It was not only theological or church questions that haunted him. . . . [T]here was also the world before his keen eyes, with its economic, social and cultural phenomena. . . .
He made a calm and harmonious impression upon the outside world. At meetings of pastors he spoke only briefly. Twice he quoted to them nothing but the words:
One man asks: What is to come?
The other: What is right?
And that is the difference
Between the free man and the slave.
He said nothing more, but those few words spoken in calmness and certainty, and out of personal freedom, found their mark. . . .
[H]e was haunted by the question about the will of God *hic et nunc*. Here he looked far afield: he was not just concerned with Germany and National Socialism, but with all nations of the world with their needs and bewilderments, but also with the new things that emerged from them.[54]

Jacobi notes that Bonhoeffer's thoughts often surprised his friends. His thoughts are still surprising. If there is anything that most people consider a basic assumption of the moral life in general, and of the Christian life in particular, it is that a person should do the right thing regardless of the consequences. Bonhoeffer, in this little statement quoted by Jacobi, not only questions this assumption, but totally reverses it. The person who asks what is right is a slave. The person who asks what is to come is free. The man whom Jacobi remembers is the Bonhoeffer of 1933, but everything here fits perfectly with the statements in the *Ethics*, written almost a decade later. For example:

> Whoever wishes to take up the problem of a Christian ethic must be confronted at once with a demand which is quite without parallel. He must from the outset discard as irrelevant the two questions which alone impel him to concern himself with the problem of ethics, "How can I be good?" and "How can I do good?", and instead of these he must ask the utterly and totally different question "What is the will of God?"[55]

Bonhoeffer does not distinguish between the "right" and the "good" as do many contemporary ethicists.[56] He uses the words interchangeably, flatly rejecting both as starting points for ethical reflection and action, and concentrates on the will of God. It is precisely consequences of action that matter. Thus the free person asks not whether an action is right, but rather what it is that will come of this action. The question has to do with what new economic, social, and cultural phenomena are emerging among all the nations of the world. The ethical question has to do with taking responsibility for the future, and one does that by asking about the will of God for the entire creation. It is, certainly at first glance, a surprising way to go about doing ethics.

The theme has been sketched in the prologue under the phrase "For the Sake of the Future." In this section the phrase "responsibility for the future" is used. "Sharing the future" will be used occasionally, particularly when the emphasis is upon partaking in the suffering of God in the life of the world. Larry Rasmussen strikes this note, for instance, in his study of Bonhoeffer that he labels an "Ethic of the Cross."[57] Jacobi's reminiscence, just quoted, is entitled "Drawn toward Suffering." The title of this book is *Shaping the Future*. That which is constant with Bonhoeffer is the look to the future. Martin Marty observes correctly that "Bonhoeffer, who dealt so much with the future, still represents promise. . . ."[58] It is important to alter the phrases with which that future is addressed, however, in order to take into account various mixes of divine initiative and human response, different degrees of passion and action, shadings of emphasis on the extent and the limit of human responsibility. It is not the case that Bonhoeffer wants to abandon God and take the world into his own hands. It is rather his conviction that God has a purpose for this world and that God works toward the future through his people, that drives Bonhoeffer to seek the will of

God, unwilling "to accept life in this world as a mere 'holding operation' until the triumph of the spirit in the second coming of Christ."[59]

He trusted God's future even as he worked for it and gave his life for it. He saw the future as God's future.[60] Yet he believed that for a person to refuse to take responsibility for that future is sheer nihilism.[61] He sometimes anguished over decisions. But once he made them he moved ahead. He did not stand as "Hercules at the crossroads,"[62] wondering forever which way to go. He knew that the command of God gave "permission to live,"[63] and allowed "the flood of life to flow freely."[64] It was not his conscience, or any other route to absolute moral certainty, that gave him the freedom to act, to make up his mind, and to "come out into the tempest of living."[65] It was rather confidence in the future of God's world.[66]

This emphasis upon the future places Bonhoeffer with those ethicists who concentrate on the consequences of actions rather than on the motives out of which the actions are done. It is not the rightness of an action but the result of an action that commends it. In terms of formal ethical models, Bonhoeffer would have to be placed among the teleologists rather than among either the "deontologists" or the "situationists." These are somewhat fluid categories, even overlapping one another in the work of some ethicists, and there will be occasion to work with these models in a more thorough way in connection with some of Bonhoeffer's specific ethical reflections. At the moment it is perhaps sufficient to distinguish them by reference to their respective approaches to the question of ethics and time. Deontologists work with the assumption that right and wrong are timeless, always and everywhere the same. Cultural differences exist, and application of right and wrong must take these differences into consideration. But right and wrong per se are timeless. Situationists assume that right and wrong cannot be timeless because life is not timeless. Life is episodic, constantly in flux, calling for decisions appropriate to changing conditions and situations. In this case, one attempts to do not the right (timeless) thing, but rather the appropriate (timely) thing. Teleologists assume that time is linear, that one thing leads to another, that actions have consequences, that some kind of cause-and-effect system operates in this world, even though it may be impossible to predict with accuracy the future from the present. Teleologists attempt to do things here and now that are likely to produce good results there and then, in future places and times. Taking responsibility for the future, consciously sharing the future, or being willing to put one's hand to shaping the future fit more closely with ethical models traditionally labeled teleological than with those labeled either deontological or situational.

Since one can never predict the future with accuracy, any person doing ethics in a teleological mode automatically gives up the assurance of being "right." One may still decide to make very bold moves, even moves that may cost one's life, but one can never do it in the security that one has done the right thing. It ought to be no surprise, then, that one of Bonhoeffer's favorite Bible passages, one that he quoted often, was 2 Chron. 20:12: "We do not know what to do, but our eyes are upon you." Bethge says that he quoted it more often than any other Bible verse in 1932, the year before Hitler came to power, and that he closed the final lecture hour of the winter 1932–33 semester with the other half of this verse: "O our God, wilt thou not execute judgment upon them? For we are powerless against this great multitude that is coming against us."[67] He preached on this same text in Berlin on 8 May 1932, Exaudi Sunday. The entire sermon is a delicate handling of the seriousness and the freedom of ethical decision making.[68] Luther talked about the certainty of faith which functions in the midst of the absence of security regarding the rightness of one's own decisions. The same mood penetrates Bonhoeffer's commitment to shaping the future as a way of making ethical decisions.

A number of Bonhoeffer interpreters comment on this theme of shaping the future, although none has made it the central interpretive key for reading and presenting Bonhoeffer's ethics. Geffrey Kelly, for instance, catches it in the following passage:

> Bonhoeffer's moral posture on the question of resistance and conspiracy, even without the support of his church or of the masses, was finally and fully appreciated only as the horrors of the Nazi regime were documented for the world at large. He saw his actions as an expression of responsibility for the shaping of history to benefit the coming generation.[69]

Kelly is writing about Bonhoeffer's theology of history rather than his ethics of the future, but the congruence of the two is obvious.

Ott comments on Bonhoeffer's prison letter of 1 February 1944, in which the phrase "shape the future" is used. Bonhoeffer laments the fact that there seems to be no way to "get hold" of a person who has no urge to shape the future. Ott comments:

> There is yet another viewpoint from which Bonhoeffer sees the ethical situation made materially concrete, it is so through the responsibility of the one who acts for the shaping of the future, that area of the future given as our responsibility. It is an ever-recurring theme in Bonhoeffer that we must act not from principles, but out of our responsibility for the future, and that success also is ethically not simply indifferent. He did not work out further how to link this thought to the christological structure of ethical action — and yet

we find an echo of it in what he says on the christological *motif* of representation; the man who was responsible acts as representative also for those for whom he takes over responsibility.[70]

Ott justifiably sees that this emphasis is traceable all the way back to *The Communion of Saints*, Bonhoeffer's first publication.

When Gustafson discusses Barth and Bonhoeffer, he talks about their "cosmic optimism." He perceives that "in each of these men of reputed darkness, there is an overwhelming shaft of light."[71] The ethic that emerges from the theological struggles of both of them is an ethic of Christian responsibility for the shaping of the future of God's world. This cosmic optimism is accompanied by anthropological realism. It embraces a robust doctrine of sin, is never naive, yet always hopeful.

Jürgen Weissbach is another Bonhoeffer interpreter who has noted this theme. He finishes his essay on Bonhoeffer with the following words:

> Bonhoeffer's *Ethics* is really an expansion of the theology of the Barmen Declaration. He cannot regard ethics as an independent discipline alongside dogmatics, but he can say with Karl Barth: "Its matter is the Word and work of God in Jesus Christ, in which the right action of man has already been performed and therefore only waits to be confirmed by our action." This shows that ethics is not a possibility for man on his own. And, as Bonhoeffer is aware, this presupposes a decision of faith. . . . This means that the world does not have to be Christianized. Instead, the dominion of Christ over all realms frees everything for its own proper concern, for genuine worldliness. . . . It is through this that Bonhoeffer gives concrete directions for a life in Christian liberty, apart from the casuistry of an ethic based on duty but free from inwardness and from a preoccupation with individual sanctification, free for the formation of the world here and now.[72]

Bonhoeffer's concentration on shaping the future occurred at a time when the Nazis were ushering in their thousand-year kingdom. The German Christians placed the swastika in church chancels and called it the German symbol of hope.[73] Frank Buchman of the Oxford Movement came to Berlin in 1936 and said "I thank heaven for a man like Adolf Hitler, who built a front line of defence against the antichrist of Communism."[74] Shaping the future was a great theme for the Nazis, and Hitler was looked to by a great many Germans as their way out of the depression, back to a position of national pride. It was a time when Christians who opposed Hitler could argue, as did Rudolf Bultmann during these years, for linking Christianity with existentialism, for interpreting Christian faith in terms of personal rather than political existence.[75] In this case Christianity has to do with the authentic existence of the individual, with being free from *my* past and open to *my* future. It has nothing whatsoever to do with world view or with the future of society or of the world. Bultmann built on the existentialism of Martin Heidegger but also argued that he was simply bringing Luther's emphasis on justification by faith "to its logical conclusion in the field of epistemology."[76] Bonhoeffer, as well as Barth, took a different tack and insisted that Christian faith has everything to do with society and everything to do with the future of the world. What was wrong with Hitler was not that there was an emphasis on the future, but that it was a false future and a demonic hope. The future must be shaped to conform not with Nazi ideology, but with the form of Jesus Christ.

In the prologue and in this introduction an attempt has been made to prepare the way for the main body of this study. What follows is an argument for understanding Bonhoeffer's contribution to Christian ethics using his entire life and work as potential data, and the theme of shaping the future as an integrative scheme. Attention will be paid, when it is thought important, to changes and developments in his position, but the emphasis will be on essential continuity.

Chapter 1 will describe Bonhoeffer's formulation of an ethical theology. He was not engaged in doing theological ethics as much as he was in doing ethical theology, a theology that at every point is penetrated by ethical concerns and questions. This ethical theology has Christ as its center, results in the rejection of two-sphere thinking, and takes reality to be the sacrament of the ethical. It is concerned with the interpenetration of relationality and responsibility, and embraces time and history as ethical concomitants.

Chapter 2 will show that although Bonhoeffer rejects spatial thinking and utilizes temporal and historical categories for reflection, he is not a radical situationist. It is clear from even a superficial reading that Bonhoeffer is very interested in structure and order, and even in law. So he works at structuring what he calls the responsible life. The structures that emerge are not typical ethical categories, yet they often have roots in traditional ethical formulations. His usual pattern is to take categories that were spatially conceived, and to place them in conceptualizations that take time and history and specifically the future seriously. Thus we find him talking not about the two kingdoms, but about the last things and the things before the last. He believed in God's ordering of his creation, in spite of the massive misuse of the orders of creation doctrine by conservative Lutherans. So he recast that phrase into orders of preservation, and later into the divine mandates. God's ordering of his creation has thus to do with our ordering of our own lives, with our shaping of the future, and with what Bonhoeffer talks about as form, formation, and conformation. Law is not alien to life, but is a gift of God for the ordering of life. The natural must also be recovered for the sake of the gospel. It is not strange that Bonhoeffer should be open to the possibility of accepting strength, power, and success as legitimate gifts of God and even as results of living the natural life. The command of God finally becomes, as Barth saw so clearly, not so much obligation as permission.

Having described Bonhoeffer's ethical theology and his structuring of the responsible life, we must ask how or whether the position "works." We shall do that in chapter 3, taking as the major test case the classic ethical problem of truth telling and how Bonhoeffer handles that in practice and in theory.

NOTES

1. *NRS*, 36.
2. Ibid., 39ff.
3. Ibid., 121.
4. Eberhard Bethge, *Dietrich Bonhoeffer: Eine Biographie* (Munich: Chr. Kaiser, 1967), 1073ff. This appendix is not included in the English edition.
5. Hellmut Traub, in *I Knew Dietrich Bonhoeffer*, ed. Wolf-Dieter Zimmerman and Ronald Gregor Smith (London: William Collins Sons, 1966), 161.
6. *E*, 10.
7. Eberhard Bethge, "The Editing and Publishing of the Bonhoeffer Papers," *The Andover Newton Bulletin* 52 (December 1959): 1–24.
8. *E*, 8–9.
9. Hanfried Müller, *Von der Kirche zur Welt* (Hamburg-Bergsted: Herbert Reich Evang, 1961).
10. Dietrich Bonhoeffer, *Ethik* (Munich: Chr. Kaiser, 1981), 398.
11. Tiemo Rainer Peters, "Orders and Interventions: Political Ethics in the Theology of Dietrich Bonhoeffer," in *A Bonhoeffer Legacy*, ed. A. J. Klassen (Grand Rapids: W. B. Eerdmans, 1981), 320.
12. *GS* IV, 505–43.
13. Traub, in *I Knew Dietrich Bonhoeffer*, 161.
14. Ruth Zerner, "Dietrich Bonhoeffer's Views on the State and History" in *Bonhoeffer Legacy*, 132.
15. Ibid., 152.
16. David Hopper, *A Dissent on Bonhoeffer* (Philadelphia: Westminster Press, 1975), 144.
17. *GS* II, 379.
18. Ibid., 133.
19. Eberhard Bethge, in *I Knew Dietrich Bonhoeffer*, 46.
20. "Stations on the Way to Freedom," in *E*, 15.
21. *TP*, 187.
22. *E*, 370.
23. Edwin Robertson has written two imaginary conversations having to do

with Bonhoeffer's decision making. The one is between Bonhoeffer and Teilhard de Chardin. It is unpublished but is mentioned in the preface to *True Patriotism*. The second is between Bonhoeffer and H. Richard Niebuhr and is included in the British edition, but not the American edition, of *The Way to Freedom*. Both conversations were broadcast by the BBC. They are creative and suggestive and make use of primary Bonhoeffer materials, but it would be inappropriate to consider them of essential importance in attempting to get at the intersection of Bonhoeffer's theory and practice of decision making.

24. The admonition in the foreword to the German edition is unfortunately omitted from the English edition.

25. *NRS*, 190ff.

26. Ibid., 212ff.

27. Ibid., 37.

28. Tiemo Rainer Peters, *Die Präsenz des Politischen in der Theologie Dietrich Bonhoeffers* (Munich: Chr. Kaiser, 1976).

29. Clifford Green, "Bonhoeffer in the Context of Erikson's Luther Study," in *Psychohistory and Religion. The Case of "Young Man Luther,"* ed. Roger A. Johnson (Philadelphia: Fortress Press, 1977); Robin Lovin and Jonathan Gosser, "Dietrich Bonhoeffer: Witness in an Ambiguous World," in *Trajectories in Faith*, ed. James Fowler, Robin Lovin et al. (Nashville: Abingdon Press, 1980); Roger A. Johnson, "Dietrich Bonhoeffer: Religionless Christianity—Maturity, Transcendence, and Freedom," in *Critical Issues in Modern Religion*, ed. Roger A. Johnson (Englewood Cliffs, N.J.: Prentice-Hall, 1973).

30. Eberhard Bethge, "The Challenge of Dietrich Bonhoeffer's Life and Theology," in *World Come of Age*, ed. R. Gregor Smith (Philadelphia: Fortress Press, 1967), 22–88.

31. Eberhard Bethge, "Turning Points in Bonhoeffer's Life and Thought," in *Bonhoeffer in a World Come of Age*, ed. Peter Vorkink II (Philadelphia: Fortress Press, 1968), 73ff.

32. *LPP*, 275–76.

33. Paul Lehmann, review of *No Rusty Swords*, *Union Seminary Quarterly Review* 21 (March 1966): 364ff.

34. John D. Godsey, "Reading Bonhoeffer in English Translation: Some Difficulties," *Union Seminary Quarterly Review* 22 (Fall 1967): 79–90; John Deschner, "Bonhoeffer Studies in English," *Perkins School of Theology Journal* XXIL (Spring, 1969): 60–68; John A. Phillips, review of *Letters and Papers from Prison*, rev. ed., *Union Seminary Quarterly Review* 22 (Fall, 1967): 115ff.

35. John A. Phillips, "Dietrich Bonhoeffer: The Letters and the Legacy," *Motive* (February 1967): 43.

36. Ibid.

37. Ibid.

38. Harvey Cox, "Using and Misusing Bonhoeffer," *Christianity and Crisis* 24 (19 Oct. 1964): 199.

39. Heinrich Ott, *Reality and Faith*, trans. Alex. A. Morrison (Philadelphia: Fortress Press, 1972); André Dumas, *Dietrich Bonhoeffer: Theologian of Reality*, trans. Robert McAfee Brown (New York: Macmillan Co., 1971); David Hopper, *A Dissent on Bonhoeffer* (Philadelphia: Westminster Press, 1975); John A. Phillips,

Christ for Us in the Theology of Dietrich Bonhoeffer (New York: Harper & Row, 1967).

40. James Gustafson, *Christ and the Moral Life* (New York: Harper & Row, 1968).

41. Edward Long, Jr., *A Survey of Christian Ethics* (New York: Oxford Univ. Press, 1967).

42. William Hamilton, *The New Essence of Christianity* (New York: Association Press, 1961); Paul van Buren, *The Secular Meaning of the Gospel* (New York: Macmillan Co., 1963); Harvey Cox, *The Secular City* (New York: Macmillan Co., 1965); Phillips, *Christ for Us in the Theology of Dietrich Bonhoeffer*.

43. Karl Barth, *Church Dogmatics* IV/2, quoted in *DB*, 372.

44. Karl Barth, "From a Letter to Superintendent Herrenbrück," in *World Come of Age*, ed. R. Gregor Smith, 89ff.

45. John Godsey, *The Theology of Dietrich Bonhoeffer* (Philadelphia: Westminster Press, 1960).

46. Clifford Green, *Bonhoeffer: The Sociality of Christ and Humanity* (Missoula, Mont.: Scholars Press, 1972).

47. Ernst Feil, *The Theology of Dietrich Bonhoeffer*, trans. Martin Rumscheidt (Philadelphia: Fortress Press, 1985); André Dumas, *Dietrich Bonhoeffer: Theologian of Reality*.

48. *LPP*, 219.

49. James Patrick Kelley, *Revelation and the Secular in the Theology of Dietrich Bonhoeffer* (unpublished dissertation, Yale University, 1980), 121.

50. *LPP*, 275–77.

51. Ibid., 369.

52. *DB*, 154; *GS*, VI, 367–68.

53. Kelley, *Revelation and the Secular*, 141.

54. Gerhard Jacobi, in *I Knew Dietrich Bonhoeffer*, 71–73.

55. *E*, 188.

56. It is very common, though not universal, among contemporary ethicists to use the word "right" in the context of deontological modes of ethical reflection, and the word "good" in the context of teleological modes. The deontologist seeks to distinguish clearly between "right" and "wrong." The teleologist seeks to make judgments between degrees of "good" results following an action, acknowledging that such "good" results are always mixed with "bad" results.

57. Larry Rasmussen, "Ethik des Kreuzes am gegebenen Ort," in *Bonhoeffer und Luther* (Munich: Chr. Kaiser, 1983), 129–66.

58. Martin Marty in the foreword to Benjamin Reist, *The Promise of Bonhoeffer* (Philadelphia: J. B. Lippincott, 1969), 8.

59. Paul Lehmann, in *I Knew Dietrich Bonhoeffer*, 44.

60. *GS* IV, 27.

61. *TP*, 133.

62. *E*, 283.

63. Ibid., 281.

64. Ibid., 283.

65. Ibid., 16.

66. *GS* I, 50.

67. Bethge, *DB*, German ed., 264. This section is omitted in the English translation of the biography.

68. *GS* I, 133–39.

69. Geffrey B. Kelly, "Bonhoeffer's Theology of History and Revelation," in *Bonhoeffer Legacy*, 117.

70. Heinrich Ott, *Reality and Faith*, trans. Alex A. Morrison (Philadelphia: Fortress Press, 1972), 272–73.

71. James Gustafson, *Christ and the Moral Life* (New York: Harper & Row, 1968), 31.

72. Jürgen Moltmann and Jürgen Weissbach, *Two Studies in the Theology of Bonhoeffer* (New York: Charles Scribner's Sons, 1967), 151.

73. *DB*, 191.

74. Ibid., 446.

75. Cf. Rudolf Bultmann, "Autobiographical Reflections," in *Existence and Faith* (New York: Meridian Books, 1960), 283–88.

76. Rudolf Bultmann, "Bultmann Replies to His Critics," in *Kerygma and Myth*, ed. Hans Werner Bartsch (London: SPCK, 1953), 211.

1 | Formulating an Ethical Theology

Ethical Theology as Bonhoeffer's Task

One way to gather up the many strands of Bonhoeffer's ethical actions and reflections is to say that he was at work throughout his adult life on the formulation of an "ethical theology." The term is not in common use, and Bonhoeffer himself nowhere employs it. It does, however, call attention to the nature of Bonhoeffer's contribution to Christian ethics.

The term "theological ethics" is regularly used to suggest that there are other kinds of ethics, for instance, philosophical ethics, from which theological ethics is to be distinguished. The claim of the term is that there is a method or style or content, a *kind* of ethics, or a *way of doing* ethics, which is specifically grounded in theology and which cannot be properly understood apart from this ground. Theological ethics is ethics thoroughly penetrated by theology rather than by some other cluster of materials or methods or concerns.

The term "ethical theology" is used here to suggest that Bonhoeffer, perhaps unconsciously, struggled to formulate a theology that is penetrated at every point by ethical concerns and issues and questions. The term suggests that there are other kinds of theology, for instance, philosophical theology or fundamental theology or biblical theology, from which ethical theology can be distinguished. Assuming that there is such a thing and that Bonhoeffer was at work formulating a version of it, one can say that ethical theology knows the difference between believing and behaving, between confessing and acting, but attempts at every point to demonstrate the connections. Ethical theology insists that concern for one's neighbor can never be set aside while one does "theology proper." The doctrine of justification can never be explored without linking it to questions of justice. God cannot be thought about or proclaimed apart from action in and reflection upon the world God made and cares for. That does not mean that biblical exegesis, historical research on Christian origins, analysis of the interplay between theology and philosophy, become less important. It means that all such enterprises become more important, because they are at no point intellectual games or abstract speculations. They have to do with the whole of life lived in this whole real world.[1]

Ethical theology is not ethics in place of theology. During the "Death of God" movement in the sixties, there were those who sought to translate theology into ethics in such a way that it was actually replaced by ethics. William Hamilton, for instance, claimed that Bonhoeffer "has forced us to move from theology to ethics."[2] Hamilton is not saying that Bonhoeffer moves us from an overemphasis on theology to a much needed emphasis on ethics; he is saying that Bonhoeffer moves us to an abandonment of theology in exchange for ethics. Hamilton argues for the ethicizing of theology because he thinks God is really dead, and he claims Bonhoeffer as inspiration for this idea. The position taken here is very different. Bonhoeffer believed that God is alive and that talk about God is necessary. Bonhoeffer is a theologian who honors and does theology, but it is a theology intrinsically ethical at every point.

On the other hand, ethical theology as done by Bonhoeffer does not mean the swallowing up of ethics by theology. There are those who interpret Bonhoeffer in this way also, who read him as one who does only theology even when he claims to be doing ethics. It is not difficult to understand this reading of Bonhoeffer. He does give the impression at times that he is rejecting everything that has ever been understood to be ethics. Reference has already been made to the following passage.

> Whoever wishes to take up the problem of a Christian ethic must be confronted at once with a demand which is quite without parallel. He must from the outset discard as irrelevant the two questions which alone impel him to concern himself with the problem of ethics, "How can I be good?" and "How can I do good?", and instead of these he must ask the utterly and totally different question "What is the will of God?"[3]

Rather than claiming Bonhoeffer as an advocate of the substitution of ethics for theology, it is possible to read him as doing the opposite, substituting theology for ethics. This latter interpretation is easier to support.

When Bonhoeffer attempted to introduce the theology of Karl Barth to his fellow students at Union Seminary in New York, he said:

The revelation of God in Christ is not a revelation of a new morality, or new ethical values, a revelation of a new imperative, but a revelation of God's real action for mankind in history, a revelation of a new indicative. It is not a new "you ought" but a new "you are."[4]

Yet Bonhoeffer tended to stress this theme so strongly that even Barth found it a bit difficult to take. When they talked together in Bonn for the first time in July 1931, the conversation turned to ethics very quickly. Bonhoeffer wrote about it in a letter to his friend, Erwin Sutz:

We very soon came to the problem of ethics and had a long discussion. He would not make concessions to me where I expected that he would have had to. Besides the one great light in the night, he said, there were also many little lamps, so-called "relative ethical criteria"; he could not, however, make their significance and application and nature comprehensible to me—we didn't get beyond his reference to the Bible. Finally, he thought that I was making grace into a principle and killing everything else with it. Of course I disputed his first point and wanted to know why everything else should not be killed.[5]

If it is possible to interpret Bonhoeffer as abandoning theology for the sake of ethics, it is more possible to interpret him as abandoning ethics for the sake of theology. He is not the first, of course, to run this risk. Every theologian who insists on the priority of grace, or who sees legalism as the primary heresy to be attacked systematically, runs the same risk. Both Luther and Barth, the two theologians to whom Bonhoeffer was most indebted, are accused of the same thing. One could make a very long list of such people from the apostle Paul to Rudolf Bultmann. All would reject the notion that they had abandoned ethics, and would insist that they are doing a different kind of ethics from that for which their accusers are looking. Our task is to get at, as clearly as possible, the special contribution of Bonhoeffer to this broad tradition. Bonhoeffer cannot do theology and then ethics, or vice versa, nor can he substitute one for the other. He must do them together and at the same time. But as he does that, he is driven by his radical commitment to Jesus Christ to allow theology to be the noun and ethics the adjective, which is why he is more legitimately misunderstood as abandoning ethics for theology than as abandoning theology for ethics.

One way to get at the novelty of Bonhoeffer's approach, and to understand the reasons why some ethicists consider his ethics to be pre-ethics at best, is to see Bonhoeffer's work in relation to a position that is in some ways similar to his own, but that in a very important yet subtle way is exactly the opposite. The reference point for this comparison will be Donald Evans.[6]

In his investigation of "the inner dynamics of religion and morality," Evans asks the question, Which starts first, religion or morality? and concludes, largely on the basis of an Eriksonian manner of reading psychological origins, that religion and morality begin together. Later, according to Erik Erikson and Evans, both religion and morality "transcend their origin" and become distinct, religion focusing on God and morality on people.[7] The religion/morality distinction used here is parallel to, and related to although not identical to, the theology/ethics distinction. Religion and morality are "first order" matters; theology and ethics are parallel "second order" matters.

After deciding that it would be incorrect to talk about *temporal priority* of religion to morality, or vice versa, Evans asks whether one might have a *rational priority* to the other. He concludes that this is possible and decides to call that approach in which morality is rationally prior a "neo-Kantian" philosophy, and that in which religion is rationally prior an "existentialist" philosophy. Evans is clear about choosing the former.

> In this book I have been assuming that religious beliefs are implied by attitudes which are themselves justified as constituents of human fulfillment. This approach places the book within an intellectual tradition which was initiated mainly by Immanuel Kant. He broke with an approach in which we first appeal to reason and perhaps to revelation to establish truths concerning God independently of any consideration of human fulfillment and its constituents, and then ask what implications the alleged truths concerning God may have concerning human fulfillment. Instead, Kant claimed that a certain kind of respect for the moral law is essential to being a human person and then he asked what religious beliefs are presupposed by this attitude.[8]

Evans caricatures the approach against which Kant wrote. But his own leanings are very clear.

> In my overall approach, as in that of Gregory Baum, neither human beings nor God can be properly understood in abstraction from each other. Nevertheless it is true that in this book my theology (beliefs concerning God) depends to a great extent on my anthropology (beliefs concerning human nature).[9]

If Bonhoeffer had reflected on his work in this same manner, he would have been just as clear as is Evans on the intimate interrelationship of religion and morality (or theology and ethics) and would have agreed that one must be rationally prior, but would have come down, finally, on the opposite side. He would not have labeled it "existentialist," as Evans does. But Bonhoeffer's opposition to the Kantian tradition is clear and explicit and relentless. Neither God nor world can be understood in abstraction from the other. Yet theology is rationally prior to ethics. Theology is the noun, ethics the adjective. It is the Man for others who leads his followers to be for others. "The problem of Christian ethics is the realization among God's creatures of the revelational reality of God in Christ."[10]

At least two interpreters of Bonhoeffer have made use of the phrase "ethical theology." Ernst Feil has suggested that Bonhoeffer's theology is an "ethical theology" much more than it is a "dogmatic theology."[11] Benjamin Reist makes an extended statement on Bonhoeffer's ethics, using this phrase as a key term. It is said so well and coincides so closely with the theme of shaping the future that it is worth quoting at length.

> From the perspective of our discussion, the promise of Bonhoeffer's theology has to do with the development of what might be called *ethical theology* . . . . This is where Bonhoeffer was going. . . . An *ethical theology* has to do with neither the replacement of theology by ethics nor the absolutizing of the social-action syndrome. It involves, rather, the ethical intensification of *all* theological concepts. This alone responds to and corresponds with the task of claiming for the Christ a world come of age and the task of discerning in the world come of age the reality of the Christ who is the Lord. It is the way in which obedient faith and faithful obedience thinks about the reality of Christ in a world come of age. All the rich treasury of Christian thought, from (and including) the Bible forward, must be re-thought with this in mind. This is what Bonhoeffer was actually doing. . . . An ethical theology concentrates on the pressure on today of the imminent tomorrows—not the distant tomorrows, but the ones close in, in which the God who is real in Jesus Christ is immanent. This is where God is, in the world come of age as it moves on toward its imminent tomorrows. The God who is real in Jesus Christ is on the move, then. He truly transcends us, for our tomorrows are filled with only one certainty, namely, that he will be there. To discern him one must look not "up" but "forward." Obedient faith and faithful obedience knows that our todays always stand under the sign of the resurrection. For the today that was Good Friday could not contain the God who there in his weakness drew near to man, so that man even in torment could be before him.
>
> To discern the God who is real in Jesus Christ in the mist of the fast-approaching tomorrows is an ethical task. Concreteness, earthiness, humanity are its mark, and his. This is why no man can hear the gospel of Christ except through the events that conspire to constitute his own time. The theme of the ethics of the reality of Christ is therefore always comprised of the search for an ever-renewing fulfillment. The Kingdom of God is always at hand. An ethically presented eschatology replaces a mystical one. For the fulfillment of the purposes of the God who is real in Jesus Christ coincides with the liberation of the men who are commanded to be free before him.[12]

Jürgen Weissbach has already been quoted as saying that "Bonhoeffer's *Ethics* is really an expansion of the theology of the Barmen Declaration."[13]

It can also be said that the Barmen Declaration is in significant ways an expression of Bonhoeffer's ethical theology. The declaration reflects Barth more directly than it does Bonhoeffer. Yet this confession, this theological statement, was hammered out on the anvil of vital ethical issues. It was formulated specifically against the Nazi racist ideology. And it was specifically against the Nazi nature religion of blood, race, and soil that Barmen insisted that Christian faith must have its center in Jesus Christ, and nowhere else. The Barmen Declaration of 1934 was the charter document of the Confessing Church and it stands today alongside the Augsburg Confession in the hymnbook of the church of Berlin-Brandenburg as one of the historic confessions of that church. It is an example of ethical issues driving and compelling theology to be clearly attentive to those issues. It is theology that is intrinsically ethical.

Today, when Christian churches and global groupings of Christian churches are deeply involved in statements and actions on a broad spectrum of ethical issues, most notably peace and human rights issues, it is not yet clear whether leaders will have the courage and the sophistication to work in the public arena on ethical issues while retaining the church's identity as Christian. Bonhoeffer was sure that it was only as the church retained its identity as Christian that it would be able to exercise its identification with the world. For Bonhoeffer, this meant that Jesus Christ must be the radical center of its confession and its caring.

The Radical Centrality
of Jesus Christ

On the wall of the village church in Flossenbürg, near the concentration camp where Bonhoeffer was executed, there is a commemorative plaque that reads simply "Dietrich Bonhoeffer—Witness for Jesus Christ among His Brothers." It could not have been better stated, unless it had said "Sisters and Brothers." For whatever else Dietrich Bonhoeffer was, he was throughout his adult life one who asked the question about Jesus Christ and continually pointed to him as the center not only of the church's life and work, but of all creation and of all history.

To say that Jesus Christ is the center of Bonhoeffer's life and work is different from saying that Christology is its center. In his 1933 Christology lectures, Bonhoeffer says that the real question is not how, but who.[14] The how question must be asked. The church must continue to reflect on how Jesus of Nazareth comes to be the Christ of the church. Christology is done by Bonhoeffer not only in his 1933 university lectures but periodically throughout his life. Yet it is always the person Jesus Christ, rather than reflections or speculations about him, that is the radical center of Bonhoeffer's life and of his efforts toward the formulation of an ethical theology. Seen from this perspective, the continuity is overwhelming. Whether he is preaching or lecturing or exegeting biblical texts or writing about the church or God or the world or the life of discipleship or the history of the West or the nature of suffering, one seldom goes very far with Bonhoeffer without hearing that Name. In his *Ethics*, Bonhoeffer says it in many ways. The following passage is typical:

> There is earnestness neither in the idea of a pure Christianity in itself nor in the idea of man as he is in himself; there is earnestness only in the reality of God and the reality of man which became one in Jesus Christ. What is earnest and serious is not some kind of Christianity, but it is Jesus Christ himself. And in Jesus Christ there is neither radicalism nor compromise, but there is the reality of God and men. There is no Christianity in itself, for this would destroy the world; there is no man in himself, for he would exclude God. Both of these are merely ideas; only the God-Man Jesus Christ is real, and only through Him will the world be preserved until it is ripe for its end.[15]

As a rule those interpreters who recognize the radical centrality of Jesus Christ in Bonhoeffer's life and work also tend to see him pursuing an essentially consistent course. André Dumas, for instance, says that the *Ethics* of Bonhoeffer is simply an unfolding of his 1933 Christology lectures.[16] He says that the content of the *Ethics* is such that it could have been written immediately after the *Creation and Fall* lectures, also given in 1933.[17] Focusing on the radical centrality of Jesus Christ for Bonhoeffer, Dumas says that this central conviction remains unchanged throughout.[18]

Feil is another interpreter who emphasizes continuity in Bonhoeffer's life and work and who sees that continuity in Bonhoeffer's constant stress on the *cantus firmus*, namely, on Jesus Christ.[19] Not even in the prison letters is there a break, according to Feil, because the unfolding of the nonreligious Christianity formula is a spelling out of an emphasis that Bonhoeffer worked with from the beginning. Rainer Mayer also sees the radical centrality of Jesus Christ as a link that ties the earliest Bonhoeffer to the Bonhoeffer of the prison letters.[20] If one understands, writes Mayer, that for Bonhoeffer there is only one way to talk about transcendence and that is by talking about Jesus, then it becomes immediately clear that the final "this-worldly transcendence" formula in the prison letters is entirely consistent with Bonhoeffer's talk about transcendence in *Act and Being*.[21] The references that follow are not designed to prove that the radical centrality of Jesus Christ is *the* thread of continuity in Bonhoeffer, but to illustrate the claim that the emphasis is continuously present, and that it is the person of Christ, not Christ as idea or doctrine or symbol or experience, that controls Bonhoeffer's work toward an ethical theology.

In *The Communion of Saints*, Bonhoeffer defines the church in a striking phrase: "Christ existing as congregation." This book, Bonhoeffer's doctoral dissertation written at age twenty-one, is about the church. But there is no way for him to talk about the church other than by talking about Jesus Christ.

> The church is established in reality in and through Christ — not in such a way that we can think of the church without Christ himself, but he himself "is" the church. He does not represent it, for only what is not present can be represented. But in God's eyes the church is present in Christ.[22]

Clifford Green has established in great detail that for Bonhoeffer the church is understood in terms of the sociality of Christ.[23] The total impact of Bonhoeffer's early dissertation is that the conceptuality of Christ requires the conceptuality of the church. The reverse, however, is also true. There is no way to understand the communion of saints apart from Jesus Christ who exists in our midst as congregation.

Act and Being, Bonhoeffer's inaugural dissertation of 1931, is a very complex discussion of fundamental conflicts between opposing theological and philosophical orientations. The church is the solution to the act/being problem. But again, for Bonhoeffer, the church means Jesus Christ. The final section of the book deals with "Being in Adam" and "Being in Christ." The final words of the book locate the solution in Christ, and tie that solution to Bonhoeffer's emphasis on the future.

> Home is the communion of Christ, which is always "future," the present "in faith," because we are children of the future; always act, because being; always being, because act.

> Here in faith becoming a reality, there in vision perfected, this is the new creation of the new man of the future, who no longer looks back on himself but only away from himself to the revelation of God, to Christ; the man who is born out of the narrowness of the world into the breadth of Heaven, who becomes what he was or, it may be, never was: a creature of God — a child.[24]

The 1933 Christology lectures are throughout an attack on what Bonhoeffer calls liberalism or Greek thinking, and an affirmation of what he considers to be biblical or "Chalcedonian" thinking. There is repeated reference to Luther's conviction that if one wants to speak of God it is necessary to point to the man Jesus. Bonhoeffer insists with Luther that "the child in the manger is wholly God."[25] Christian ethics focuses on Jesus Christ, who is never simply a moral teacher or leader or example. Ethics that has to do with Jesus necessarily has to do also with God. Thus *Christian* ethics must be ethical *theology.*

> We may also have to come face to face with Goethe or Socrates. That is part of our culture and our ethos. But far more depends upon our confronting Christ — life or death, salvation or damnation. This cannot be known outside, but in the Church it is seen that all rests upon the sentence, "And there is salvation in no one else" (Acts 4:12). The encounter with Jesus is fundamentally different from that with Goethe or Socrates. One cannot avoid encounter with the person of Jesus because he is alive. With some care Goethe can be avoided, because he is dead.[26]

Jesus is the one on whom "everything rests." He is the center of all time and all space. And he is also there for me. "The man for others" formula of the prison letters is rooted in the *pro me* of Lutheran Christology and is present, at least in embryonic form, in the 1933 university lectures.

> It is the nature of the person of Christ to be in the centre, both spatially and temporally. The one who is present in Word, Sacrament and Church is in the centre of human existence, of history and of nature. It belongs to the structure of his person to be in the centre. When we turn the question, "Where?" back into the question, "Who?", we get the answer. Christ is the mediator as the one who exists *pro me*. That is his nature and his mode of existence. In three ways, he is in the centre: in being there for men, in being there for history, in being there for nature.[27]

Perhaps more than any theologian in the history of the church Bonhoeffer combines a cosmic Colossians-style Christology with a relentless emphasis on the man Jesus of Nazareth who is there-for-others. He sees the fatal flaw of liberalism to be its docetic tendency to separate Jesus from the Christ,[28] and to move away from the man Jesus toward universal moral and religious norms and values. Ebionitism, says Bonhoeffer, "is superior to docetic liberalism, because it fixes its eyes upon the specific Jesus, the real man."[29] With Luther and against Calvin, Bonhoeffer insists that the finite (whether Jesus of Nazareth, or the bread and wine of the sacrament, or the here-and-now of a moral decision) is capable of bearing the infinite.[30] With Luther, Bonhoeffer says, "I do not know who the man Jesus Christ is unless I can at the same time say, 'Jesus Christ is God'; and I do not know who the God Jesus Christ is, unless I can at the same time say, 'Jesus Christ is man.' "[31]

Bonhoeffer's work on Genesis 1—3, *Creation and Fall*, also done in 1933, coincided with the initial impact of Adolf Hitler on Germany. The radical centrality of Jesus Christ for Bonhoeffer is again clear. It is not difficult to read between the lines an intense involvement with what was happening in Germany. He writes: "But the church is naturally in tumult when these children of the world that has passed away lay claim to the church, to the new, for themselves."[32] Yet his exposition of these chapters in Genesis is throughout an ethical theology with Jesus Christ at the center. He is almost embarrassingly clear in his claim that Genesis 1—3 can be read only *sub specie Christi*.[33] He says that the creation story must be read in the church in the first place *from* Christ and only then as leading to Christ. He is clear in his rejection of natural theology.[34] There is nothing in the creation which makes us recognize the creator. It is only the Word.[35] Christ is for Bonhoeffer, as for Luther and Barth, so much the radical center that there is no way to move toward God or toward the world other than through him. There is, however, the possibility and necessity of moving from him to God and to the world. "We do not have God in any way except in his name. This is true today as well: 'Jesus Christ' is the name of God. This is highly anthropomorphic and highly objective at the same time."[36] The final section of the lectures on Genesis 1—3 connects the tree of life with the cross of Christ and moves the reader in the direction of the hope of the resurrection and toward the responsible shaping of the future.

> Christ on the Cross, the murdered Son of God, is the end of the story of Cain, and thus the actual end of the story. This is the last desperate storming of the gate of paradise. And under the flaming sword, under the cross, mankind dies. But Christ lives. The stem of the Cross becomes the staff of life, and in the midst of the world life is set up anew upon the cursed ground. . . . What a strange tree of life, this tree on which God himself must suffer and die—but it is in fact the Kingdom of Life and of the Resurrection given again by God in grace; it is the opened door of imperishable hope, of waiting and of patience. The tree of life, the cross of Christ, the middle of the fallen and preserved world of God, for us that is the end of the story of paradise.[37]

The radical centrality of Jesus Christ in the ethical theology of Bonhoeffer is just as clear in *The Cost of Discipleship*, based on work done originally during the Finkenwalde period. The remarkable thing about Bonhoeffer's interpretation of the Sermon on the Mount is that he refuses to allow the words of Jesus to be detached from his person, set adrift in the abstractions of ethical discourse. Some of the passages are so christocentric that it may sound to someone looking for moral advice as though Bonhoeffer is in fact abandoning ethics for theology. When commenting on the Beatitudes, Bonhoeffer says that the sentence "Blessed are the poor" (Luke) or "Blessed are the poor in spirit" (Matthew) has nothing to do with a particular kind of behavior. The point of the phrase is rather the call and promise of Jesus alone.[38] Again, he says that the point is not simply to seek goodness and justice and truth for their own sake and to suffer for them. The point is that everything depends on loyal obedience to Jesus who is the source and spring of all goodness and justice and truth.[39] In case some reader is still not clear about it, he repeats:

> Again it is no universal law. Rather is it the exact opposite of all legality. It is nothing else than bondage to Jesus Christ alone, completely breaking through every programme, every ideal, every set of laws. No other significance is possible, since Jesus is the only significance. Beside Jesus nothing has any significance. He alone matters.[40]

He even says that it is wrong to speak about "the Christian life." We should speak rather of Christ's living in us.[41] Discipleship is Bonhoeffer's theme in this exposition of the Sermon on the Mount, and he hammers away relentlessly on the fact that discipleship means Jesus Christ.

> Discipleship means adherence to Christ, and, because Christ is the object of that adherence, it must take the form of discipleship. An abstract Christology, a doctrinal system, a general religious knowledge on the subject of grace or on the forgiveness of sins, render discipleship superfluous, and in fact they positively exclude any idea of discipleship whatever, and are essentially inimical to the whole conception of following Christ. With an abstract idea, it is possible to enter into a relation of formal knowledge, to become enthusiastic about it, and perhaps even to put it into practice; but it can never be followed in personal obedience. Christianity without the living Christ is inevitably Christianity without discipleship, and Christianity without discipleship is always Christianity without Christ.[42]

And again:

> The life of discipleship can only be maintained so long as nothing is allowed to come between Christ and ourselves — neither the law, nor personal piety, nor even the world. The disciple always looks only to his master, never to Christ *and* the law, Christ *and* religion, Christ *and* the world. He avoids all such notions like the plague.[43]

It is a mistake to read this passage, and others similar to it in *The Cost of Discipleship*, as indicating a negative attitude toward the world, replaced later by a robust affirmation of the world. Even in the prison letters Bonhoeffer rejects the "world" insofar as it opposes Christ and rejects also the idea that Christ and the world are two independent but related sources for truth and appropriate behavior. The point is that in no case is the radical centrality of Jesus Christ to be compromised. The *emphasis* on church in *The Cost of Discipleship* and on world in the prison letters is to be sure a shift in emphasis. But there is no rejection in the prison letters of the centrality of Christ, so prominent in *The Cost of Discipleship*. That centrality remains. This is why, although Bonhoeffer in Tegel prison sees certain "dangers" in *The Cost of Discipleship*, he still "stands by" it.[44] The identification of Christ with the church is as strong here as it is in *The Communion of Saints*. Again, he says, "Christ is the Church."[45] But that means that he suffers in his members for the world.[46] The Tegel theme of "participating in the sufferings of God in the secular life"[47] is already present, at least in embryonic form, in *The Cost of Discipleship*.

Life Together, also from the Finkenwalde period, is equally christocentric. The greatest danger to Christian community, that which poisons it at its very root, is "the danger of confusing Christian brotherhood with some wishful idea of religious fellowship."[48] The contrast between "Christian" and "religious" is every bit as sharp and as deep as it is in the "non-religious Christianity" formula of the prison letters. "Christianity means community through Jesus Christ and in Jesus Christ. No Christian community is more or less than this."[49] Everything in this book follows from this commitment to the radical centrality of Jesus Christ. It leads Bonhoeffer in many directions, for instance, to the sharp distinction (though not separation) between sin and sickness, confession and counseling.

> It is not experience of life but experience of the Cross that makes one a worthy hearer of confessions. The most experienced psychologist or observer of human nature knows infinitely less of the human heart than the simplest Christian who lives beneath the Cross of Jesus. The greatest psychological insight, ability, and experience cannot grasp this one thing: what sin is. . . . In the presence of a psychiatrist I can only be a sick man; in the presence of a Christian brother I can dare to be a sinner. . . . It is not lack of psychological knowledge but lack of love for the crucified Jesus Christ that makes us so poor and inefficient in brotherly confession.[50]

Bonhoeffer was describing and explaining the practice of "brotherly confession" which was a part of the Finkenwalde experiment. Confession makes no sense unless one understands sin and the forgiveness of sin declared in the name of Jesus.

Temptation, Bonhoeffer's exposition of the temptation of Adam in comparison with and in contrast to the story of the temptation of Christ, also evidences the radical centrality of Jesus Christ in Bonhoeffer's attempt to formulate an ethical theology. The key sentence states that all temptation is temptation in Jesus Christ and all victory is victory in Jesus Christ.[51] The position is so stark that it is again clear why someone looking for a universal ethical system would find the material too theological. The following passage is typical:

> The Bible is not like a book of edification, telling us many stories of men's temptations and their overcoming. To be precise, the Bible tells only two temptation stories, the temptation of the first man and the temptation of Christ, that is the temptation which led to man's fall, and the temptation which led to Satan's fall. All other temptations in human history have to do with these two stories of temptation. Either we are tempted in Adam or we are tempted in Christ. Either the Adam in me is tempted — in which case we fall. Or the Christ in us is tempted — in which case Satan is bound to fall.[52]

Not to be missed is the very nice shift from first person singular to first person plural in the last two sentences. It is consistent with Bonhoeffer's conviction that true community is found in Jesus Christ, and in him alone. "In Adam" one is alone. "In Christ" one is in community.

Jesus Christ as center continues on into the *Ethics* and the prison letters. There will be opportunity in the following pages to make that clear. At the moment, it is necessary only to repeat that for Bonhoeffer it is not Christology, but Jesus Christ himself who is the radical center of all of creation and all of history, and therefore the radical center of his attempt to formulate an ethical theology.

> The ancient Church meditated on the question of Christ for several centuries. It imprisoned reason in obedience to Jesus Christ, and in harsh, conflicting sentences gave living witness to the mystery of the person of Jesus Christ. . . . The Christology of the ancient Church really arose at the cradle of Bethlehem, and the brightness of Christmas lies on its weather-beaten face.[53]

Like Luther, Bonhoeffer wants nothing to do with the terrible invisibility of a far-away God. God is for him always the God buried deep in the flesh of Jesus of Nazareth, and that conviction has everything to do with what Bonhoeffer's ethical theology is about.[54]

In his criticism of American theology, Bonhoeffer says that God founded his church beyond religion and beyond ethics.[55] The problem with American theology, according to Bonhoeffer at that time, was that Christianity had been transformed into religion and ethics. The problem was precisely that American theology had failed to make Jesus Christ the center of its work. When Jesus Christ becomes the center, then it is necessary to begin

to work in a "non-religious" way. This fact is expressed in many ways by
Bonhoeffer. One of the most striking and clear ways is in his total rejection
of what he calls two-sphere thinking.

The Rejection of Two-Sphere Thinking

The passage where Bonhoeffer's work toward an ethical theology comes
most clearly into focus is the section in the *Ethics* entitled "Thinking in
Terms of Two Spheres." Anyone coming to the *Ethics* for the first time
could not do better than to begin with a careful reading of that section.
Jesus Christ as radical center of time and space leads Bonhoeffer into direct
conflict with an entire way of thinking about God and world which many
Christians take to be identical to Christianity itself. But it is a way of thinking that must be rejected if one is going to allow Jesus Christ to be the
center of life. The passage reads, in part, as follows:

> In Jesus Christ the reality of God entered into the reality of this world. The
> place where the answer is given, both to the question concerning the reality
> of God and to the question concerning the reality of the world, is designated
> solely and alone by the name Jesus Christ. God and the world are comprised
> in this name. In Him all things consist (Colossians 1:17). Henceforward one
> can speak neither of God nor of the world without speaking of Jesus
> Christ. . . .
>
> In Christ we are offered the possibility of partaking in the reality of God
> and in the reality of the world, but not in the one without the other. The real-
> ity of God discloses itself only by setting me entirely in the reality of the
> world, and when I encounter the reality of the world it is always already sus-
> tained, accepted and reconciled in the reality of God. This is the inner mean-
> ing of the revelation of God in the man Jesus Christ. Christian ethics enquires
> about the realization in our world of this divine and cosmic reality which is
> given in Christ. . . . Its purpose is, therefore, participation in the reality of
> God and of the world in Jesus Christ today, and this participation must be
> such that I never experience the reality of God without the reality of the
> world or the reality of the world without the reality of God. . . .
>
> As soon as we try to advance along this path, our way is blocked by the
> colossal obstacle of a large part of traditional Christian ethical thought. Since
> the beginnings of Christian ethics after the times of the New Testament the
> main underlying conception in ethical thought, and the one which con-
> sciously or unconsciously has determined its whole course, has been the con-
> ception of a juxtaposition and conflict of two spheres, the one divine, holy,
> supernatural and Christian, and the other worldly, profane, natural, and un-
> Christian. . . .
>
> It may be difficult to break the spell of this thinking in terms of two
> spheres, but it is nevertheless quite certain that it is in profound contradiction
> to the thought of the Bible and to the thought of the Reformation, and that
> consequently it aims wide of reality. There are not two realities, but only one

reality, and that is the reality of God, which has become manifest in Christ in the reality of the world. Sharing in Christ we stand at once in both the reality of God and the reality of the world.[56]

The rejection of two-sphere thinking is at the heart of Bonhoeffer's ethical theology. But that rejection is a direct result of the affirmation of Jesus Christ as radical center of space and time. The rejection is for the sake of and because of the affirmation. Being clear about what one rejects can give greater freedom in the elaboration of what one affirms. Jesus rejected the Pharisaic teaching about the law in order to make clear his own freedom in relation to the law. Paul fought the Judaizers in order to clarify his understanding of the gospel. Luther rejected works-righteousness in order to affirm justification by grace alone through faith. Bultmann rejected nineteenth-century historicism in order to affirm the *kerygma*. Bonhoeffer rejected two-sphere thinking in order to affirm Jesus Christ as radical center of time and space.

The phrase "two-sphere thinking" is Bonhoeffer's own, but very few people who have been in the church for any length of time will fail to recognize what he is talking about, whether or not they agree that it should be rejected. Two-sphere thinking has taken innumerable forms in the church's history, and Bonhoeffer describes many of them. The basic content of this conceptuality is, however, extremely simple and clear. Two-sphere thinking defines God in terms of separation from world. To be "godly" is by definition to do everything in one's power to avoid being "worldly." To be "worldly" is by definition to be "ungodly." Two-sphere thinking thus leaves a person with the alternative of seeking God and abandoning the world, or of embracing the world and abandoning God. Bonhoeffer is convinced that the church throughout its history has been plagued by variations of this kind of thinking, and that both the church's theology and its ethics have been adversely affected by it. He rejects two-sphere thinking, however, not because he believes that its effects are bad or because it offends his philosophical sensitivities, but because he believes it to be directly contrary to the central Christian affirmation that God and the world come together in Jesus Christ.

It sounds as though Bonhoeffer's ethical theology could be described as incarnational. Such a designation would not be inaccurate, but it would be inadequate. Incarnational theologies can very easily be set adrift from the person of Jesus Christ, using "incarnation" merely as an interpretive principle. In the *Ethics*, Bonhoeffer speaks repeatedly of Jesus Christ as "incarnate, crucified, and risen." Incarnation as a principle will not do for Bonhoeffer. His insistence throughout is that God and world come together in the babe in the crib and the man on the cross. Not Christology, not even incarnation, but Jesus Christ himself requires the rejection of two-sphere thinking.

Bonhoeffer's contribution does not lie in the fact that he is the first to have seen that God and world come together in Jesus Christ. It lies in the thoroughness with which he affirms it and the consistency with which he follows through on its implications. There are some surprising turns in his line of argument. It is obvious that two-sphere thinking can lead to a separation of the Christian from the world. But it can lead to the exact opposite, an uncritical embracing of the world with no awareness of God whatever.[57] Bonhoeffer uses the medieval monk and the modern Protestant secularist as typifying these two possibilities.

> The whole of medieval history is centered upon the theme of the predominance of the spiritual sphere over the secular sphere . . . and the modern age is characterized by an ever increasing independence of the secular in its relations with the spiritual. So long as Christ and the world are conceived as two opposing and mutually repellent spheres, man will be left in the following dilemma: he abandons reality as a whole, and places himself in one or other of the two spheres. He seeks Christ without the world, or he seeks the world without Christ. In either case he is deceiving himself. Or else he tries to stand in both spaces at once and thereby becomes the man of eternal conflict, the kind of man who emerged in the period after the Reformation and who has repeatedly set himself up as representing the only form of Christian existence which is in accord with reality.[58]

Two-sphere thinking leads a person inevitably, Bonhoeffer thinks, to seek God without the world or the world without God or, on the other hand, to live as a schizophrenic, a person of eternal conflict, seeking God and the world at the same time even though the person thinks that the two are by definition mutually exclusive.

Although his sharp rejection of two-sphere thinking sounds at times as though he is moving into religious pantheism or philosophical monism, Bonhoeffer checks himself repeatedly against being interpreted in this way. God and world come together in Jesus Christ, but God does not become world and world does not become God. Mayer has a felicitous term for what Bonhoeffer is doing. He calls it "unity in duality."[59] The unity of God-and-world-together-in-Christ demands and embraces a duality of God and world as distinguishable entities. The term does not make a logical claim, as do terms such as "paradox" or "coincidence of opposites," but an ontological one. It does not have to do with how sentences fit or do not fit together. The claim has to do, as we shall see in the next section, with what

Bonhoeffer thinks is actually the case, the "real." It has to do with the christological claim about one person but two natures which are "without confusion and yet distinct," in the words of the Chalcedonian formula. Bonhoeffer uses the Chalcedonian formula, in fact, in attempting to clarify his relating of the *cantus firmus* to the counterpoint, in the prison letter of 20 May 1944.[60]

If "two-sphere thinking" has dominated Christian theology and ethics for centuries, as Bonhoeffer claims, and if it must be rejected in order to embrace a thoroughly Chalcedonian way of thinking, then a great many theological and ethical formulations have to be recast. Chapter 2 of this study will be devoted to some of Bonhoeffer's attempts to recast these traditional formulations. At this point it must suffice to look briefly at what the move from two-sphere thinking to Chalcedonian thinking implies in just one area of Bonhoeffer's interest, namely, the understanding of the church.

Orthodox Lutheran and Reformed ecclesiology distinguishes between the church invisible and the church visible. The distinction is a dichotomy based on what Bonhoeffer calls two-sphere thinking. It assumes that the invisible church is the true and real church, that it is in the "spiritual realm," known only to the mind of God. The visible church is the congregation on the corner, the people whose names are on the membership rolls, the people who come to worship and pray, who serve on boards and committees, who sing in the choir. The two are related in that the visible congregation is a reflection and representation of the invisible reality.

It is obviously necessary to find some way to distinguish between the church "properly speaking" and the church "improperly speaking." Not every person whose name is on the membership roll of a congregation is necessarily a member of the Body of Christ. The problem, however, is that the invisible/visible dichotomy purchases this distinction at too high a price. Using pure Platonic categories, it floats the "real" church out into the "spiritual realm" and demeans the local congregation and clusters of congregations by encouraging the use of pejorative designations such as "the institutional church." Bonhoeffer was convinced, on biblical and confessional grounds, that the local congregation *is* the true and real church. "Christ exists as congregation!"[61] The church is not an ideal to strive after but a reality in which to participate.[62] He agreed with the Augsburg Confession (Article 7) that the church *is* the people who gather around Word and Sacrament.

The necessary distinction, then, still has to be made, and it can be made in a number of ways. In *The Cost of Discipleship* Bonhoeffer uses "visible" and "hidden" rather than "visible" and "invisible." The shift may seem overly subtle, even arbitrary. But it is of very decisive importance. It is the difference between a Chalcedonian understanding of the Body of Christ and an understanding of the church that equates reality with invisibility. He makes the distinction in his exposition of the juxtaposition of chapters 5 and 6 of Matthew. He writes:

> "Let your light so shine" . . . and yet: Take care that you hide it! There is a pointed contrast between chapters 5 and 6. That which is visible must also be hidden. . . . precisely because the Christian life is of its very nature extraordinary, it is at the same time ordinary, natural, and *hidden*. If not, it is not the Christian life at all, it is not obedience to the will of Jesus Christ.[63]

The categories are similar to Luther's *Deus revelatus* (God revealed) and *Deus absconditus* (God hidden). God is always both, always both at the same time. It is again an implication of Chalcedonian thinking as over against two-sphere thinking. Jesus is entirely visible, haveable, graspable. Yet the fact that he is the Christ is "hidden," recognized only by eyes of faith. The bread and the wine of the sacrament are entirely visible. There is nothing at all invisible about them. They are seen and smelled and tasted. But it is precisely "in, with, and under" this visible bread and wine that the one who eats and drinks receives the hidden body and blood of Christ. There are not two realities related to one another as spirit to matter, or as invisible to visible. There is one reality, but it is a unity-in-duality, both visible and hidden at the same time, "without confusion and yet distinct."

Nowhere does Bonhoeffer employ the visible/invisible dichotomy as a key to understanding anything. His rejection of two-sphere thinking is total. This quite clearly means the rejection of idealism (whether Platonic or Kantian), that vision which focuses on "spiritual and unseen realities," both religious and moral. It also means, however, the rejection of positivism, that cluster of perspectives that reduces reality to observed data, apart from their ground in God. The ethical concomitant of idealism is moral absolutism, the ethics of timeless rights and wrongs. The ethical concomitant of positivism is raw situationism, the ethics of episodic responses to changing circumstances. Bonhoeffer rejects them both. Although he fights idealistic ethics more energetically, his occasional checks against the ethics of positivism are crisp and clear. For example:

> There is a way of basing ethics upon the concept of reality which differs entirely from the Christian way. This is the positive and empirical approach, which aims at the entire elimination from ethics of the concept of norms and standards because it regards this concept as being merely the idealization of

factual and practically expedient attitudes. . . . This conception is undoubtedly superior to the idealist conception in that it is "closer to reality." Good
does not consist here in an impossible "realization" of what is unreal, the
realization of ethical ideas. It is reality itself that teaches what is good. The
only question is whether the reality that is intended here is capable of satisfy-
ing this demand. It now transpires that the concept of reality which underlies
the positivistic ethic is the meretricious concept of the empirically verifiable,
which implies denial of the origin of this reality and the ultimate reality, in
God. . . . [A]ll it demands is complete surrender to the contingent, the casual,
the adventitious and the momentarily expedient, because it fails to recognize
the ultimate reality and because in this way it destroys and abandons the
unity of good.[64]

Bonhoeffer's task of formulating ethical theology is focused on his affirmation of the radical centrality of Jesus Christ. Since this name brings God
and world together, and since God and world together in Christ is what
constitutes reality, it follows that every expression of two-sphere thinking
must be rejected. That means the rejection of both moral absolutism and
raw situationism. Bonhoeffer is interested in constructing an ethics that
will take very seriously what actually is the case, what is real. As he struggles with this project, he coins the phrase "reality as the sacrament of the
ethical."

Reality as the Sacrament
of the Ethical

Bonhoeffer's Use of the Phrase

To anyone who tends to think in terms of two spheres, the phrase "sacrament of the ethical" sounds as strange as do some of Bonhoeffer's later formulations, such as "holy worldliness" or "this-worldly transcendence." It
seems incongruous to place the words "sacrament" and "ethical" together.
"Sacrament" refers to a purely gracious act of God. "Ethical" refers to a
purely human act. "Sacrament of the ethical" is a surprising, even a
strange, phrase. It is not unusual to inquire about the ethical implications
of the sacrament. One can move rather easily, for instance, from the fact
that God uses water for a holy purpose in baptism to the conclusion that
we should regard the stewardship of the earth's water as an unqualified
moral obligation. It is also not unusual to use the word "sacrament"
metaphorically, to speak of a "sacramental universe," as some Anglican and
Orthodox theologians do. Ethical impulses follow, of course, from such
talk. Or, it is not unusual to refer to God's gracious act in the sacrament
as motivation for ethical action. God demonstrates his love for us uncondi-

tionally; we ought to do the same toward others. Bonhoeffer is doing something quite different from any of these attempts to relate the sacrament and the ethical. He is struggling to formulate an ethical theology based on God and world together in Christ. The phrase "reality as the sacrament of the ethical" is one of the most creative formulations to emerge from this struggle.

The phrase begins to make sense when one realizes that the new question that Bonhoeffer is asking is pressed upon him by his embracing Jesus Christ as the center of all creation and of all history, and by the thoroughgoing rejection of two-sphere thinking which follows directly from it. What seems incongruous and strange to people who think in terms of two spheres seems so obvious and natural to Bonhoeffer that these kinds of juxtapositions flow from his pen quite effortlessly. He writes to Bethge:

> But I feel how my resistance to everything "religious" grows. Often as far as an instinctive revulsion, which is certainly not good. I am not religious by nature. But I always have to be thinking of God and of Christ, and I set great store by genuineness, life, freedom, and compassion.[65]

The sequence of the two sentences "I am not religious by nature" and "I always have to be thinking of God and of Christ" seems to be incongruous to any "religious" person. How can he be not religious and at the same time always thinking of God? The answer, as we have seen, is that for Bonhoeffer Jesus Christ means precisely the rejection of two-sphere, or "religious," thinking. It is not that there is a causal relationship between the two factors in the quotation. The one does not necessitate the other. It is rather that the two factors are, for Bonhoeffer, completely and totally congruent. The confession of Christ is the confession of God and the world together, which is the opposite of the "religious" claim that God and world are known by their separation from one another. Of course, all religious people do make a connection between God and world, but the connection is necessitated by the separation, and the connecting of these two separated entities is precisely what religion is about.

Also remarkable about the statement is what follows: "and I set great store by genuineness, life, freedom, and compassion." His always having to be thinking about God is specifically and at the same time also setting great store by these human qualities. The two are totally congruent, not because of any religious or moral connection, but because of the congruence of God and world in Christ. There is no translation necessary, no spelling out of implications, no deduction from general principles, no casuistic application of timeless norms to cases, no move from theology to ethics. The radical centrality of Jesus Christ means that world and God have not something, but everything to do with one another. The phrase "reality as the sacrament of the ethical" is one way in which Bonhoeffer seeks to capture that conviction. It is a particularly crisp phrase which he unfortunately uses only a few times. One occasion is in August 1932, in a letter to Sutz.

> Basically it all hangs on the problem of ethics, that is, specifically on the question of the possibility of the proclamation of the concrete command through the church. And it seems to me a real lacuna in Brunner's ethic that he does not bring this question to the center of his discussion. . . . It seems to me that for theological thought this is the first question and the starting point of everything else. Brunner simply does not talk about the church very much, and in the whole book there is very little about what it means to the church that it can or cannot preach the concrete command. The big question is the problem of concretion in the proclamation, and this is what constantly bothers me. It is simply not enough, it is even false, to say that the principle of the concretion can only be the Holy Spirit itself, as a number of students were always saying in my seminar. The concretion of the proclamation of grace is certainly the sacrament. But what is the sacrament of the ethical, of the command? About this we have to speak when we see one another.[66]

The phrase occurs in this letter as a question, but it is clear that the formulation was on his mind during those weeks.

In a paper read on 26 July 1932 to a youth peace conference in Czechoslovakia, he worked through it in some detail. The title of the speech was "A Theological Basis for the World Alliance?"[67] He began by asserting that "there is still no theology of the ecumenical movement." The emphasis was upon practical work and it was very common to hear people in ecumenical circles say, "Thank God we don't have to bother about theology here. We are at last free from those problems which so hamper Christian action." Bonhoeffer insists that ecumenical thought has become powerless and meaningless because of the political upsurge of nationalism, but that this problem cannot be combated by Christian action alone. Theology is required. So he begins to ask basic theological questions, as basic as "What is Christianity?" Remarkable, unless one understands Bonhoeffer, is the fact that he asks those theological questions in a thoroughly ethical way. He addresses theological questions by asking what the state, business, and social life have to do with Christianity. His response to those questions is that "the Church as the one community of the Lord Jesus Christ who is Lord of the world has the commission to say his word to the whole world. The territory of the one church of Christ is the whole world . . . it is not a holy, sacred part of the world which belongs to Christ but the whole

world." The exclusivity of the name and the inclusivity of the claim are as integral to one another here in 1932 as they are in the *Ethics*. The latter passage reads: "The more exclusively we acknowledge and confess Christ as our Lord, the more fully the wide range of His dominion will be disclosed to us."[68]

The stress on the "concrete command," which later becomes a dominant theme in the *Ethics*, is also already present in 1932 in this address and in the letter to Sutz. The question that Bonhoeffer asks is how can the gospel and how can the commandment of the church be preached with authority, that is, in quite concrete form. The commandment must be definite and it must be concrete or else it is not God's commandment. The word of the church must encounter the world in all its present realities from the deepest knowledge of the world if it is to be authoritative. The command of God can never come from timeless universalizable truth imposed on actual situations. Because God and world are together in Christ, the command of God must come out of the reality of the situation, and this requires that the church know something about those situations of which it speaks. Otherwise, it cannot speak with any authority. It is obvious, however, that the church cannot know everything about any situation. It is faced, then, with two possibilities. The first is to evade the situation and turn to general principles, making grand demands for love and peace, fatuous declarations about how the world should solve its problems by tomorrow afternoon. The second option is to take as serious a look at the data as possible and then, in spite of all the risks and uncertainties, to act. Bonhoeffer flatly rejects the first option of moving to general principles. Where it cannot speak concretely, the church must keep a qualified and intentional silence. When it does speak it must dare to put the commandment concretely. The key is located once again in Jesus Christ, this time in the reality of Christ present in his church in the forgiveness of sins. In every case, we have the choice of exercising a qualified silence or of speaking concretely. When we speak concretely we know that we do so without total knowledge or complete information. The reality that makes the concrete command possible in spite of that fact is the forgiveness of sins.

> In so doing the church will recognize that it is blaspheming the name of God, erring and sinning, but it may speak thus in faith in the promise of the forgiveness of sins which applies also to the church. Thus the preaching of the commandment is grounded in the preaching of the forgiveness of sins. The church cannot command without itself standing in faith in the forgiveness of sins and without indicating this in its preaching of the forgiveness of sins to

all those whom it commands. The preaching of the forgiveness of sins is the guarantee of the validity of the preaching of the commandment.[69]

Bonhoeffer then goes on to say that the forgiveness of sins is grounded in the sacrament, that is, "bound up with water, wine, and bread." At this point in the lecture comes the comment about reality as the sacrament of the command.

> What the sacrament is for the preaching of the Gospel, the knowledge of firm reality is for the preaching of the sacrament. *Reality is the sacrament of command.* Just as the sacraments of Baptism and Communion are the sole forms of the first reality of creation in this age, and just as they are sacraments because of this their relation to the original creation, so the "ethical sacrament" of reality is to be described as a sacrament only insofar as this reality is itself wholly grounded in its relationship to the reality of creation. Thus just as the fallen world and fallen reality only exist in their relationship to the created world and created reality, so the commandment rests on the forgiveness of sins.[70]

Reflecting within the categories of law and gospel, Bonhoeffer sees that there is something wrong about a theology that insists that the gospel or grace be communicated through empirical reality, namely, the water and the bread and the wine, and that then casts the law or the command into the timelessness of the nonempirical ideal. Because Bonhoeffer's ethical theology is grounded in the incarnate, crucified, and risen Christ, because for him God and world come together in Jesus Christ, there must be a sacrament for the command as there is a sacrament for the promise, and that sacrament of the command is reality.

Implications for the Is/Ought Problem

"Reality as the sacrament of the command" is a piece of ethical *theology*. It is statement about the sacraments. But because it is *ethical* theology, it is also a statement about decision making. The meanings that flow from the formula bear directly on some classic issues in philosophical and theological ethics. One such issue is the relation of the "is" to the "ought."[71]

Bonhoeffer was aware of the implications of what he was doing even at the time he wrote *The Communion of Saints*. There he wrote, "In the sphere of Christian ethics it is not what ought to be that effects what is, but what is that effects what ought to be."[72] The sentence is so remarkable because it is so clearly and flatly stated. Bonhoeffer is opposing conventional wisdom. One of the most sacred assumptions of ethicists along a very broad spectrum of positions is that it is impossible to derive an "ought" from an "is." The dictum is virtually axiomatic among ethicists, but its classic formulation is often attributed to G. E. Moore. Moore was of the opinion that ethical norms are "simple," that is, he thought that they are intuitively grasped and that they are undifferentiated. "Good," for instance, has the quality of "yellow." One simply recognizes something that is yellow as being yellow. One does not collect data on it and then arrive by induction at the conclusion that something having these qualities also has a high probability of being yellow. The same pertains to the good. It is intuitively grasped and is undifferentiated. One does not do research and collect observations in order to arrive from a data base at a more probable understanding of the good. One simply knows what the good is, and the good that one knows is simple, that is, it is neither complex nor ambiguous. One does not derive an "ought" from an "is." One moves rather from the "ought" that one knows to the "is" to which that "ought" must be applied.

This movement from the "ought" to the "is" is characteristic of all ethical deontology and of all ethical intuitionism. The movement from "ought" to "is," or from norm to case, or from rule to situation, rests philosophically on the idealist tradition that sees the true, the good, and the beautiful as timeless ideas of which temporal phenomena can be only shadows or copies or representations. The ethical dictum that one cannot derive an "ought" from an "is" has its philosophical concomitant in Lessing's statement, quoted so significantly by Kierkegaard, that it is impossible to derive eternal truths from historical facts. The argument in ethics parallels the realist/nominalist controversy in medieval philosophy and the deduction/induction distinction in logic. Theologically, it has to do with the location of God. If God and the good are somehow coordinated, and if God is known by his separation from the world, then the good will also be located in the nonempirical and the task of ethics will be to work toward some application of the nonempirical (timeless) good to each new empirical (temporal) situation. For this mode of reflection (another manifestation of two-sphere thinking) it is as abhorrent to attempt to move from an "is" to an "ought" as it would be to move from a contingent historical fact to a universal truth.

Bonhoeffer places himself squarely against this entire formidable tradition. Nonempirical ethics is rejected along with two-sphere thinking because of the radical centrality of the incarnate, crucified, and risen Christ. Theologically, the Christian moves from the contingent historical fact of Jesus, who was born "when Quirinius was governor of Syria" and who suffered "under Pontius Pilate" to the universal truth that the only true God is the God who raised Jesus from the dead. Ethically, the Christian moves from the indicative of God's act in Christ to the imperative of discipleship to the risen Christ, from this "is" to this "ought."

This is why it is not at all strange for Bonhoeffer to say that "God is in facts," strange as that may sound to many "religious" people. The passage reads: "Whatever weaknesses, miscalculations and guilt there is in what precedes the facts, God is in the facts themselves."[73] Bonhoeffer does not mean that God is in the facts in some metaphorical sense. He does mean that God is "in" the facts, just as and because God is "in" the flesh of Jesus of Nazareth, and the body and blood of Jesus is "in" (and "with" and "under") the bread and wine of the sacrament. The Christian believes that this is really the case, that it is what is real. Reality, then, has everything to do with "facts," and the "is" has everything to do with the "ought." This reality serves as the sacrament of the ethical.

That God is in the facts means that *God* is in the facts. Not to recognize that is as wide of reality as not to recognize that God is in the *facts*. Bonhoeffer covers both misinterpretations with allusions to Don Quixote and Sancho Panza. He read *Don Quixote* in Spanish while a vicar in Barcelona and the power of these figures stayed with him the rest of his life. In a letter to Bethge on 21 February 1944, Bonhoeffer talks about Don Quixote as "the symbol of resistance carried to the point of absurdity, even lunacy" and of Sancho Panza as "the type of complacent and artful accommodation to things as they are."[74] Don Quixote is the idealist, Sancho Panza is the positivist. Or, as Heinrich Ott puts it: "Don Quixote and Sancho Panza both have an unreal attitude to reality. The former, 'in theoretical fantasy,' passes by reality, while the latter on the other hand accepts at once as the real what is in a pedestrian sense 'given.' "[75] Bonhoeffer is clear in defining his position against both of these aberrations. Both idealism and positivism are canceled out when one brings God and the world together in Jesus Christ. In the letter of 21 February 1944, Bonhoeffer further refines his conviction that God is "in the facts."

> I think we must arise to the great demands that are made on us personally, and yet at the same time fulfill the common place and necessary tasks of daily life. We must confront fate — to me the neuter gender of the word "fate" [*Schicksal*] is significant — as resolutely as we submit to it at the right time. One can speak of "guidance" only on the other side of that twofold process, with God meeting us no longer as "Thou," but also "disguised" in the "It"; so in the last resort my question is how we are to find the "Thou" in this "It" (i.e., fate), or, in other words, how does "fate" really become "guidance"? It is therefore impossible to define the boundary between resistance and sub-

mission on abstract principles; but both of them must exist, and both must be practiced. Faith demands this elasticity of behavior. Only so can we stand our ground in each situation as it arises, and turn it to gain.[76]

When Bonhoeffer talks about finding the "Thou" in the "It," he is saying something parallel to his comment that "God is in the facts."

It is not that all of this is clear even to himself. It is not that it yields automatically a by-the-numbers ethical methodology. It is in the last resort a question. Yet that question may be more important for the church today than many answers currently available. If everything about finding the "Thou" in the "It" is not entirely clear, the emphasis is at least consistent. With all of his remarkable emphasis upon the person and specifically upon person-to-person sociality, which will be explored in the next section on relationality and responsibility, Bonhoeffer never makes the mistake of attempting to abstract personal life from material existence. From the creation of all things to the resurrection of the physical body, Bonhoeffer knows that throughout the full range of Christian doctrine there is the repeated assertion that we are creatures of the earth as well as creatures of God, that the earth is our mother as God is our Father.[77] God in the flesh of Jesus of Nazareth means that the "Thou" can never be construed apart from the "It." God can never be known apart from his world. Reality including both the "It" and the "Thou" is the sacrament of the ethical.

Reality as the sacrament of the ethical continues to be methodologically constitutive of Bonhoeffer's ethical theology in the *Ethics*. Although the full phrase does not occur in the *Ethics*, the term "reality" is so central that many interpreters have used the word in the titles of their books on Bonhoeffer, designating it as a key category for unlocking the entire Bonhoeffer phenomenon. Ott, for example, talks about reality as Bonhoeffer's theme and ours.

> Bonhoeffer was the first to sense with such clarity and such passion the hidden fundamental question of our era which troubles us, the question difficult to formulate, perhaps up to now not formulated at all, yet always unavoidably and disturbingly there and concerning us as our destiny, *the question about reality*. . . . Bonhoeffer lived and thought under the influence of this hidden, but mighty, stream.[78]

Reality as the sacrament of the ethical means that ethical action must be action in "correspondence with reality." Such action will not look beyond the world to ideal norms, but will look rather to the future of the world which it is called upon to shape. That shaping takes place within the limits of one's responsibility. About this Bonhoeffer is very specific.

The "world" is thus the sphere of concrete responsibility. . . . Our responsibility is not infinite; it is limited, even though within these limits it embraces the whole of reality. It is concerned not only with the good will but also with the good outcome of the action, not only with the motive but also with the object. . . . One must risk looking into the immediate future; one must devote earnest thought to the consequences of one's action; and one must endeavor to examine one's own motives and one's own heart. One's task is not to turn the world upside-down, but to do what is necessary at the given place and with a due consideration of reality.[79]

Reality, construed as God and world together in Christ, spreads out ethical opportunity and obligation both temporally and spatially into the dimensions of relationality and responsibility.

Relationality and Responsibility

Although he never uses the term, Bonhoeffer was engaged his entire life in the task of formulating what we have called here an ethical theology. It grows out of the thoroughness with which he focuses on Jesus Christ as the radical center for Christian action and reflection. Since God and world come together in Jesus Christ, the rejection of two-sphere thinking follows, along with an abhorrence for all religious dualisms. Not the ideal, but the real, is what Christianity is about. It is reality, in fact, which is the sacrament of the ethical. And that visible sign of the command of God brings the Christian into a multitude of relationships which make up the nexus of ethical responsibility. We live both with one another (relationality) and for one another (responsibility). Bonhoeffer makes this coordination very explicit in his first dissertation.

We must now ask what the concrete acts are of the communion of saints acting as a community of love. . . . Two groups of ideas summarize these acts: 1. The God-appointed structural "togetherness" [Miteinander] of the church and each of its members; 2. The fact that the members act for one another [Füreinander], and the principle of vicarious action.[80]

Bonhoeffer's ecclesiology is always an ethical ecclesiology, just as his theology is always an ethical theology. "In this state, established by Christ, of being 'with one another,' which is shared by the church and its members, the being 'for one another' is also given."[81]

Bonhoeffer insists in his original dissertation, as he does later in *Life Together*, that community can never be found if sought for its own sake. Unless one is willing to enter the realm of responsibility, there is no way to experience relationality. In *The Communion of Saints*, Bonhoeffer concludes his exposition of the willingness of Moses and Paul to incur God's

wrath for the sake of the other (Exod. 32:32; Rom. 9:1ff.) with the statement that "love ultimately seeks not communion, but the 'other'; . . . the
less it seeks communion, the more surely it will find it."[82] That this is a
major theme in *The Communion of Saints* is clear from the fact that Bonhoeffer spells it out across a wide spectrum of issues including intercessory
prayer and suffering, and with a great number of biblical references (e.g.,
Gal. 6:2, "bear one another's burdens") and quotations from Luther. One
quotation from Luther which Bonhoeffer regards as making this point
with "incomparable beauty" is from the *Tesseradecas*.

> My burden is borne by the others, their strength is my strength; when I falter
> and fail the faith of the church comes to my aid. And even when I come to
> die, I should be assured that not I, or at least not I alone, am dying, but that
> Christ and the communion of saints are suffering and dying with me. We go
> the way of suffering and death accompanied by the entire church.[83]

Relationality and responsibility are also brought together in Bonhoeffer's early study of the church under the phrase "ethical collective persons." Beginning with a question which carries the same creative flair as
does his question about the sacrament of the ethical, Bonhoeffer goes to
work on this issue.

> If the subject of sin is at once the individual and the race, what is the form
> of sociological unity suitable for the mankind of Adam? This reintroduces the
> question of the ethical personality of collective persons which we previously
> left open and which determines whether there is any meaning in the idea of
> a collective person. Is it possible to regard the collective person as an ethical
> person, that is, place it in the concrete situation of being addressed by a
> Thou? If so, then we shall have proved that it is a center of action.
>   The meaning and reality of such a call can be comprehended only by one
> who, as a part of an empirical community, has experienced it. It is the Israel-
> ite concept of the people of God, which arose solely through being thus
> challenged by God, by the prophets, by the course of political history and by
> alien peoples. The call is to the collective person, and not to the individual.[84]

The fact that the call is to the collective person and not to the individual,
however, does not mean that the individual is eradicated or made irrele-
vant. Corporate relationality does not cancel out personal responsibility.
"God does not only have eyes for the nation; he has a purpose for every
smallest community, for every friendship, every marriage, every family."[85]
The question of the relation of the individual to the collective person is a
difficult one, and Bonhoeffer does not avoid it. There is responsibility for
the individual person, but only in the context of relationality in the collective person.

The community which is from God to God, which bears within it an eschatological meaning — this community stands in God's sight, and does not dissolve
into the fate of the many. It has been willed and created, and has fallen into
guilt; it must seek repentance, it must believe in and experience grace at the
limits of time. It is clear that this can happen only "in" the individual. Only
thus can the hearing of the call be concretely comprehended, and yet it is not
the individuals, but the collective person [*Gesamtheit*] who, in the
individuals, hears, repents and believes. The center of action lies in the collective person.[86]

It has been appropriate to spend considerable time with Bonhoeffer's
first book, *The Communion of Saints*. The emphasis on relationality and
responsibility is clear and specific at that point. But it does not stop there.
The themes move throughout the Bonhoeffer literature. In *Act and Being*,
the church is the solution to the act/being problem, and when Bonhoeffer
moves to ethics in that book, he discusses responsibility in the context of
the collective person in Adam and the collective person in Christ. The same
cluster of emphases is the subject of the lectures published under the title
Temptation. In the 1933 Christology lectures, he insists at considerable
length that the *pro me* (the "for me" of the sacrament) is not at all an individualistic concept. He combats a major stream of Lutheran tradition
when he insists on speaking of Christ as community, and about Christ not
only as the center of human existence and of history, but as the mediator
between God and nature. In much the same way that he later treats grace
as both free and costly (relationality of God to person, responsibility of
person for neighbor), he says in the Christology lectures that the "for me"
of the word of justification is always one that implies both relationality and
responsibility. The themes continue into the *Ethics* and the prison letters.
There is a direct line, in fact from Bonhoeffer's dealing with relationality
and responsibility in *The Communion of Saints* to his description in the
prison letters of the Christian life as sharing the suffering of God in the life
of the world.[87]

All of this has a great deal to do with Bonhoeffer's understanding of reality, introduced in the last section. It is not as though the description of reality is a purely objective or impersonal task, even though "God is in the
facts" in such a way that we must "look for the Thou in the It." The move
is not only from reality to relationality and responsibility but the latter two
feed back into the understanding and structuring of reality in such a way
that it cannot be grasped apart from them. The moves are never simple but
always complex, never unidirectional but always multidimensional. The
grasping of reality requires personal involvement, and that involvement
always has to do, for Bonhoeffer, with Jesus Christ.

In order to be able to understand how Bonhoeffer, from his starting-point, the ethical problem, arrives at his radical equation of Christ and reality, we must form a picture of the particular place in his thought of the ethical event. That place is responsible action. Ethical "principles" miscarry. They are not after all able to master reality at the decisive moment. Reality, meaning what is at stake in the situation of decision, is only mastered by responsible action in the concrete situation. And yet action, too, in Bonhoeffer still has about it a certain ambiguity. It, too, still has its boundaries, and is only in keeping with reality when it is embraced by Jesus Christ and contained in him.[88]

The point in this section has not been to deal exhaustively with relationality and responsibility in Bonhoeffer. What detailing is possible will be done in the next chapter under the heading "Structuring the Responsible Life." The point here has been rather to note the logical necessity, within Bonhoeffer's conceptuality, of a thoroughly corporate understanding of reality. Theological and ethical idealists can with inner logic embrace individualistic systems. Bonhoeffer's rejection of Idealism necessitates the rejection of individualism and the embracing of corporate existence. What Green calls "the sociality of Christ" in Bonhoeffer encompasses interpretations of relationality and responsibility.[89] As soon as one begins to take this kind of corporate life seriously, it is obvious that time and history have already become constitutive elements in one's way of understanding and dealing with life, both theologically and ethically.

Time and History as Ethical Constituents

In his introduction to the American edition of the drama and novel fragments written by Bonhoeffer in Tegel prison, Green makes the point that this *Fiction from Prison* and the *Letters and Papers from Prison* are companion pieces, the first oriented chiefly to the past and the second oriented chiefly to the future.[90] It is a nice insight, particularly because the two orientations are not taken to be mutually exclusive. The subtitle of the American edition of the fiction fragments, "Gathering up the Past," is taken from comments in a letter to Bethge in which Bonhoeffer talks about the fiction attempts. In the same letter and in three other letters to Bethge, he mentions that he has written an essay on "The Feeling of Time." The essay has not survived, but Green is undoubtedly correct in believing that the notes dated 8 May 1943 are Bonhoeffer's notes for this essay.[91] They are the kind of musings that a person might jot down when the mind is allowed to wander freely, associating ideas, sayings, impressions, feelings.

The essay on time was written by Bonhoeffer while he was gathering up the past and facing the future. Its occasion was an attempt to deal with the feeling that life spent in prison was a waste. He mentions that one of his predecessors had scribbled over the cell door, "In 100 years it will all be over."[92] That was one way to deal with the situation, but it was clearly not Bonhoeffer's way. Time and history were much too important for him, personally, theologically, and ethically, to be handled in this fashion. We can only guess what the essay contained. What we know for certain is that time and history were never inconsequential for him, either early in life or in his final years. It has already been stated that Bonhoeffer's entire task of formulating an ethical theology centered in Christ was a repudiation of the idealist notion that God and the good are by definition timeless. In this section the extent to which time and history enter the fabric of Bonhoeffer's ethical theology will be explored in somewhat greater detail.

The paradigmatic proponent of timeless ethics and morality is taken by Bonhoeffer to be the great German idealist of the eighteenth century, Immanuel Kant. Kant epitomizes the assumption that right and wrong must be universalizable. His classic formula is the "categorical imperative": "So act so that you can will your action as a universal law for all humankind." However they actually behave, most people assume that this is the way they ought to behave. It is, in a significant way, a commonsense idea. Parents who have never heard of Kant regularly put the Kantian question to their children, "What if everybody did that?" What is at stake in this question is the principle of fairness, of consistency of behavior, of dependability, of treating others as one would like to be treated. Kant, however, pushes this principle into the absolute. The point for Kant is that circumstances change but right and wrong do not change. What morality is about is that every person in every place and every time should do the right and avoid the wrong. To say that moral laws must be universalizable is, finally, to say that morality is intrinsically timeless.

This common assumption, worked out in classic form by Kant, was always in the background as Bonhoeffer struggled with the question of what an ethical theology would look like if it embraced time and history as essential ingredients. The struggle went on continuously until the end.

The connection between ethics and history was there at the beginning of his academic career. While a vicar at Barcelona, he wrote to Reinhold Seeberg that he had another work in mind on "Consciousness and Conscience in Theology." Seeberg responded suggesting that "the history of ethics and still more of morality is a sphere in which a young man might well make a corner for himself today, perhaps with the aim of writing a history of ethical dogma from the Sermon on the Mount up to our own day.''[93] Bonhoeffer did later write on the Sermon on the Mount and entitled it *The Cost of Discipleship*. He did study the history of ethics. But instead of writing on the history of ways in which Christians have reflected upon timeless ethical principles, Bonhoeffer attempted rather a systematic methodology of ethics that embraced time and history at the very core of its way of thinking and doing.

It was also in Barcelona when he was twenty-one years old that he wrote to Helmut Rössler about "real people" and the "limits of responsibility." Not only the themes, but the sentences in this letter could appear, and virtually do appear, in the *Ethics* and the prison letters written a decade and a half later.

> I'm getting to know new people every day; here one meets people as they are, away from the masquerade of the "Christian world," people with passions, criminal types, little people with little ambitions, little desires and little sins, all in all people who feel homeless in both senses of the word, who loosen up if one talks to them in a friendly way, real people; I can only say that I have gained the impression that it is just these people who are much more under grace than under wrath, and that it is the Christian world which is more under wrath than under grace.[94]

While in that Barcelona parish, Bonhoeffer gave a lecture on Christian ethics to the members of the congregation. It is a very important document for many reasons.[95] For our purposes in this section it is necessary only to note the thoroughness with which Bonhoeffer makes time and history constitutive for his ethical theology, even at this early stage of development.

> We will speak today of the basic questions raised by the demand for a Christian ethic, not by making the attempt to lay down generally valid, Christian norms and precepts in contemporary ethical questions — which is in any case completely hopeless — but rather by examining and entering into the characteristic trend of contemporary ethical problems in the light of fundamental Christian ideas. The reason for a limitation of this nature lies in the fact, still to be elaborated in detail, that there are not and cannot be Christian norms and principles of a moral nature; the concept of "good" and "evil" exist only on the completion of an action, i.e., at any specific present, and hence any attempt to lay down principles is like trying to draw a bird in flight. But more of this later.
>
> Ethics is a matter of history, it is not simply something which has descended from heaven to earth, but is rather a child of the earth. For this reason it changes its appearance with the trends of history and the shift of generations. There is a German ethic and a French ethic, just as there is an American ethic and none is more ethical or less ethical than the others, but all are firmly fixed in the nexus of history. . . .
>
> We said that there was a German, a French, and American ethic, for ethics

is a matter of blood and of history. But in that case how does the idea of a so-called Christian ethic stand? Are these two words, Christian and ethic, not perhaps completely disparate? Does not the idea "Christian" in this way become secularized, and a so-called Christian ethic become one alongside many, one of many, perhaps rather better or perhaps rather worse, but still in any event completely implicated in the relativity of history? In that case there is a Christian ethic as well as a German ethic, and neither of them is allowed to lay claim to superiority. It is therefore extremely hazardous to speak of a Christian ethic and at the same time to maintain the absolute claim for such an ethic.[96]

Throughout this lecture, Bonhoeffer struggles with the problem of how to claim authority for an ethic embedded in the relativities of time and history. It seems as though one can have it either way. One can claim absolute authority for an absolute ethic, that is, an ethic not subject to the relativities of history. Or one can claim relative authority for an ethic embedded in those same relativities. Bonhoeffer wants an ethic embedded in time and history, and yet wants to make an absolute claim for it. The problem is parallel to making a universal claim about a contingent fact of history, or to deriving an "ought" from an "is." It is inescapable for anyone who decides to make Christ the center of all things, as does Bonhoeffer.

Ethical clarity does not come from adherence to timeless principles, even the principle of love. "The nature of the will of God can only be clear in the moment of action."[97] The great moral renewal through Jesus Christ means the renunciation of principles. Yet for Bonhoeffer, the will of God is never something that is intuitively grasped, whether through conscience or feeling or "answer" to prayer or "promptings" of the Holy Spirit. Neither is it something that is directly and immediately derivable from the reading of Scripture or the accumulation of observed data. Ethics is rather a matter of the concrete situation and that means that the will of God is discernible only upon completion of the act. One never knows for sure beforehand that one is doing the right thing. One may look back and decide that one has done the right thing. The Christian lives in the certainty of faith that God will accomplish his purpose, but apart from the security that absolute ethics claims to give.

During the period of training pastors for the Confessing Church, the same commitment to time and history continued. On the altar at Finkenwalde, where a painting or a statue would normally be placed, there was simply the word *hapax*. That word, used three times in the Epistle to the Hebrews, reminded the worshiping community that Jesus Christ is not a timeless truth or ideal, but the *once-for-all* revelation of God. Bonhoeffer's contention is that there have been innumerable ways in which the church has strayed from this one basic point and attempted to understand Jesus Christ in nonhistorical ways. But Jesus Christ is a person of time and place. And because God was in Christ in that time and that place, he can be and is in every new time and every new place. Time and history thus become constitutive for Christian believing and doing. Bonhoeffer thinks that this fact has never been taken with sufficient seriousness, and thus he sees himself setting ethics on a new course. He is very self-conscious and specific about what he is doing.

> The place which in all other ethics is occupied by the antithesis of "should be" and "is," idea and accomplishment, motive and performance, is occupied in Christian ethics by the relation of reality and realization, past and present, history and event (faith), or to replace the equivocal concept by the unambiguous name, the relation of Jesus Christ and the Holy Spirit.[98]

Offensive as this harsh diastasis is to some people, Bonhoeffer nevertheless states it flatly and clearly because he believes that everything is at stake precisely at this point. A key passage, already quoted twice, is worth looking at again from this perspective.

> Whoever wishes to take up the problem of a Christian ethic must be confronted at once with a demand which is quite without parallel. He must from the outset discard as irrelevant the two questions which alone impel him to concern himself with the problem of ethics, "How can I be good?" and "How can I do good?", and instead of these he must ask the utterly and totally different question "What is the will of God?"[99]

It is only as one reads Bonhoeffer with some thoroughness that it becomes clear that "the will of God" is for him a category stretching out into the future, not limited to the moment of hearing and obeying. He repeatedly makes clear the fact that the time and history of which he is speaking is not the time and history of the existentialists. With some notable exceptions, such as his exegetical method in *Creation and Fall*, he insists that time and history are stretched out on a continuum that has to do with past, present, and future. He frequently talks about God as "Creator, Reconciler, and Redeemer." In the *Ethics* he regularly attaches to the name of Jesus the words "incarnate, crucified, and risen." Often he talks about the world as "loved, condemned, and reconciled." He describes human beings in terms of their "origin, essence, and goal." From the systematic critique of existentialism in the two dissertations to the offhand remarks about "psychotherapists and existentialists" in the prison letters, Bonhoeffer makes it abundantly clear that the time which is constitutive for his ethical theology has to do with the whole history of the whole creation. Nothing less than this could provide him with the vision of God and the world that allowed him to make unpopular decisions and daring moves as he worked at shaping the future with the coming generations in mind. Geffrey Kelly captures it in the opening paragraph of his treatment of "Bonhoeffer's Theology of History and Revelation."

> Dietrich Bonhoeffer had an extraordinary sense of the future implications for both church and society of those historical events which unrolled in the period of his active life as minister, teacher, and conspirator within Nazi Germany. At times his perceptiveness seemed to mark him among his contemporaries as a pesky, no-compromise agitator, stirring up trouble when people hankered after nothing more than security. He was, in many respects, a prophet of doom and hope, a pace ahead of his colleagues and with a cause few embraced and still fewer were willing to die for. His reading of history was often clear — his own actions, after some initial wavering, decisive. His theological justification of those actions which led him inevitably to the conspiracy, however, was at once as torturous and inspiring as it was deeply undergirded by his christocentric faith.[100]

Dumas, G. Clarke Chapman, Jr., and Hans Schmidt argue in various ways that Bonhoeffer thought "spatially" and did not have a sufficiently robust understanding of time and history.[101] The position taken here is that he does embrace space as well as time, nature as well as history, but that the movement is consistently from time to space, from history to nature. So thoroughly is he opposed to spatial (or "religious") two-sphere thinking that the problem arising out of his ethical theology is whether there is any continuity at all to moral behavior. So insistent is he on the "fresh every morning" character of God's command that the real danger is not conservatism, but moral chaos. There have been hints along the way that Bonhoeffer works hard to combat the arbitrariness of raw situationism. In the following chapter we shall see that he does exhibit a very great interest in ethical structures. He rarely uses them, however, in a traditional manner. In order to employ them, he finds it necessary to recast them in such a way that they fit a temporal, rather than a spatial, mold and serve to assist the Christian who seeks to do God's will and thus participate in God's shaping of the future.

NOTES

1. The similarity to common themes in liberation theology is immediately obvious. Two differences can be suggested at this point. Liberation theology takes a single ethical theme, the liberation of oppressed peoples, and does theology allowing that theme to penetrate at every point. Bonhoeffer's ethical theology has a much broader scope, allowing the full range of ethical concerns to penetrate. Secondly, liberation theology tends, in its emphasis on "orthopraxis," to make specific moral decisions and actions criteria for determining who is and who is not Chris-

tian. Bonhoeffer is always clear that confessing the name of Jesus makes one a Christian, and that the act of confessing brings with it the responsibility of obeying.

2. William Hamilton, "Bonhoeffer: Christology and Ethics United," *Christianity and Crisis* (19 October 1964): 198.

3. *E*, 188.

4. *NRS*, 362.

5. Ibid., 121.

6. Donald Evans, *Struggle and Fulfillment* (Philadelphia: Fortress Press, 1979).

7. Ibid., 170.

8. Ibid., 172–73.

9. Ibid., 173.

10. *E*, 190.

11. Ernst Feil, *The Theology of Dietrich Bonhoeffer*, trans. Martin Rumscheidt (Philadelphia: Fortress Press, 1985).

12. Benjamin Reist, *The Promise of Bonhoeffer* (Philadelphia: J. B. Lippincott, 1969), 118–20.

13. Jürgen Moltmann and Jürgen Weissbach, *Two Studies in the Theology of Bonhoeffer* (New York: Charles Scribner's Sons, 1967), 151.

14. *CC*, 30ff.

15. *E*, 128–29.

16. André Dumas, *Dietrich Bonhoeffer: Theologian of Reality*, trans. Robert McAfee Brown (New York: Macmillan Co., 1971), 33.

17. Ibid., 154.

18. Ibid., 167.

19. Ernst Feil, "Dietrich Bonhoeffer's Understanding of the World," in *Bonhoeffer Legacy*, ed. A. J. Klassen (Grand Rapids: Wm. B. Eerdmans, 1981), 247.

20. Cf. Rainer Mayer, "Christology: The Genuine Form of Transcendence," in *Bonhoeffer Legacy*, 179–92.

21. *LPP*. In the letter of 30 April 1944, Bonhoeffer writes, "God's 'beyond' is not the beyond of our cognitive faculties. The transcendence of epistemological theory has nothing to do with the transcendence of God. God is beyond in the midst of our life," 282.

22. *CS*, 115.

23. Clifford J. Green, *Bonhoeffer: The Sociality of Christ and Humanity* (Missoula, Mont.: Scholars Press, 1972).

24. *AB*, 184.

25. *CC*, 104.

26. Ibid., 34.

27. Ibid., 60.

28. Ibid., 69.

29. Ibid., 84.

30. Ibid., 92. Cf. James H. Burtness, "As Though God Were Not Given," *dialog* 19 (Fall 1980): 249–55.

31. *CC*, 45.

32. *CF/T*, 11.

33. Ibid.

34. Ibid., 12.
35. Ibid., 22–23.
36. Ibid., 45.
37. Ibid., 93–94.
38. CD, 118.
39. Ibid., 22.
40. Ibid., 63.
41. Ibid., 343.
42. Ibid., 63–64.
43. Ibid., 192.
44. *LPP*, letter of 21 July 1944, 369.
45. *CD*, 270.
46. Ibid., 342.
47. *LPP*, letter of 18 July 1944, 361.
48. *LT*, 26.
49. Ibid., 21.
50. Ibid., 118–19. There is no evidence that Bonhoeffer ever had anything but the greatest respect and admiration for his father and the work in psychiatry done by his father. The derogatory remarks in the prison letters about psychotherapists have to do with what Bonhoeffer considered to be an irresponsible and degrading invasion of privacy. His father's work was on the neurological aspects of psychiatry, a very different enterprise from psychotherapeutic methods associated with Freud and Jung. Cf. *DB*, 11–12.
51. *CF/T*, 127.
52. Ibid., 101.
53. *TP*, 29.
54. *GS* I, 62–65.
55. *NRS*, 117.
56. *E*, 194–97.
57. Ibid., 196–97.
58. Ibid., 197. Instead of talking about God and the world brought together in Christ, Bonhoeffer talks here about Christ and the world. It would be a mistake to make anything of this inconsistency. Trinitarian faith allows the believer to slip unconsciously, whether in prayer or in reflection, from one to another person. There is ample evidence that Bonhoeffer was entirely clear in his own mind about the necessary distinctions between the words "God" and "Christ."
59. Mayer, "Christology: The Genuine Form of Transcendence," in *Bonhoeffer Legacy*, 185.
60. *LPP*, 303.
61. *CS*, 85 and passim. The English translation reads "church." The German, "*Gemeinde*," however, is better translated "congregation."
62. *LT*, 30.
63. *CD*, 175–76.
64. *E*, 193–94.
65. *DB*, 626; *GS* II, 420; *GS* VI, 568.
66. *GS* I, 33. A few paraphrases have been employed in this translation in order to make the text read more smoothly.

67. *NRS*, 157ff.

68. *E*, 58.

69. *NRS*, 164.

70. Ibid.

71. *The Is-Ought Question: A Collection on Papers of the Central Problem in Moral Philosophy*, ed. W. D. Hudson (New York: St. Martin's Press, 1979).

72. *CS*, 146.

73. *LPP*, 191.

74. Ibid., 217. On other occasions he paints these two extremes with the figures of Brand and Peer Gynt from Henrik Ibsen.

75. Heinrich Ott, *Reality and Faith*, trans. Alex. A. Morrison (Philadelphia: Fortress Press, 1972), 253.

76. *LPP*, 217–18.

77. *CF/T*, 46.

78. Ott, *Reality and Faith*, 316–17.

79. *E*, 233.

80. *CS*, 126–27; also *GS* II, 331.

81. *CS*, 129.

82. Ibid., 131.

83. Ibid., 127–28.

84. Ibid., 82–83.

85. Ibid., 83.

86. Ibid.

87. *LPP*, letter of 18 July 1944, 361–62.

88. Ott, *Reality and Faith*, 246.

89. Green, *Bonhoeffer: The Sociality of Christ and Humanity*.

90. Dietrich Bonhoeffer, *Fiction from Prison* (Philadelphia: Fortress Press, 1981), ix.

91. Ibid., viii.

92. *LPP*, letter of 15 May 1943, 39.

93. *NRS*, 36.

94. Ibid., 37.

95. Two versions appear in the *GS*. The first (*GS* III, 48–58) is an abridged version which omits, for example, some very nationalistic material. The second (*GS* V, 156–80) is complete. The translation in *NRS* (39–48) is from the abridged version.

96. *NRS*, 39–40.

97. Ibid., 43.

98. *E*, 190.

99. Ibid., 188.

100. Geffrey Kelly, "Bonhoeffer's Theology of History and Revelation," in *Bonhoeffer Legacy*, 89.

101. Dumas, *Dietrich Bonhoeffer: Theologian of Reality*; G. Clarke Chapman, Jr., "Bonhoeffer and Liberation Theology," in *Ethical Responsibility*, ed. John D. Godsey and Geffrey B. Kelly (New York and Toronto: Edwin Mellen Press, 1981); Hans Schmidt, "The Cross of Reality," in *World Come of Age*, ed. R. Gregor Smith (Philadelphia: Fortress Press, 1967).

2 | Structuring the Responsible Life

Working at the Intersection of Situations and Structures

Situations and Structures as a Classic Problem in Ethics

Every ethical deontologist is aware that exceptionless rules must somehow be applied to actual situations, and every ethical situationist is aware that differences between situations cannot justify arbitrary behavior. The study of a particular position or an individual ethicist becomes interesting when one begins to see the nuances with which a major ethical option is qualified. In this sense, Bonhoeffer is no exception. He often sounds like a pure situationist. But his position becomes increasingly interesting as one notices the persistent drive toward some way of acknowledging and even creating ethical structures.

We have seen that the most striking thing about Bonhoeffer's ethical theology is his massive rejection of the entire tradition of idealistic ethics, which he considers to be the mainstream of ethical reflection in the West. To say that it is necessary to forget everything that has gone before in order to start afresh sounds extremely arrogant and naive. He says this, however, not because he takes himself so seriously, but because he wants to take Jesus Christ seriously as the center of all life. It is precisely that focus on the incarnate, crucified, and risen Christ that leads Bonhoeffer to reject all two-sphere thinking, to look at reality as the sacrament of the ethical, and to embrace time and history as ethical constituents. Although the position taken here is that Bonhoeffer's ethical theology can best be classified as "teleological" or "consequentialist" and grasped under the rubric "shaping the future," it is true that a great deal of the Bonhoeffer material could lead one to think of him as a thoroughgoing situationist.

He is so strongly opposed to absolute ethical principles that for him even the phrase "Christian ethics" is problematic.[1] He is aware that the phrase might lead one to think that there is a set of moral rules or a pattern of ethical behavior that can be labeled "Christian." The problem is that "the Christian life" can then be separated from Jesus Christ and can be followed by anyone attracted to that "lifestyle," whether that person has anything to do with Jesus Christ or not. But then everything is lost. Something very specific has been made very general. A particular revelatory event has become a universal moral rule. Ethics has become a substitute for theology. Human behavior has become all-important. Jesus Christ has become optional. It is because of this danger that Bonhoeffer wonders whether the term "Christian ethics" should even be used.

Bonhoeffer is, of course, not the first to voice these concerns nor is he unique in this emphasis. The apostle Paul insists that the line of demarcation between a good and a bad deed is simply whether it has been done "out of faith."[2] His obsession to fight legalism seems to lead him to excesses that sound antinomian.[3] The advice of Augustine to "love God, and then do as you please"[4] seems to be the same kind of totally unhelpful comment. It seems to say that there are no even relatively objective criteria for judging behavior or adjudicating differences in moral disputes. Luther said that good works do not make a person good, but a good person does good works.[5] Jesus said that there is no point in putting good fruit on a bad tree because the tree must first become good and then it will automatically produce good fruit.[6] Paul Lehmann states that Christian ethics has to do not with an imperative, but rather with an indicative, not with the question concerning what we ought to do, but rather with the question about what God is doing.[7]

All of these positions, like that of Bonhoeffer, are radically theocentric or christocentric. They are all diastatic, stressing the distinction rather than the similarity between Christian and non-Christian ethics. They all insist upon the priority of faith to life. They all consider legalism and moralism to be the great dangers that must be avoided at almost any cost.

These positions also tend to stress spontaneity rather than rationality in decision making. In *Agape and Eros*, a classic document in this tradition, Anders Nygren lists spontaneity as the first characteristic of agape.[8] On an entirely different theological base, Joseph Fletcher does the same in *Situation Ethics*. He insists that there is only one absolute and that absolute is love. Even justice equals love.[9] In that book, there is only one question to ask of moral behavior and that is whether in the situation at hand the most loving thing was done. The chapter on "The New Morality" in Bishop John Robinson's *Honest to God* says essentially the same thing.[10] Rudolf Bultmann's existentialist interpretation of the New Testament reduces Christian ethics to "radical obedience."[11] For him to say more than that is to lose the spontaneity that faith delivers and to risk the legalism that faith abhors.

There is a rather obvious objection that can be brought to any of these positions, including that of Bonhoeffer. One way of stating it is that this kind of talk leads to a totally arbitrary ethic which is for all practical purposes without content. How is it possible even to begin conversation about moral issues if any behavior whatsoever can be defended with the argument that it has been done "out of faith," or that it was "the most loving thing" to do in that situation, or that a deed was done in obedience to Jesus whose demand is so radical that it cannot be determined or understood or defended rationally? If good deeds cannot be talked about as such, but only as "fruits of faith" done by people who have been made "good" by the act of justification, then has not ethics been abandoned for the sake of theology? Any person who reflects on moral behavior runs the risk of self-deception, of justifying whatever behavior that person finds most attractive. This family of positions seems to run that risk more than do those that stress the timeless or universal nature of moral behavior. If there is no even relatively fixed content in ethics, then any content one wants to bring seems to be at least theoretically justifiable.

Another way of putting the criticism is to say that this way of doing ethics seems to be more negative than positive. It is very clear that all of these people are against legalism and moralism. They are against defining "good" or "right" in terms of universalizable moral actions or timeless ethical rules. They all focus on the moral agent or the moral act rather than on moral criteria for adjudicating differences in moral judgment. They are all aware of the fact that people are often hurt by mechanical obedience to strict rules. When one asks the positive question, however, what they are for rather than what they are against, both the passion and the argument often become very thin. It is possible to read Bonhoeffer also and to respond, "I understand what he is against, but what is he for?"

A third way of stating the objection is that this kind of ethics is not ethics at all, or is at best pre-ethics, a preparation for the actual work of doing ethics. It does accomplish the clearing away of debris. It demolishes legalism, and that is a necessary thing for any ethic, certainly for any Christian ethic, to do. But does this family of positions ever get started on the necessary task of constructing relatively objective criteria for evaluating moral behavior?[12] If it does not, can it be taken seriously as an option for those who are seeking to receive or to give moral guidance? It all seems too soft, too arbitrary, too subjective, too poorly equipped to adjudicate moral differences. It is one thing to say everything depends on the *situation*. It is quite another to say *everything* depends on the situation. Those who say the latter seem to be ruling out the doing of ethics altogether.

On the other hand, it is important to note that none of the positions mentioned above is as simplistic as it first appears. Jesus laid down a great many moral imperatives, some with very specific content. The apostle Paul laces his letters with specific moral exhortations and in some cases argues moral issues with considerable subtlety. The entire first letter to Corinth is essentially Paul's argued response to problems of behavior in that congregation. He does not even hesitate to use non-Christian moral codes current among the people with whom he worked. Augustine, who said, "Love God and then do as you please," also worked out in intricate detail the ethical criteria of "just war theory." Luther made major contributions to ethical theory with his "doctrine of the two realms" and his understanding of vocation. One may disagree with the ethics of Karl Barth, but it would be exceedingly strange for anyone to read *Church Dogmatics III/4*, for instance, and to conclude that Barth is not doing ethics at all. Lehmann's *Ethics in a Christian Context* is an indicative, rather than an imperative, ethic. Yet the constructive work that Lehmann does on conscience is impressive, and his grounding of Christian ethics in the *Koinonia* is a specific move away from purely subjective or individualistic ethics. Fletcher has much more to say than "Do the most loving thing" as soon as he begins to work on a specific problem in medical ethics.

As was said at the beginning of this section, every ethical situationist is aware that differences between situations cannot justify arbitrary behavior. Yet it is almost always the case that the constructive work of ethicists on the situationist side of the ethics spectrum is more elusive than is the constructive work of those on the absolutist side. But it may be elusive because it is complex, subtle, delicate. An example is the work of Stanley Hauerwas.[13]

Hauerwas flatly rejects what he calls the "standard account," his name for idealistic ethics and in particular the ethics of Kant. His objection to this classic deontological position is that it has little to do with community and therefore little to do with real life. He is at work attempting to develop an ethic that would take very seriously not only the moral agent but also the communal character of ethical decision making. If one is looking to Hauerwas for a neat "system," one can become quickly discouraged. He is well aware of that fact, and in a reference to a zoo keeper in Dublin, he illustrates the problem.[14] The keeper was able to breed lions in captivity, and this was such a rare feat that he was often asked how he was able to do it. He responded that the trick was "understanding lions." If anyone pressed the point and asked what that meant, he would then reply, "Every one is different." He knew a great deal about lions in general, yet was able to treat each one individually. When one examines the finesse with which Hauerwas works through the self-deceptions of Albert Speer, or the obligations of parents toward handicapped children, it is obvious that his massive rejection of the "standard account" in ethics does not mean that he is unable or uninterested in doing constructive work in ethics. It is the case with most ethicists on the situationist end of the ethics spectrum that they do pay attention to structures, and this is the case also for Bonhoeffer.

Bonhoeffer's Place in the Handling of the Problem

It should be clear that Bonhoeffer's rejection of the idealist tradition in ethics and his embracing of time and situations does not mean that he has no interest in ethical structures. The fact that he treats generalizations as lies[15] does not mean that there are no relatively objective procedures for decision making. In fact, Bonhoeffer is criticized by some for his too conservative attachment to structures. Like other ethicists on the situationist side of the ethics spectrum, Bonhoeffer's position may seem elusive, but it is neither contentless nor arbitrary. He is constantly working at the intersection of situations and structures, and a number of interpreters have seen this clearly. It is the specific way in which he does it, not the mere fact that he does it, that makes reading Bonhoeffer worth the effort. The structures for ethical reflection that Bonhoeffer constructs are built on his commitment to time and history as ethical constituents, and to the shaping of the future as the heart of the ethical task.

André Dumas is one who has made a great deal of the emphasis on structures in Bonhoeffer.[16] The English translation of Dumas renders Bonhoeffer's German word *Gestalt* as "structure" throughout,[17] even though this is not done consistently in the English translations of Bonhoeffer's works. Dumas even claims that Christ as structure is the key to Bonhoeffer's entire work.[18] He spells this out with references to the whole Bonhoeffer literature. One such reference is to *Creation and Fall.*

According to Bonhoeffer, the decisive impact of the word is the appearance of structure or form [Gestalt].

"That God speaks, and speaking, creates, the Bible strangely only mentions first where it is concerned with the creation of form, the wresting of form out of the formless. Form corresponds to the Word. . . . As the formless night becomes form by the light of the morning, as the light creates and unveils form, so that primeval light had to order the chaos, create, and unveil form" [CF, 24].

Structure and not intention constitutes the goodness of the created work. By his work, by what he realizes and not by a spirit or an ideal, God reveals himself in the midst of his creation. Bonhoeffer's commentary on Genesis 1 is an analysis of the various structures by which the unstructured, unformed world is transformed into God's creation for man.[19]

When Dumas later, in a section entitled "Jesus Christ as Structure and as Place," emphasizes structure to the point of stressing Bonhoeffer's commitment to spatiality rather than to temporality, he allows this emphasis on structure to move to the point of virtually losing the dynamic of Bonhoeffer's position. Nevertheless, Dumas's work is instructive because of the thoroughness with which he sees the importance of structure as an interpretive key to Bonhoeffer. The ramifications are extensive. God's structuring of the world around us occurs in the context of freedom for the neighbor. The effect of sin is to "de-create" the world, which means to "de-structure" it, to throw it into chaos. Adam destroyed the structures of the world by refusing to accept freedom in relationship and responsibility. Dumas understands that this conceptuality is entirely different from the Greek myth of the fall of Prometheus who steals fire from the gods and becomes a progenitor of the human race.

Another interpreter who focuses a great deal on structure is Heinrich Ott. In an important conversational note with Jürgen Moltmann, Ott talks about what Moltmann calls the "Christocratic structure of reality" in Bonhoeffer.

Jürgen Moltmann . . . has described the essence of Bonhoeffer's thought very aptly. Thus he speaks of the "Christocratic structure of reality" . . . , of Bonhoeffer's peculiar insight of "an *anhypostasia* of the reality of the world in the incarnation of God" . . . [Moltmann says further:] "That this reality discloses itself in the word of Christ as revelation alone does not mean that it only exists in the act of recognition of revelation and in faith. Rather the whole of reality in which faith comes into existence, in which it takes part and in the history of which it becomes implicated, is before belief or unbelief the reality surrounded and accepted by God" . . . All this is very relevant. It is also apt when . . . quoting Bonhoeffer's *Ethics*, he speaks of a "movement of [sc. the world's] being accepted and becoming accepted by God in Christ." The immanence of God in the reality of the world is not something "static" or "substantial," but has the character of a movement.[20]

In another passage Ott talks about Bonhoeffer's Christology as looking for the structure of the "where" within that of the "who."[21] He explains that Bonhoeffer remains within the structure of the person when he says that everything depends upon Christ being present to his church as a person in space and time. The place of the present Christ is the center of existence, of history, and of nature. Ott sees the importance of structure for Bonhoeffer as clearly as does Dumas, but he does not make Dumas's mistake of losing sight of the importance of time and history. In the final pages of his book on Bonhoeffer, Ott makes all of this very explicit.

> . . . [P]recisely this theological affirmation was the right one for him, that Jesus Christ is everywhere the true reality, the determining structural component of all that is real. But the Christological ontology which seeks to understand reality as such by endeavouring to discover Jesus Christ as its essence must necessarily become ethics, and further . . . must become a *Christologically determined situation ethic.* . . .
>
> In this unending task of the consideration of reality, there are, it is true, thanks to the person of the Mediator and to the solidarity of the men who are determined by him, those recurring *situations* and *structures* of which we have already spoken. . . .
>
> The trend towards the universal certainly has this effect, that our reflection upon the presence of Jesus Christ in all reality shows not only certain recurring situations of human existence but also certain recurring structural components of the presence of Christ. . . . But even these it will not be possible to include in a complete catalogue and thus bring into a system. The recognition of these structural components, which one might call "Christological existentials," not of course in the sense that they always and everywhere belong to human being as *such*, but rather in the sense that they do in fact belong to the being which has been captured by Christ, rather has a significance related to the day; they prepare us beforehand for the discovery and the theological demonstration of the presence of Christ in ever new existential situations.[22]

Bonhoeffer is certainly an ethical "situationist" in that he opposes ethical absolutes of all kinds and emphasizes concrete times and places. Yet to label him a situationist without qualifying that term is to misconstrue him completely. The Jesus Christ of time and history is also the one in whom the reality of God and the reality of the world come together. Reality, always on the move, is structured by Jesus Christ. Thus the Bonhoeffer who asked who Jesus is for us today, and who wanted to know what following

Jesus means, was as interested in structures as he was in situations, and worked his entire life at the intersection of the two.

The Last Things and the Things Before the Last

One of the important ways in which Bonhoeffer seeks to structure the responsible life is by providing a temporal framework within which to recognize the ambiguity of ethical situations. The phrase "the last things" suggests eschatology, and the seriousness of that suggestion is incorporated into the title of this book, *Shaping the Future*. However, it would be inappropriate to speak too quickly of Bonhoeffer's ethics as "eschatological," because for him it is specifically the duality of the formula which is the title of this section that makes it useful. In the title of chapter IV of the *Ethics* the phrase "the things before the last" follows the phrase "the last things." When Bonhoeffer was thinking about a title for his ethics book he considered "the preparing of the way and the entry into possession."[23] The parallel to the title of this section, and to the title of chapter IV of the *Ethics*, is obvious.

The point has been made that Bonhoeffer stands in a long line of people whose position on Christian ethics appears to many to be elusive. To a sympathetic reader the same materials appear rather to be immensely suggestive, arresting, probing, creative of chain reactions of new possibilities for reflection. James Woelfel places the subtitle "Classical and Revolutionary" on his book *Bonhoeffer's Theology*.[24] This subtitle captures the way in which Bonhoeffer works. The materials he uses are classic Christian materials. In order to make effective the revolutionary power of these materials, however, Bonhoeffer often finds it necessary to reformulate them. "The last things" suggests eschatology. It also suggests justification to Bonhoeffer, because the justification of the sinner is God's "final" act. Thus from one point of view, "the things before the last and the last things" is a reformulation of the doctrine of justification.[25] In *Act and Being* Bonhoeffer states it programmatically with regard to classic philosophical materials.

> In the Christian doctrine of being, all metaphysical ideas of eternity and time, being and becoming, living and dying, essence and appearance must be compatible with ontological concepts of sin and grace, or they must be entirely recast.[26]

Bonhoeffer is clear that he is not simply abandoning metaphysical ideas. He is not even claiming that they all necessarily need recasting. What he says is that if they are incompatible with sin and grace, then they must be recast. It is this recasting that takes place repeatedly as Bonhoeffer works at structuring the responsible life.

Often neglected in traditional treatments of sin and grace is the inescapable ethical concomitant that every facet of life exists in the context of fundamental ambiguity. Sin is a word that describes the whole creation as distorted and grace is a word that claims this distorted creation as object of God's redemptive work in Christ. The ambiguity arises in the fact that these two conditions exist at the same time and that both conditions penetrate the total reality. Luther's phrase was *simul iustus et peccator*, at the same time justified and sinner. Sin and grace therefore mean that there is no place (church authority, civil law, moral expert) to which to go, no part of one's own person (conscience, intuition, reason) to which to go, to find simple guidance for pure behavior. In a pastoral letter from Finkenwalde to former students, Bonhoeffer strikes this note.

> It was all unpure through sin and all is now pure through grace. Through Jesus Christ the creature of God is good. The goodness of the creature lies no longer in its naturalness, it is not good in itself, but through the gift which comes through the word and through prayer.[27]

It has been customary for Christian ethics to assume the existence of some "pure" way of determining right and wrong. Whether that way is through the conscience, or through an inerrant Scripture text, or through reason, or through certain knowledge of the will of God through the Holy Spirit, or through sanctified intuition, or through clear and direct answer to prayer, the idea persists that somehow being a Christian, or perhaps simply a human being, gives one access to information that is in some simple way morally "correct." Bonhoeffer rejects this idea specifically because it is not compatible with sin and grace. In a 1932 lecture he makes clear that this duality is true specifically also of the church.

> The church is a bit of the world, a lost, godless world, under the curse, a complacent, evil world. And the church is the evil world to the highest degree because, in it, the man of God is misused, because in it God is made a plaything, man's idol. Indeed it is simply the eternally lost, anti-Christian world if it emerges from its ultimate solidarity with the evil world and sets itself up, boasting against the world. But the church is a bit of the qualified world, qualified by God's revealing, gracious Word which, completely surrendered and handed over to the world, secures the world for God and does not give up. The church is the presence of God in the world. Really in the world, really the presence of God. The church is not a consecrated sanctuary, but the world, called by God to God; therefore there is only *one* church in all the world.[28]

Bonhoeffer's categories of the things before the last and the last things are ways of structuring the duality of the whole creation under sin and grace at the same time. They are a way of talking about the fundamental ambiguity of human and Christian life. One can make a case for saying that Bonhoeffer is simply recasting some very traditional categories in order to emphasize a point that should have been obvious in the first place. It is also possible, however, to look at these categories as entirely new ethical structures. What is certain is that they are extremely important for Bonhoeffer, that they occur in some very early literature, and that they are essential for an understanding of the *Ethics*.

The categories appear as early as Barcelona. In a sermon on 1 John 2:17, delivered by the twenty-two-year-old vicar in August 1928, Bonhoeffer worked on the distinction between the ultimate (the last things) and the penultimate (the things before the last).[29] In a radio address on 1 February 1933, two days after Hitler came to power, Bonhoeffer used the categories to attack the "Leadership principle" (Hitler as *der Führer*). The authorities cut him off before he was able to finish, but he later gave the full address in a public lecture in Berlin.

> The Leader serves his office. But this service of his office is itself only penultimate. The individual experiences in the authority of an office his commitments, his restrictions, but at the same time his responsibility. Even here, however, man is not yet seen as he is. Only when a man sees that office as a penultimate authority in the face of an ultimate, indescribable authority, in the face of the authority of God, has the real situation been reached. . . .
>
> The fearful danger of the present time is that above the cry for authority, be it of the Leader or of an office, we forget that man stands alone before the ultimate authority. . . . Thus the Leader points to the office, but Leader and office together point to the final authority itself, before which Reich or state are penultimate authorities.[30]

There are many places where the terms "penultimate" and "ultimate" do not occur as such, but in which the categories are clearly operative. An example is the discussion in *The Cost of Discipleship* of Luther's "Sin boldly, but believe more boldly still."

> If we are to understand this saying of Luther's, everything depends on applying the distinction between the data and the answer to the sum. If we make Luther's formula a premise for our doctrine of grace, we are conjuring up the spectre of cheap grace. But Luther's formula is meant to be taken, not as the premise, but as the conclusion, the answer to the sum, the coping-stone, his very last word on the subject.[31]

It is in the *Ethics*, however, that these categories become full-blown ethical structures. In the section entitled "The Last Things and the Things Before the Last," Bonhoeffer begins by talking about "Justification as the Last Word." The opening lines could have been written by Luther or by Barth.

> The nature of the Christian life is disclosed not by what the man is in himself but by what he is in this event. The whole length and breadth of human life is here compressed into a single instant, a single point. The totality of life is encompassed in this event. What event is this? It is something final, something which cannot be grasped by the being or the action or the suffering of any man. The dark pit of human life, inwardly and outwardly barred, sinking evermore hopelessly and inescapably in the abyss, is torn open by main force, and the word of God breaks in. In the rescuing light man for the first time recognizes God and his neighbor. The labyrinth of the life he has so far led falls in ruin. Man is free for God and his brothers.[32]

Justification is here a single point, not a process or a movement. "The past and the future of his whole life are merged in one in the presence of God. The whole of the past is comprised in the word forgiveness. The whole of the future is in safekeeping in the faithfulness of God."[33] Yet this punctilious language is always qualified by talk that is clearly temporal, historical, stretched out toward the future of God's world. "He becomes aware that there is a God who loves him; that a brother is standing at his side, whom God loves as he loves him himself and that there is a future with the triune God, together with His Church. He believes. He loves. He hopes."[34] There is talk about the church, the creation, and the triune God. Jesus Christ is talked about in terms of "life, death, and resurrection." Justification is the last word, but it is last in both a qualitative and a temporal sense.

Justification as final in a qualitative sense means that it is "the complete breaking off of everything that precedes it, of everything that is before the last," that it is "never the natural or necessary end of the way which has been pursued so far, but it is rather the total condemnation and invalidation of this way."[35] That justification is a qualitatively final word means for Bonhoeffer that there can never be any method of achieving it, that there can never be a "way" to that final word, a work or a deed that will bring one to it. That excludes the way of Paul, the way of Luther, the way of the adulterous woman, the way of the thief on the cross, the way of Peter, the way of Mary Magdalene. In Bonhoeffer's ethical theology all legalisms and moralisms are totally excluded. There is no way to the final word.

Justification is also final, however, in a temporal sense. It does not appear out of nothing. There is something that does precede it, something that does go before it. "It is always preceded by something penultimate, some action, suffering, movement, volition, defeat, uprising, entreaty or hope, that is to say, in a quite genuine sense by a span of time, at the end of which it stands."[36] What Bonhoeffer is saying here is very similar to what he was saying in *The Cost of Discipleship.* "Only the one who believes obeys," but also "only the one who obeys believes."[37] The first sentence signals the qualitative finality of justification, the second the temporal finality. The insistence on holding to both simultaneously is what makes Bonhoeffer's theology *ethical* theology and his ethics ethical *theology.* He elaborates this delicate relationship in clear and simple terms.

> Luther had to pass through the monastery, and Paul through his bigoted zeal for the law; even the thief had to go through guilt to the cross: for only thus could they hear the last word. A way had to be trodden; the whole length of the way of the things before the last had to be traversed; each one had to sink to his knees under the burden of these things, and yet the last word was then not the crowning but the complete breaking off of the penultimate. In the presence of the last word the situation of Luther and Paul was in no way different from that of the thief on the cross. A way must be traversed, even though, in fact, there is no way that leads to this goal; this way must be pursued to the end, that is to say, to the point at which God sets an end to it. The penultimate, therefore, remains, even though the ultimate entirely annuls and invalidates it.
>
> The word of the justifying grace of God never departs from its position as the final word; it never yields itself simply as a result that has been achieved, a result that might just as well be set at the beginning as at the end. The way from the penultimate to the ultimate can never be dispensed with. The word remains irreversibly the last; for otherwise it would be reduced to the quality of what is calculable, a merchandise, and would thereby be robbed of its divine character. Grace would be venal and cheap. It would not be a gift.[38]

The entire passage is virtually interchangeable with sections from the "Costly Grace" essay in *The Cost of Discipleship.* The ultimate is not "calculable," nor is the penultimate. One cannot calculate one's way to grace, nor can one calculate one's way to morality.

Yet it is precisely for the sake of the ultimate that it is necessary to speak of the penultimate. It is particularly interesting that when Bonhoeffer begins to talk about the things before the last, he repeatedly talks about time. He asks "whether faith can, so to speak, be extended into time, or whether faith does not rather always become real in life as the ultimate phase of a span of time or of many spans of time." He talks about "living faith which justifies a life." He asks whether "this faith is and ought to be realizable every day, at every hour, or whether here, too, the length of the penultimate must every time be traversed anew for the sake of the ultimate." He asks whether "the word, the gospel, can be extended in time."[39]

The duality of the qualitative finality and the temporal finality of justification leads Bonhoeffer to describe two ethical errors, each one an extreme way of trying to eradicate the duality. The one extreme he calls "the radical solution." It sees only the ultimate and specifically the ultimate as a complete breaking off from the penultimate. In this case:

> Christ is the destroyer and enemy of everything penultimate, and everything penultimate is enmity toward Christ. Christ is the sign that the world is ripe for burning. There are no distinctions. Everything must go to the judgment. There are only two categories: for Christ, and against him. "He that is not with me is against me" (Matthew 12:30). Everything penultimate in human behavior is sin and denial.[40]

The other solution Bonhoeffer calls "compromise." Here the ultimate and the penultimate are also separated, but it is the penultimate that dominates. The world is taken "as it is." Ibsen's *Brand* exemplifies the radical solution; Dostoevsky's Grand Inquisitor exemplifies the way of compromise. In other passages Don Quixote stands for the first, Sancho Panza for the second. Compromise means in this case dismissing completely the ultimate and simply "going with the flow."

Bonhoeffer rejects both extremes. He sees clearly that "the radical cannot forgive God his creation"; it is always "hatred towards the world." Compromise, on the other hand, always springs from "hatred of the ultimate"; it is hatred of the justification of the sinner by grace alone.

> Radicalism hates time, and compromise hates eternity. Radicalism hates patience, and compromise hates decision. Radicalism hates wisdom, and compromise hates simplicity. Radicalism hates moderation and measure, and compromise hates the immeasurable. Radicalism hates the real, and compromise hates the word.[41]

The great problem with both of these extremes is that both are opposed to Christ, and fail to see that he alone is the solution to the problem of the relation between the ultimate and the penultimate. It is Jesus Christ who structures the responsible life in the duality of the ultimate and the penultimate which excludes the extremes of radicalism and compromise.

> Christian life, therefore, is a matter neither of radicalism nor of compromise. There is no point in debating the relative earnestness of these two conceptions; for there is earnestness only in Jesus Christ, and his earnestness reveals that neither of these solutions is earnest. There is earnestness neither in the idea of a pure Christianity in itself nor in the idea of man as he is in himself;

there is earnestness only in the reality of God and the reality of man which became one in Jesus Christ. What is earnest and serious is not some kind of Christianity, but it is Jesus Christ himself. . . . [O]nly through him will the world be preserved until it is ripe for its end.[42]

This set of categories gives Bonhoeffer the ethical-theological sanction for the preservation of the world. The penultimate exists for the sake of the ultimate, and not the other way around. Yet the penultimate is essential. "The state in which grace finds us is not a matter of indifference, even though it is always by grace alone that grace comes to us."[43] The thorny problem, debated endlessly at church conferences and ecumenical assemblies, of the relation between proclamation and development, or evangelism and liberation, is handled with clarity and precision by Bonhoeffer because he knows both the connection and the distinction between the penultimate and the ultimate.

> The hungry man needs bread and the homeless man needs a roof; the dispossessed need justice and the lonely need fellowship; the undisciplined need order and the slaves need freedom. To allow the hungry man to remain hungry would be blasphemy against God and one's neighbor, for what is nearest to God is precisely the need of one's neighbor. It is for the love of Christ, which belongs as much to the hungry man as to myself, that I share my bread with him and that I share my dwelling with the homeless. If the hungry man does not attain the faith, then the guilt falls on those who refused him bread. To provide the hungry man with bread is to prepare the way for the coming of grace.
>
> But what is happening here is a thing before the last. To give bread to the hungry man is not the same as to proclaim the grace of God and justification to him, and to have received bread is not the same as to have faith. Yet for him who does these things for the sake of the ultimate, and in the knowledge of the ultimate, the penultimate does bear a relation to the ultimate. It is pen*ultimate*. The coming of grace is the ultimate.[44]

Sin and grace, recast by Bonhoeffer in a temporal mold so that both the qualitative and the temporal finality of justification can be made clear, are expressed in terms of the things before the last and the last things. Those categories do not yield immediate moral advice. In fact they point to the ambiguity of all moral action. But they do provide a structuring function for responsible living which at the very least sets limits for and gives direction to appropriate behavior.

Many interpreters of Bonhoeffer have recognized the importance of these terms. Ernst Feil, for instance, says that the ultimate and the penultimate are Bonhoeffer's attempts to replace two-sphere thinking with a positive proposal for a specifically historical way of doing things. Feil is exactly correct when he says that in order to understand Bonhoeffer's concept of the world (space) it is necessary to understand that Bonhoeffer was a historical (temporal) thinker. He believes that Bonhoeffer attempted to think historically "to an ever increasing extent" and that this was a counter-move to Idealism on Bonhoeffer's part.[45]

> Bonhoeffer's efforts to make reality concrete are evident in his earlier writings as well as in his prison letters, in that he preferred to work with historical categories. . . . He relinquishes any abstract understanding of secularization, as we can see from a comparison with F. Gogarten, who relied on the same books Bonhoeffer did . . . but apparently came to entirely different conclusions. Gogarten represents a Diltheyan, ultimately idealistic acosmicism and a corresponding inwardness. Bonhoeffer guards against such a "religious"— in the sense of pantheistic-subjective — concealment of the true godlessness of such a world-come-of-age, which in itself is ambivalent.[46]

Tiemo Peters also focuses on these categories. He begins his important statement on the political ethics of Bonhoeffer with a discussion of the penultimate and the ultimate.

> The ethical consequences are obvious. . . . The ultimate and the penultimate belong together. Mankind is rendered creative through his believing recognition of his bondage regarding the "ultimate"; at the same time he is made free in the "penultimate," free "from the world before God," even while remaining in the midst of the world. In other words, all relativities of the penultimate receive their ethical qualification through the ultimate.[47]

There can be no question about the centrality of the categories of penultimate and ultimate for Bonhoeffer's ethical theology, nor about their effectiveness in his attempt to give some structure to the responsible life. This is, however, only one set of categories. There are many other ways that Bonhoeffer goes about working at the intersection of situations and structures, and we shall proceed to look at some of them.

God's Ordering of His Creation

Order and Freedom

"The New Morality" chapter of Robinson's book, *Honest to God,* is characteristic of the situation ethics of the sixties, and is based, according to Robinson, on Bonhoeffer as well as on Paul Tillich and Bultmann.[48] It was a period during which "Do your own thing" became an almost sacred duty and "law and order" became a nasty phrase denoting power used to repress freedom. For those whose acquaintance with Bonhoeffer is restricted to associations with the situationism of the sixties, it may be surprising to discover the strong commitments that Bonhoeffer had to both law and order. Even after Hitler had been in power for a decade, Bonhoeffer wrote, "It is only as the Redeemer in Jesus Christ that responsible action will be able to recognize the God who holds the world in order by His law."[49] Bonhoeffer's lifelong attack on legalism and moralism never brought him to the point of attacking either law or order per se. In fact, order was an extremely important factor in his life and in his ethical theology, as was law. The God who brought order out of chaos in the beginning continues to preserve that order through law. In this chapter we shall examine Bonhoeffer's ways of using ethical structures that reflect God's ordering of his creation. Later in this chapter we shall look at Bonhoeffer's understanding of law.

The role of order in Bonhoeffer's intellectual work fits very closely with the importance of order in his own life. He was raised in a very disciplined household where orderliness, punctuality, respect, and responsibility were taken for granted. Those values, pervasive in the German bourgeoisie, were particularly important in maintaining the large and complicated Bonhoeffer home. A bell rang at six o'clock signaling the time for the children to wash their hands for dinner. At the table the children spoke only when spoken to by their parents. There was lively conversation, but it was always controlled. At night Dietrich knocked on the wall of his sisters' bedroom when it was time to think about God for a while before going to sleep. The musical evenings in which various members of the household participated grew out of accumulated years of music lessons and disciplined practice. All of this was not thought of as repressive. In fact, it provided a context for freedom and even surprise.[50] The autobiographical poem "Stations on the Way to Freedom" begins with a stanza entitled "Self-discipline." The final line of the stanza is, "None learns the secret of freedom save only by way of control."[51]

Order as a context for freedom is one clue to Bonhoeffer's entire life. Lehmann uses "Paradox of Discipleship" as a title for a remembrance of Bonhoeffer. He talks about Dietrich's "contagious freedom" but also points to his orderliness. "With people, he was as ready to listen as to speak, to identify as to analyse, to participate as to investigate. One did not notice the solitude which prepared him for fellowship, the discipline which sustained his abandon, the quiet piety which nourished the acumen of his lively mind."[52] Prior to returning to Germany in 1935 to take charge of the Confessing Church seminary at Finkenwalde, he visited three Anglican monasteries in England. He was clearly attracted to the ordered life, even in its monastic expression. When he incorporated some of these rubrics into the life at Finkenwalde, many of the students were shocked and even angry. Yet he soon won over the students as they played ping-pong with him, enjoyed the beach together, shared the kitchen chores, sang the spirituals he had learned in Harlem. They had not been accustomed to seeing such disciplined order and such contagious freedom brought together. Otto Dudzus, another Finkenwalde student, makes the point with the memory of a tiny incident.

> He was a man who would rather have helped to build a whole and sound order of things than to remove a perverted, destroyed order. Small events illustrate this more clearly than long reflections. On our return journey from the ecumenical conference in Fanø we had to change trains at the Danish frontier station, Süderlügum. The train to Hamburg was waiting on the opposite platform. We students took the easy way and just crossed over the rail. Bonhoeffer was the only one who took the rather long and tedious way down to and across the wooden bridge which spanned the rails. He made us feel that he had no patience for our disregard of a meaningful order. The smallest offense against order shocked him. For the sake of the order which had been destroyed on a grand scale, he became a revolutionary.[53]

It was at the Benedictine monastery at Ettal, where he wrote to his parents that the ordered life there suited him very well,[54] that Bonhoeffer wrote the section in the *Ethics* on "The Recovery of the Natural." The combination of order and freedom is not unique to Bonhoeffer. It is commonplace to anyone acquainted with the apostle Paul, Augustine, or Luther. The point is simply that no reader of Bonhoeffer should be misled by his massive attack on legalism into thinking that he had any basic antipathy for order. The opposite is true. Order was a major factor in both his life and his reflection.

From "Orders of Creation" to
"Orders of Preservation" to
"Divine Mandates"

One of the classic formulas with which God's ordering of his creation has been discussed in post-Reformation theology and ethics is the orders of creation. It is a way of thinking deeply set within the Reformed and Lutheran traditions and has served there somewhat the same function served by natural law theory in the Roman Catholic tradition. It has brought both continuity and community to ethical reflection, as well as the insistence that human life must be brought into harmony with the created order. Emil Brunner's book on ethics, *The Divine Imperative*, was entitled in German *Das Gebot und die Ordnungen* (The Command and the Orders). Bonhoeffer was thoroughly familiar with Brunner's book and refers to it a number of times. But the formula was not unique to Brunner. The orders of creation were treated at that time in every major Protestant text on ethics, and continue now to be an arena for lively debate in German theology and ethics.

Although there are varieties of orders of creation talk, the orders dealt with always include the family, the state, and the church. The positive contribution of this formulation has already been mentioned. The negative danger is that the orders can be absolutized to the point of becoming demonic, which is what happened during the Nazi years in Germany, in particular with regard to the state. Rom. 13:1, "Obey the powers that be, for they are ordained by God," was used effectively against resisters. They were reminded that the state was an order of creation instituted by God and therefore not to be questioned. Other things followed, including race as an order of creation, not to be tampered with. As early as 6 June 1932, the Faith Movement of the "German Christians" listed among its "Guiding Principles" the following:

> We see in race, folk, and nation, orders of existence granted and entrusted to us by God. God's law for us is that we look to the preservation of these orders. Consequently miscegenation is to be opposed. For a long time German Foreign Missions, on the basis of its experience, has been calling to the German people: "Keep your race pure," and tells us that faith in Christ does not destroy one's race but deepens and sanctifies it.[55]

It would have been difficult enough to combat this racism if it had been promoted only by the government. Making the struggle much more difficult was the fact that the church, at least a strong movement within the church, was preaching racism as Christian doctrine, based on its notion of how God ordered his creation. Bonhoeffer had a deep commitment to order and against chaos. His task was to attack the way in which order was misused by the Nazis and the "German Christians" and to find new ways to create and preserve order that would allow for that freedom so essential to human life.

As early as his Youth Peace Conference lecture of 1932, Bonhoeffer makes specific reference to the orders of creation. He is already dealing with them critically, prior to the time that Hitler was in power. The following quotation proceeds after a paragraph in which he asks, "Whence does the church know God's command for the moment?" The first answer would be "the biblical law," but Bonhoeffer replies that God's command for the moment is not necessarily heard in the biblical law.

> The second answer would find God's commandment in the orders of creation. Because certain orders are evident in creation, one should not rebel

against them, but simply accept them. One can then argue: Because the nations have been created different, each one is obliged to preserve and develop its characteristics. That is obedience towards the Creator. And if this obedience leads one to struggles and to war, these too must be regarded as belonging to the order of creation. Here too, the commandment of God is thought of as something which has been given once and for all, in definite ordinances which permit of discovery. Now there is a special danger in this argument; and because it is the one most used at the moment, it must be given special attention. The danger of the argument lies in the fact that just about everything can be defended by it. . . .

[T]he mistake lies in the fact that in the solution of this apparently so simple equation the great unknown factor is overlooked, the factor which makes this solution impossible. It is not realized in all seriousness that the world is fallen and that now sin prevails and that creation and sin are so bound up together that no human eye can any longer separate the one from the other, that each human order is an order of the fallen world, and not an order of creation. There is no longer any possibility of regarding any features per se as orders of creation and of perceiving the will of God *directly* in them. The so-called orders of creation are no longer per se revelations of the divine commandment, they are concealed and invisible. Thus the concept of orders of creation must be rejected as a basis for the knowledge of the commandment of God. Hence, neither the Biblical law as such nor the so-called orders of creation as such are for us the divine commandment which we perceive today.

The commandment cannot stem from anywhere but the origin of promise and fulfillment, from Christ.[56]

It is important to note that Bonhoeffer is not rejecting order. Even his rejection of the orders of creation is qualified. The orders of creation as used at that time overlooked completely that the creation is fallen and that the orders per se do not provide occasion for perceiving the will of God *directly*. What he rejects is that the orders *as such* were used to defend the worst excesses of German nationalism. Instead of seeing that God's order now exists in a fallen world, the orders of creation, specifically the state, were absolutized and tied directly to the will of God, with disastrous results. Later in that same lecture, Bonhoeffer says, "Any order—however ancient and sacred it may be—*can be dissolved* and must be dissolved when it closes itself up in itself, grows rigid and no longer permits the proclamation of revelation."[57] The proclamation of revelation means for Bonhoeffer specifically Jesus Christ, from whom alone is the origin of promise and fulfillment, the one from whom alone the commandment of God can be known.

The problem is how to recast and transform the distorted and misused doctrine of the orders of creation, taking into account sin and grace, the fact that the creation is fallen, and that Jesus Christ is now present. The task is to restructure this notion so that it is dynamic rather than static, redemptive rather than repressive, oriented to the future rather than to the past.

Bonhoeffer begins to talk about orders of preservation. He first defines the restructuring. "Preservation is God's act with the fallen world, through which he guarantees the possibility of the new creation. Orders of preservation are forms of working against sin in the direction of the Gospel."[58] His elaboration makes clear the christological focus.

> Which orders can best restrain this radical falling of the world into death and sin and hold the way open for the Gospel? The church hears the commandment only from Christ, not from any fixed law or from any eternal order, and it hears it in the orders of preservation. The commandment of Christ is therefore quite simply the critical and radical commandment, which is limited by nothing else, by no so-called "orders of creation." It can demand the most radical destruction simply for the sake of the one who builds up. For the church to venture a decision for or against an order of preservation would be an impossibility if it did not happen in faith in the God who in Christ forgives even the church its sins. But in this faith the decision must be ventured.[59]

There is no rejection of order, or of God's ordering of his creation, or even of the notion of orders. The question is *which* orders. Bonhoeffer's answer at this point is the orders of preservation.

The place where the orders of preservation receive their most explicit and comprehensive treatment is in the 1932–33 university lectures published as *Creation and Fall*. It is precisely because the creation is fallen that orders of creation is a misleading and dangerous term. "The preservation of the original creation and the preservation of the fallen creation are two entirely different things."[60] Again, Bonhoeffer's insistence on the recognition of the creation as fallen is linked to his sharp focus on Jesus Christ. What he is at work doing is "recasting" an old ethical structure to bring it into congruence with sin and grace, into correspondence with reality.

> The Creator is now the Preserver. The created world is now the fallen, preserved world. In the world between curse and promise, between *tob* and *ra*, good and evil, God deals with man in his own way. *He made them garments*, says the Bible. That means that God accepts men as they are, as fallen. He affirms them as fallen. He does not expose them before one another in their nakedness, he himself covers them. God's action is concerned with man, but the deciding point is that it now orders and restrains. . . .
> All the orders of our fallen world are God's orders of preservation on the way to Christ. They are not orders of creation but of preservation. They have

no value in themselves. They are accomplished and have purpose only through Christ.[61]

Bonhoeffer later abandons the phrase orders of preservation, but the same content appears in the *Ethics* in a new formulation, the divine mandates. One reason for dropping the orders of preservation language was that Paul Althaus of Erlangen began to use it, and Bonhoeffer wanted to run no risk of being identified with Althaus, who was sympathetic to the Nazis. He does, however, continue to use the word preservation, even in the *Ethics*, as a key category. The conviction remains that ethical decisions must be made in the context of God's ordering of his creation, and that this ordering results in social structures such as family, state, and church, which are positive gifts of the God who brings order out of chaos. The insistence upon the recognition of these social structures, which provide continuity and community to moral behavior and ethical reflection, is the primary intention of Bonhoeffer's formula of the divine mandates just as it was the primary intention of the formula orders of preservation. Writing about the mandates in the *Ethics*, he says it clearly.

> We cannot now escape the question where and in what historical form God makes His commandment known. For the sake of simplicity and clarity, and even at the risk of a direct misunderstanding, we will begin by answering this question in the form of a thesis. God's commandment, which is manifested in Jesus Christ, comes to us in the Church, in the family, in labour and in government.[62]

The same things that distinguished the orders of preservation from the orders of creation are also characteristic of the divine mandates. There is, for instance, a notable tentativity about the mandates, a fluidity even in their number and designation, which could never be true for those who regarded the orders of creation as absolute and changeless created structures. In one place, Bonhoeffer includes marriage along with family and adds culture before government. It is not clear whether culture is in addition to government or part of government. The fluidity of the mandates is further confirmed in the prison letters where he reflects on the possibility of friendship as a mandate.[63]

Another distinctive feature of the divine mandates, as it was of the orders of preservation, is that they are tied to the concrete command. Responsible action is *mandated*, commanded. It is not just that the orders "exist" as created. Family, state, and church are the places where one hears the command of God in the here and now. The focus is not God's past creation but his present will for the future of his creation. The shift is significant and consistent.

Also characteristic of both the orders of preservation and the divine mandates is their setting in a christological framework. Classic Lutheran ethics has always considered the orders of creation as a first-article rubric. Particularly for Lutherans, it has to do with creation, not with redemption, and this distinction is taken to be as clear and as important as is that between law and gospel. Jesus Christ as radical center of Bonhoeffer's ethical theology, however, is also the focus of his structuring of the mandates. He defines "mandate" as "the concrete divine commission which has its foundation in the revelation of Christ and which is evidenced in Scripture."[64] He is, as always, uncompromising on this point. "The divine mandates are dependent solely on the *one* commandment of God as it is revealed in Jesus Christ."[65] Again it is the relentless rejection of all dualisms, necessitated by the reality of God and world together in Christ, that brings Bonhoeffer to see the mandates as structures for re-creating a de-created world. The language of the opening paragraph on the mandates is punctuated by words such as "unity," "the whole," "undivided claim," "reconciling love."[66]

The topics and issues discussed in the section on the mandates in the *Ethics* are similar to those traditionally discussed in ethics texts under the rubric of orders of creation. Bonhoeffer talks about the nature and function of social institutions. He even says that the word "institution" could be used instead of "mandate," and that it "would no doubt be capable of expressing very effectively what is here intended" if it could be purged of misinterpretation.[67] He talks about "earthly agent" of "divine authority," using the term "deputy" to capture that cluster of ideas. He discusses "office," and works with the problem of conflicts and overlapping loyalties in the several mandates. He is very clear that he is restructuring, rather than abandoning, traditional categories. "For lack of a better word, therefore, we will for the time being retain the term 'mandate,' but it is still our purpose, by dint of clarifying the concept itself, to help to renew and to restore the old notion of the institution, the estate, and the office."[68] Bonhoeffer recognized the gross misuse of the orders of creation by the Nazis and the "German Christians," who absolutized the state and cut it off from its grounding in God's purpose. He knew that it was impossible to find moral guidance in "theoretical speculation or in private inspiration" or in "historical forces or sublime ideals."[69] The ethical structures of family, state, and church must be taken with utmost seriousness. Yet there must be a recognition that they are now part of a fallen creation, subject to demonic distortion and perversion; that they must be subject to the will of God rather than detached from it; and that they must be congruent with the reality of all things brought together in Jesus Christ. Participating in God's ordering of his creation is expressed by Bonhoeffer in a number of ways, not only in his formulation of the orders of preservation and the divine mandates, but also in his handling of the traditional doctrines of vocation and of the two realms.

"Vocation" and "The Two Realms"

Two formulas of traditional Lutheran ethics, which fit together with the orders of creation, and with which Bonhoeffer also deals, are the doctrine of vocation and the doctrine of the two realms. Both have to do with the way in which God orders his creation.

The doctrine of vocation is rooted in the fact that God's call (in Latin, *vocare*) comes to each person in a concrete place of responsibility. It does not come in abstraction or only in a "spiritual" way. The church (in Greek, *ekklesia*) is made up of those who are called out (in Greek, *ek-kaleo*) to serve God "in the place in which they have been called" (1 Corinthians 7). Thus one serves God where one is, not where one is not. The Reformation doctrine of vocation is a specific honoring of secular occupation and of secular life. The problem comes when the fallenness of the creation is forgotten, and the place in which one is called is absolutized, so that one must, in order to serve God, "know one's place" and "keep one's place." The result is a static and inflexible understanding of vocational stratifications, which tend in some societies to continue generation after generation.

Bonhoeffer affirms the doctrine of vocation and uses it directly. In one of his catechism drafts, to the question "What should I do?" he gives the answer, "Do what your calling gives you to do."[70] In the *Ethics* he uses the word "vocation" to elaborate "the place of responsibility." He does, however, as one would expect, point to "disastrous misunderstandings," one of which he calls the "secular Protestant" one, the other the "monastic" one.[71] One must say both yes and no to the traditional structures, including the doctrine of vocation. In the following paragraph the same features are present as are operative in Bonhoeffer's work with the orders.

> Responsibility in one's calling obeys only the call of Christ. There is a wrong and a right restriction and there is a wrong and a right extension of responsibility; there is an enthusiastic breaking-down of all limits, and there is a legalistic setting-up of limits. It is difficult, or even impossible, to judge from

outside whether in a particular concrete instance an action is responsible or whether it is enthusiastic or legalistic; there are, however, criteria for self-examination, though even these cannot afford complete certainty about one's own ego.[72]

A related formula is the doctrine of the two realms. It was an original construction by Luther. On the positive side, it is an ethical translation of the law/gospel formula, and carries the same "distinction without separation" dynamics. On the negative side, Luther saw it as a way of combating what he considered to be the naive enthusiasms of the radical reformers and also the double-standard morality of the Roman Catholics. It is probably the single most distinctive contribution of Luther to ethical theory.

Again, there is an obvious problem. What was intended as a duality became for many a dualism; what was intended to be a dialectic became a dichotomy. Luther stated very clearly that God rules in both realms, but that he rules in different ways. In the "kingdom on the left" he rules through power which restrains evil, when necessary even by means of the sword. In the "kingdom on the right" he rules through love and forgiveness. As does the orders of creation doctrine when rightly used, or that of vocation, the doctrine of the two realms honors secular occupation without compromising Christian vocation. The judge, when functioning in the kingdom on the left, appropriately sees that justice is done. The same person, when functioning in the kingdom on the right, in some personal or family situation, may appropriately simply forgive a wrongdoing, something which he or she may not do when on the judicial bench. The distinction does not make ethical decision or moral behavior simple, but it does provide a structure within which to reflect in a helpful way on the problem. If, however, the two realms are separated and particularly if God's activity is restricted to the "kingdom on the right," the results are disastrous. Theological sanction is then given to the state to go its own way, and for the church to retreat into an individualistic and nonpolitical quietism. This is precisely what happened among many Protestants in Germany during the Nazi years, not least among Lutherans.

Thus, as one would expect, Bonhoeffer is highly critical of the way in which this formula was used, but he also has some appreciation for its original intent. He refers in the *Ethics* to the separation of the two realms as "pseudo-Lutheran"[73] and makes clear his positive appreciation of the doctrine. "It is only in this sense, as a polemical unity, that Luther's doctrine of the two kingdoms is to be accepted, and it was no doubt in this sense that it was originally intended."[74] This positive use of the doctrine is explicit at least as far back as the Christology lectures of 1933.

Christ is present to us in the forms both of Church and State. But he is this only for us, who receive him as Word and Sacrament and Church; for us, who since the cross must see the state in the light of Christ. The state is God's "rule with his left hand" (Luther, WA 36, 385, 6–9; 52, 26, 20–6). So long as Christ was on earth, he was the kingdom of God. When he was crucified the kingdom broke up into one ruled by God's right hand and one ruled by his left hand. Now it can be recognized in a twofold form, as Church and as State. But the complete Christ is present in his Church. And this Church is the hidden centre of the state. The state need not know that the Church is this centre, but in fact it lives from this centre and has no effective existence without it.[75]

In his 1939 statement about American Christianity, which he called "Protestantism without Reformation," Bonhoeffer is very clear that he opposes the misinterpretation of the two realms doctrine.

The secularisation of the church on the continent of Europe arose from the misinterpretation of the reformers' distinction of the two realms; *American secularisation* derives precisely from the imperfect distinction of the kingdoms and offices of church and state, from the enthusiastic claim of the church to universal influence on the world. That is a significant distinction. While for the churches of the Reformation the doctrine of the two realms needs a new examination and correction, the American denominations today must learn the necessity of this distinction, if they are to be rescued from complete secularisation.[76]

Heated debate continues in the churches about this complex Lutheran ethical theory, and it no doubt will for many years. This brief statement merely indicates Bonhoeffer's own ambiguous relation to it.

Whether talking about the orders of preservation or the divine mandates, or about vocation, or the two realms, Bonhoeffer consistently expresses a strong commitment to God's ordering of his creation. He is careful to avoid a static and inflexible understanding of that ordering. He works hard to create ethical structures that are consistent with time and history as ethical constituents. For the sake of the incarnate, crucified, and risen Christ, he struggles against the misuse and destruction of order by Hitler for the purpose of restoring that order of God which gives rise to true freedom.

Conformation with Reality

Conformation

Another way in which Bonhoeffer seeks to guard against a contentless ethic and arbitrary moral judgments is by suggesting that the responsible life should correspond to reality. Since reality is focused in Jesus Christ, behavior that corresponds to reality is behavior in conformation with Christ. Anyone familiar with the English Bible, upon hearing this suggestion, is apt to think of the words of Paul to the church at Rome, "Do not be conformed to this world but be transformed by the renewal of your mind, that you may prove what is the will of God, what is good and acceptable and perfect."[77] Both the apostle Paul and Bonhoeffer are interested in discerning the will of God. Yet their words of counsel seem to be quite different. "Conformation" is negative for Paul, positive for Bonhoeffer. The "world" is negative for Paul, positive for Bonhoeffer. Paul seems to be admonishing his readers to some radical personal change. That emphasis does not seem to be strong in Bonhoeffer. One has to search in Bonhoeffer for language that suggests radical personal change.

On the other hand, Paul and Bonhoeffer are remarkably similar. Both pursue an ethical theology that insists on tying behavior and faith intimately together. Both see legalism and moralism as the primary ethical heresies. Both are thoroughly christocentric. The task of this section is to understand Bonhoeffer's structuring of responsible life in terms of conformation with Christ, and to see how this fits with or recasts traditional Christian themes going back as far as the apostle Paul. There is a chapter in the *Ethics* entitled "Ethics as Formation" and a section in that chapter entitled "Conformation." The play on words in these passages is fascinating. "The point of departure for Christian ethics is the body of Christ, the form of Christ in the form of the Church, and formation of the Church in conformity with the form of Christ."[78] The word "form" together with its cognates is used extensively by Bonhoeffer as he works to structure the responsible life in such a way that there can be participation in the shaping of the future of God's world.

We have already seen that in the book by Dumas, Bonhoeffer's word *Gestalt* is translated throughout as "structure."[79] It is not consistently translated so in the English edition of the *Ethics*. Dumas entitles one chapter of his book "Jesus Christ as concrete 'spatiality' " and begins that chapter with the astonishing sentence, "Bonhoeffer speaks of Jesus Christ both as a place and as a structure of the world around us, and almost never refers to him as an event in history."[80] Supporting his conclusion with a reference to the table of contents of the Christology lectures, Dumas says, "This vocabulary based on spatial imagery seems to me fundamental to a correct interpretation of Bonhoeffer."[81] Furthermore, Dumas adopts the word "structure" as the key to Bonhoeffer's lectures on Christology.[82] It is perhaps not insignificant that Dumas refers twice in this chapter to Claude

Levi-Strauss. "Structuralism," the movement associated with Levi-Strauss and others, which has enjoyed a modest success in literary criticism and linguistic studies, has now also invaded biblical interpretation. The use of the word structure in structuralism, however, is very different from Bonhoeffer's use of terms such as structure and form. Structuralism works at finding nonhistorical, timeless, specifically universal structures of reality. Bonhoeffer is always, on the contrary, working at structures that can embrace and encompass time and history as constituents of ethical theology. There is always, therefore, a fundamental ambiguity, a flexibility and movement and drive toward change in these structures at which he works. We have seen that this is the case with his use of the categories of ultimate and penultimate, and also his structuring of the divine mandates. Conformation is also a structure in motion. It is a category used by Bonhoeffer to seek out ethical implications of the fact that the incarnate, crucified, and risen Christ is an event in history.

In the chapter on "Ethics as Formation," Bonhoeffer begins immediately to criticize traditional ethics for not paying sufficient attention to the times. It is precisely the nontemporal character of what he calls "theoretical" or "systematic" ethics that makes it impossible for it to deal with the "superabounding reality of concrete ethical problems"[83] present during the Nazi years in Germany.

> Today there are once more villains and saints, and they are not hidden from the public view. Instead of the uniform greyness of the rainy day we now have the black storm-cloud and the brilliant lightning-flash. The outlines stand out with exaggerated sharpness. Reality lays itself bare. Shakespeare's characters walk in our midst. But the villain and the saint have little or nothing to do with systematic ethical studies. They emerge from primeval depths and by their appearance they tear open the infernal or the divine abyss from which they come and enable us to see for the moment into mysteries of which we had never dreamed.[84]

Bonhoeffer states that the traditional ethical systems, with which he was very familiar, had little to say to those terrible times in which he was living. They were "unable to grasp what is real." Their ethical programs were a "waste," "empty air."[85] He walks through a catalog of traditional ethical stances: the "reasonable person," the "fanatic," the "person of conscience," the "person of duty," the "person of absolute freedom," the "person of silent virtue." They are all "great achievements of noble humanity," but they are "rusty swords" when it comes to dealing with current and real problems.[86] The rusty swords must be replaced with sharp ones. There must be simplicity and wisdom, rather than ethical principles. The commandments, the judgments, and the mercies of God must be heard every day afresh. And the only way to do that is by beholding the man Jesus, who is not an ideal person, but rather the truly human person, humankind as it really is. Jesus Christ is not the transfiguration of sublime humanity. He is real humankind. The name Jesus contains within itself the whole of humanity and the whole of God. Looking at humankind instead of at Jesus Christ inevitably leads to either contempt for humankind or idolization of humankind, both of which are short of reality. It is only in Jesus Christ that we know what reality is about.

It is difficult to imagine how Dumas can say that Bonhoeffer "almost never refers to him (Jesus Christ) as an event in history,"[87] when the exact opposite is the case on almost every page of the *Ethics*. There *is* structure. There *is* form. There *is* place. But the place of which Bonhoeffer speaks is always controlled by and enmeshed in time.

> But there is a place at which God and the cosmic reality are reconciled, a place at which God and man have become one. That and that alone is what enables man to set his eyes upon God and upon the world at the same time. This place does not lie somewhere out beyond reality in the realm of ideas. It lies in the midst of history as a divine miracle. It lies in Jesus Christ, the Reconciler of the world.[88]

To the question of how to structure responsible life, how to keep an emphasis on situations from turning chaotic, Bonhoeffer responds that actions that conform to Jesus Christ will correspond with reality.

The word "formation" was used by the Nazis a great deal, and Bonhoeffer knew that very well. The word, he says, "arouses our suspicion."[89] The Nazis had all kinds of programs for "forming" people and were confident that it was they who were shaping the future. Bonhoeffer's response, again, is not to abandon, but to recast. "The word 'formation,' therefore, must be taken in quite a different sense from that to which we are accustomed."[90] Again, he goes to the Christian Scriptures and from them to the incarnate, crucified, and risen Christ.

> Their [the Christian Scriptures] primary concern is not with the forming of a world by means of plans and programs. Whenever they speak of forming they are concerned only with the one form which has overcome the world, the form of Jesus Christ. Formation can come only from this form. But here again it is not a question of applying directly to the world the teaching of Christ or what are referred to as Christian principles, so that the world might be formed in accordance with these. On the contrary, formation comes only by being drawn in into the form of Jesus Christ. It comes only as formation in His likeness, as *conformation* with the unique form of Him who was made man, was crucified, and rose again.[91]

This does not mean to "become like Jesus." Jesus is not essentially a teacher who gives "instruction in the way in which a pious and good life is to be attained. Christ is the Incarnate, Crucified and Risen One whom the Christian faith confesses. To be transformed in His image (2 Cor. 3:18, Phil. 3:10, Rom. 8:29, 12:2) — this is what is meant by the formation of which the Bible speaks."[92] So Bonhoeffer is for transformation as is the apostle Paul. And he is for transformation into the image of Christ. The specific note that Bonhoeffer sounds is that such a transformation cannot be properly understood if thought of as changing an impious person into a pious person. What the transformation accomplishes is putting a person in touch with what is really the case, with the whole creation as it really is, with God and world together in Christ. It means that existence and behavior will correspond with reality.

Ott is one who believes that Bonhoeffer's use of conformation has to do with time and history, that this structure is more temporal than spatial, that it has to do with "the maintenance of a hope transcending all that is forseeable."[93] Ott sees correctly that for Bonhoeffer the ethical situation is made materially concrete "through the responsibility of the one who acts for the shaping of the future, that area of the future given as our responsibility."[94] Bonhoeffer's commitment to the temporal context of the correspondence with reality that accompanies conformation with Christ has to do not only with the content, but also with the method, of ethics.

> The situation of the ethicist, and therefore of ethical study, is for its part historical. The ethicist cannot place himself and his thinking outside that historical context. Hence, his studies can never take on an unhistorical character, but the study is itself a historical act, a historical decision. It has its own setting, its own special place, in the historical situation, and cannot escape from that concrete place. In that case what is *once for all* good can never be worked out by concrete study or by responsible thought; our eyes have to be turned solely towards how Christ is formed among us *here and today*. But now this *hic et nunc* refers for Bonhoeffer not merely to the individual and unrepeatable ethical situation, it extends beyond it by virtue of his category of the collective person.[95]

The concrete place about which Bonhoeffer writes is itself a temporal structure. The sociality of Christ and the collective person, worked out with such force and dexterity in his first dissertation, comes into play as Bonhoeffer walks through the history of the Western world in the *Ethics.* Whatever one may think about the details and the sweeping generalizations of Bonhoeffer's analysis, it is clear that correspondence with reality means conformation with Christ in his body, the church. Collective person implies "collective situation."[96] Unrestrained individualism is prevented, says Bonhoeffer, by the fact that "by our history we are set objectively in a definite nexus of experiences, responsibilities and decisions from which we cannot free ourselves again except by an abstraction."[97]

Because conformation with Christ is correspondence with reality in one's own time and place, it has nothing to do with "vain imitation or repetition of Christ's form."[98] Although Bonhoeffer read and treasured Thomas à Kempis's *The Imitation of Christ*, that notion of imitation was foreign to his understanding of who Christ is and what he does. The Word of God which is heard fresh every morning allows a person to be who that person is or, better, to become who that person is.

> The real man is at liberty to be his creator's creature. To be conformed with the Incarnate is to have the right to be the man one really is. Now there is no more pretence, no more hypocrisy or self-violence, no more compulsion to be something other, better and more ideal than what one is. God loves the real man. God became a real man.[99]

So the life of the collective person is as hidden as is the historical life of Jesus himself. Bonhoeffer echoes the *Epistle to Diognetus* when he says that "the new man lives in the world like any other man. Often there is little to distinguish him from the rest. Nor does he attach importance to distinguishing himself, but only distinguishing Christ for the sake of his brethen."[100] In *Life Together* as in *The Communion of Saints*, Bonhoeffer stresses the fact that the church is Jesus Christ and only Jesus Christ, that neither the individual Christian nor the church exists to be constantly feeling its spiritual temperature or taking its spiritual pulse. Christian life is in no way the striving after an ideal, but is rather the participation in present reality in Christ.[101] To forget that everything revealed is also at the same time hidden is to substitute conformity to ourselves for conformity to reality in Christ.

> God does not will that I should fashion the other person according to the image that seems good to me, that is, in my own image; rather in his very freedom from me God made this person in His image. I can never know beforehand how God's image should appear in others. That image always manifests a completely new and unique form that comes solely from God's free and sovereign creation.[102]

Because of sin, the situations in which conformation with Christ is called for will always be ambiguous. Because reality is in motion, and God's Word is heard fresh every morning, the image of the conformation will never be simple repetition, even of the lifestyle of Jesus. Yet there is both continuity and community in this conformation, because conformation with Christ is correspondence with reality.

Conscience

A special case of conformation with Christ, one which deserves extensive treatment but which can be handled here only with a few brief suggestions, is Bonhoeffer's ethical theology of conscience. Beginning with *The Communion of Saints* and continuing on through the *Ethics* and into the prison letters, Bonhoeffer had a great deal to say about conscience. It is, however, sufficiently consistent and sufficiently congruent with his other structural work so that a brief summary statement will at least not be misleading.

The first thing to say is that Bonhoeffer flatly rejects the common notion that conscience is a sure guide to the will of God, or even to a knowledge of right and wrong. That understanding of conscience is so widespread that it could almost be said to be universal, and it exists in both naive and sophisticated forms. The parent who advises the child to follow the conscience has an idea that this "faculty" is somehow either a primeval moral compass still at work in the mind or soul of human beings or else a clear receiver of divine signals. Even Bonhoeffer's own dissertation advisor, Reinhold Seeberg, connected conscience to what he called "the religious a priori," universally present in human beings. And Bonhoeffer's Berlin professor Karl Holl saw conscience as the heart of Luther's life and theology. Roman Catholic theology, because of its somewhat less radical view of the work of sin on human reason and the human psyche, has always tended to regard conscience as a less ambiguous guide for conduct than have most Protestants. Bonhoeffer, however, consistently regards conscience as a sign of our inner division, a result of the fall. In his first dissertation he writes:

> Conscience did not exist in the primal state; it was only after the Fall that Adam knew what good and evil were. Conscience can just as well be the ultimate prop for self-justification as the point at which Christ strikes home at man through the law.[103]

In *Act and Being* he states that conscience is a person's own voice, not the voice of God, that it in fact interposes itself between a person and Jesus Christ.[104] That view seems to be behind his early interest in doing a study of the relation of consciousness and conscience.[105] In *Creation and Fall* Bonhoeffer is very explicit about conscience being a result of the fall and a sign of our dividedness. It is Adam's flight from God, his hiding from God.[106] In the *Ethics* the "person of conscience" is portrayed along with others as one of those types of "theoretical ethicists" who are not able to make contact with reality.

> The man with a *conscience* fights a lonely battle against the overwhelming forces of inescapable situations which demand decisions. But he is torn apart by the extent of the conflicts in which he has to make his choice with no other aid or counsel than that which his own innermost conscience can furnish. Evil comes upon him in countless respectable and seductive disguises so that his conscience becomes timid and unsure of itself, till in the end he is satisfied if instead of a clear conscience he has a salved one, and lies to his own conscience in order to avoid despair. A man whose only support is his conscience can never understand that a bad conscience may be healthier and stronger than a conscience which is deceived.[107]

The very interesting thing about Bonhoeffer's procedure is again that he does not simply abandon, but recasts this traditional ethical category. He talks eventually about the "conscience which is set free in Jesus Christ."[108] In a daring reference to the National Socialist who says "My conscience is Adolf Hitler" and to the Christian who says "Jesus has become my conscience," Bonhoeffer works on what he calls "an extremely direct and significant parallel" and "an extremely direct and significant contrast."[109] "Natural conscience, no matter how strict and rigorous it may be, is now seen to be the most ungodly self-justification, and it is overcome by the conscience which is set free in Jesus Christ and which summons me to unity with myself in Jesus Christ."[110] The conscience set free in Christ is set free for the service of God and neighbor and thus enters the fellowship of human guilt for the sake of that service. Its goal is not personal purity but life lived for others.

Coming back full circle, Bonhoeffer demonstrates that the recognition of the sharp distinction between the natural conscience and the conscience set free in Christ allows one to see also some striking similarities in content.

> It has been correctly observed that in the contents of its law natural conscience is in strikingly close agreement with that of the conscience which has been set free in Christ. This is due to the fact that it is upon conscience that the continuance of life itself depends; conscience, therefore, contains fundamental features of the law of life, even though these features may be distorted in detail and perverted in principle. The liberated conscience is still what it was as the natural conscience, namely the warner against transgression of the law of life. But the law is no longer the last thing; there is still Jesus Christ; for that reason, in the contest between conscience and concrete responsibility, the free decision must be given for Christ. This does not mean an everlasting conflict, but the winning of ultimate unity; for indeed the

foundation, the essence and the goal of concrete responsibility is the same Jesus Christ who is the Lord of conscience. Thus responsibility is bound by conscience, but conscience is set free by responsibility.[111]

As everything else in this fallen world, conscience is distorted and unreliable as a guide to moral behavior. It is, according to Bonhoeffer, a result of the fall, not a primal state. Yet also, as everything else in this fallen world, conscience is redeemable in Christ. And the conscience set free in Christ becomes useful as a guide, even a guide that in many cases will agree with the "natural conscience." The difference is that the dictates of the conscience set free in Christ will always be subject to and controlled by Christ, with whom the conscience is conformed. This does not lead to some kind of otherworldly behavior, detached from reality. On the contrary, it leads to behavior that corresponds to reality. In the previously quoted passage, Bonhoeffer mentions twice the "law of life," with which the conscience set free in Christ has to do. We turn now to his treatment of the law.

The Law and the Laws of Life

Dictionary definitions of law almost always include among primary uses some variant of "a guide or directive for human action." If law has to do with how people ought to behave, it surely has something to do with ethics. There are traditions in ethics, therefore, in which law is the operative category. There are also traditions in which freedom from law is the operative category, where law is an essentially negative term. In the section on "God's Ordering of His Creation," we saw that Bonhoeffer combined in his personal life rigorous discipline and contagious freedom, and that this was consistent with his attempt to work at structures such as the orders of preservation and the divine mandates which would enable freedom rather than repress it. Although freedom was exceedingly important to him, both personally and politically, he was careful to describe that freedom in such a way that it would not become chaotic or lawless. Bonhoeffer's ethics is not "law and order" ethics. But "law" is no more a negative term for him than is "order." When he works at structuring the responsible life, he is clear that responsibility cannot be simply obedience to law or freedom from law.

> The man of responsibility stands between obligation and freedom; he must dare to act under obligation and in freedom; yet he finds his justification neither in his obligation nor in his freedom but solely in Him who has put him in this [humanly impossible] situation and who requires this deed of him.[112]
>
> Obedience without freedom is slavery; freedom without obedience is

arbitrary self will. Obedience restrains freedom; and freedom ennobles obedience. Obedience binds the creature to the Creator and freedom enables the creature to stand before the Creator as one who is made in His image. . . . Obedience has its hands tied and freedom is creative. In obedience man adheres to the decalogue and in freedom man creates new decalogues (Luther).[113]

The dialectic of freedom and obligation in Bonhoeffer is not based on absolute law applied to fluid situations. It is based, rather, on an understanding of law which is thoroughly christocentric and therefore enmeshed in time and history. It is possible to read him as a legalist (for instance, in *The Cost of Discipleship*) or as an antinomian (for instance, in certain passages of the *Ethics*) if one forgets that christocentric focus. If one remembers, however, that for Bonhoeffer this Christ is always the incarnate, crucified, and risen one, it will not be difficult to understand why the law has to do with life and living. In *Creation and Fall* he works at this in a detailed way.

He deals with Gen. 1:11–13 under the rubric "The Living."[114] He says that, on the one hand, the bringing forth of the living is something entirely new, without any continuity. On the other hand, the living differs from the dead by the fact that it can itself create life. So, although the creation of life is *ex nihilo*, without continuity, it is also *continua*, giving rise to continuity.

Bonhoeffer equates the dead with the unchangeable. In a section that anticipates the "polyphony of life" passage in the prison letters, he writes, "[God] does not will to be Lord of a dead, eternally unchangeable world subjected to him, he wills to be the Lord of life, in all its infinite forms."[115] The world is not dead and unchangeable, nor does it run by immutable laws. Law is not unchangeable and therefore dead, and that includes the physical laws of the universe. "The living and created is not divine; it is and remains the creaturely, the creation, the work separated from the Creator which the Creator freely commands. . . . Nothing in the creation 'runs by itself.' "[116] Law, even the physical laws of the universe, has to do with life.

> Therefore the lawfulness of the course of the world and the aliveness of the creation are not identifiable with the preserving action of God; on the contrary, the law and life are alone preserved by the free Word of God. The law and life are not worthy of adoration, for they are creatures like all others, but the one who is worthy is the Lord of the law and the Lord of the living.[117]

Law and life have to do with one another because both are centered in the Lord who is for Bonhoeffer not God in general, but God in the flesh of Jesus of Nazareth. Both legalism and antinomianism are avoided by seeing both obedience and freedom in the light of Christ who is the living Lord and Lord of the living.

As was the case with other ethical categories, such as the orders of creation and the doctrine of the two realms, law was greatly misused by the Nazis and the "German Christians." Soon after Hitler came to power, the Nazis burned the Reichstag, blamed it on the communists, and then passed the "enabling laws" which gave them legal permission to do whatever was necessary to safeguard the country from communism. These laws created a situation in which it was possible for them to do everything legally, and in which those who opposed them were almost automatically involved in illegal activity. In addition to that, Hitler himself claimed to be above all laws.

In the context of this misuse of law by the Nazis, and also of Bonhoeffer's lifelong attack on legalism, one might expect him to align himself in a simple and energetic way with the Pauline-Lutheran contrast between the law which kills and the gospel which gives life. It is true that such passages exist. But Bonhoeffer does not usually contrast law and life. He consistently connects them. One of the ways he does this is by speaking of "the law of life." The word *Lebensgesetz* in the Bonhoeffer literature is translated in so many different ways ("law of living," "vital law," "basic law") that the reader of Bonhoeffer in English cannot notice its repetition. Yet the use of the term by Bonhoeffer is striking.

William F. Connor has shown that the word *Lebensgesetz* (law of life) occurs throughout the Bonhoeffer literature.[118] It occurs in the first publication, the 1927 dissertation *The Communion of Saints*, where Bonhoeffer speaks about it as the law that God establishes for the primal human community before the fall. After the fall this is broken, but it is reestablished by Christ as the law of life for the church, the new humankind, which in turn serves the future of the world.[119] In the early period the term, or equivalent phrases, also occurs in the 1929 Barcelona lecture on ethics,[120] in a 1932 baptismal sermon for the son of his brother Klaus,[121] in the 1932 lecture "Thy Kingdom Come,"[122] and in the first draft of the Bethel confession which Bonhoeffer prepared with Herman Sasse in 1933.[123] For this early period, Connor concludes:

> [The laws of life] . . . are permanent as being found *in* all times and places, but not as being *for* all times and places. . . . Little is said of their content. . . . The authority of the laws of life is subordinate to the divine freedom which breaks them; God does not thereby destroy them, rather he affirms their limited validity.[124]

In the middle years, 1935–39, the word occurs infrequently but its importance seems to grow. It is found in the second catechism attempt, prepared for a 1936 lecture at Finkenwalde.[125] Bonhoeffer asks, "Where has God revealed the law of life to his people?" The answer is, "At Sinai in the ten commandments: Exod. 20:2–17." The naming of the ten commandments as the law of life for Israel compares closely with the earlier Bethel confession of 1933. Connor believes that these examples stand in contrast "to the Barcelona lecture of 1929 which affirmed that Christians are free to make their own decalogue."[126] Yet if one understands Bonhoeffer's dialectic of obedience to and freedom from law, and his distinction of continuity and discontinuity between Old and New Testaments, these citations need not be taken as contrasts at all, but as different moments in the laws of life which are not timeless, but timely. The term occurs also in *The Cost of Discipleship*, published in 1937, and in the meditation on Psalm 119. According to Connor, in this middle period little new is added except that in the first step of obedience in *The Cost of Discipleship*, the question about natural law may perhaps be raised.

In the later writings (1940–44) the word occurs in a few significant places. The most explicit occurrence is in the *Ethics*:

> The decalogue is the law of living, revealed by God, for all life which is subject to the dominion of Christ. It signifies liberation from alien rule and from arbitrary autonomy. It discloses itself to believers as the law of the Creator and the Reconciler. The decalogue is the framework within which a free obedience becomes possible in worldly life. It affords liberty for free life under the dominion of Christ.[127]

It is a passage consistent with the confidential reply to William Paton's book, *The Church and the New Order*, which sought to provide a theological basis for the peace after Hitler's defeat and included the following statement. The reply was written by Bonhoeffer and Visser 't Hooft.

> The foundation of a new order of the world can only be sought in the will of God revealed in Jesus Christ. Because the world subsists only "in Christ" and is "directed to Christ" (Colossians 1), therefore every view of man "in himself" or of the world and its order "in themselves" is an abstraction. Everything stands in relation to Christ according to the will of God, whether it knows of this or not. *God has revealed the limits which may not be transgressed if Christ is to be Lord in the world . . . a secular order which maintains itself within the decalogue will be open for Christ, i.e., for the proclamation of the church and for life according to his word.* Such an order, of course, is not "Christian," but it is a just earthly order according to God's will.[128]

Consistent with the entire development of his ethical theology, Bonhoeffer ties all divine and human reality together in Christ. Nothing exists in itself, but only in relation to Christ, whether it knows it or not. There is thus a congruence between the law of God and the laws which hold together a just social order. Any responsible look to the future has to work at establishing laws that will make for a just social order, and that order will have to include the freedom to proclaim Christ.

Bonhoeffer refers to the law of life again in his 1942 essay "After Ten Years." There is also an appearance of the term in the fiction fragments from Tegel. The last explicit reference is in the 1944 prison writing "The First Table of the Ten Commandments."

> In all ages men have thought about the fundamental orders of life, and it is an exceedingly noteworthy fact that the results of almost all such reflections agree extensively with each other and with the ten commandments. . . . The Christian rejoices that he holds so many important things in common with other men. He is ready to work and to struggle alongside these men, where it is the matter of the realization of common goals. It does not surprise him that men in every age have come to understandings of life that agree extensively with the Ten Commandments, because the Giver of the Commandments is indeed the Creator and Preserver of life.[129]

According to Connor, Bonhoeffer here speaks openly and freely of the agreement between the laws of life and the decalogue, although he had sharply distinguished between them in 1933, and spoke cautiously in the *Ethics* of their "providential congruity." Connor's conclusion is instructive.

> Here at the last, Bonhoeffer expresses the full immanence of the laws of life and grants reason's role as their proper mode of perception. To speak in this way is not to give reason a right of its own, independent of the divine source and sustainer of life. For Bonhoeffer such autonomy remains impermissible; to affirm it would have placed him on the side of natural theology, which he never was. . . . The attainment of the deepest Christological foundation gives Bonhoeffer the greater freedom to affirm the place of reason in perceiving the laws of life.
>
> If we have been faithful to Bonhoeffer's thought in tracing his concept of the laws of life, we will have recognized the care with which he approached a subject so susceptible to distortion by the historical events of his time. He played the theme very softly at such times. When Germany faced collapse, however, and the future of western civilization hung in the balance, Bonhoeffer allowed the theme of the laws of life to reach its fullest amplitude. All of this he did, of course, in the name of Him whose Lordship embraces the worldliness of human life. The theme we have followed belongs neither to natural law, nor to natural theology, but to what we might better designate a theology of the natural.[130]

Connor's work on Bonhoeffer's use of the term *Lebensgesetz* serves as a window through which to view the approach to law throughout the Bonhoeffer literature.

Of particular interest is Bonhoeffer's long attachment to Psalm 119. His own study Bible is underlined and marked off in sections at this point and there are penciled-in notes on virtually every page. Although massively opposed to legalism, he loved this long hymn of praise to the law of God. He begins his section entitled "The Law" in *Psalms: The Prayerbook of the Bible* with the sentence "The three Psalms (1, 19, 119) which in a special way make the law of God the object of thanks, praise, and petition seek to show us, above all, the blessing of the law."[131] Bonhoeffer goes on to say that under law "is to be understood usually the entire salvation act of God and the direction for a new life in obedience. Joy in the law and in the commands of God comes to us if God has given the great new direction to our life through Jesus Christ."[132] In a closing paragraph Bonhoeffer refers to Psalm 119 and talks about how the "apparent repetitions are always new variations on one theme, namely the love of God's word."[133] He says that the words should accompany us all through life and that "they become in their simplicity the prayer of the child, of the young person, and of the old person."[134] In Bethge's introduction to Bonhoeffer's exposition of Psalm 119, he emphasizes the great care that was taken preparing this material for the winter 1939–40 group of vicars. Entirely consistent with the essay on "costly grace" in *The Cost of Discipleship*, Bonhoeffer insists that God's deed of redemption, and God's command and promise, go together. He says that no one understands the law of God who does not know the event of redemption and the future promise.[135] The question about the law of God is not first of all a moral question at all, but has to do rather with a complete act of God, including God's promise for shaping the future.

Bethge has appended to the *Ethics* an essay by Bonhoeffer on the first use of the law according to the Lutheran Confessions. This is a particularly important essay because in Lutheran theology the first use of the law, or the civil use, is a kind of equivalent to natural law in Roman Catholic and Reformed theology. It is generally thought that the decisive difference between the Lutheran first use of the law and the natural law of Roman Catholic and Reformed theology is that in Lutheran theology the first use of the law is purely negative. Werner Elert calls it "the law of retribution."[136] The first use of the law, then, functions as a limit for human conduct, because breaking the law brings its own punishment. It does not say what we ought to do but rather what we ought not to do. It is soon clear, however, when one reads Bonhoeffer on the first use of the law, that he understands it as being more complex than this. He says that there is no systematic handling of the first use of the law in the Formula of Concord or in the Confessions as a whole but that it is used both positively and negatively.[137] The gospel adds nothing to the decalogue or to the law as a whole. The problem of the relation of natural law, or better, the law of nature, to the decalogue returns here. There is an amazing congruence between the decalogue and the law of nature. Yet, natural law or the law of nature adds nothing to the decalogue and everything that is necessary to know is there in the Ten Commandments. In relation to the gospel, the first use is both superseded and preserved by the gospel in faith in Jesus Christ. It is both broken down and fulfilled.[138]

One must say both "gospel and law" and "law and gospel," even though the "law and gospel" order predominates in the Confessions. Both orders are confessional, according to Bonhoeffer. The important thing is that there is both a connection and a distinction between the law and gospel.

> It excludes a purely formal interpretation of the law. It is not concerned with the situation of the responsible man in the conflict of duties, but with the realization of particular conditions; it is not concerned with the place of the Christian in secular institutions, but with the form of secular order in accordance with the will of God; it is not concerned with the Christianization of worldly institutions or with their incorporation in the church, but with their genuine worldliness, their "naturalness" in obedience to God's word.[139]

Although Bonhoeffer is interested in doing a critique of the doctrine of the uses of the law, it is clear that he does not simply reject this doctrine. As is his practice, Bonhoeffer does not throw out the notion but seeks to recast it in a temporal mold. He sees some problems in the treatment of law in the Confessions. One is that the relation between the first use and natural law is not clarified. Another is that it is not clear whether there is a third use or not. It is difficult to understand how Hans Pfeifer could conclude that Bonhoeffer rejects the first use of the law[140] when he is very specific about the necessity of recasting it. After pointing to the lack of clarity in the Confessions about the first use, Bonhoeffer gives his suggestions for recasting it.

> A revision of the doctrine of *usus* would have to avoid any distinction between classes of hearers and represent the one law in its threefold form as the preaching of works, as the preaching of the acknowledgement of sin, and as the preaching of the fulfillment of the law. Alternatively, or in addition, it would have to treat the validity and effect of the whole law of God (in its threefold form) as a question which is to be systematically separated from the foregoing one. It would have to deal with the validity of the law in its two

aspects, in relation to unbelievers and to believers, and with its effect, in the four aspects of righteousness of works, the example of Christ, despair and the guidance of grace. The old Lutheran dogmatics hesitated between *duplex, triplex,* and *quadruplex usus legis* because it mixed together all these questions regarding the law; the question of its form requires treatment under three headings, that of its validity under two and that of its effect under four. Any attempt to reduce one of these questions to terms of another necessarily leads to confusion. The term *usus* itself, however, involves the danger of this confusion.[141]

In summary, Bonhoeffer deals with the law in much the same way that he deals with other traditional ethical categories. He is attached to and sympathetic with his Lutheran commitments. He works with law in the context of the law/gospel dialectic. He struggles with the natural law question. He deals at length with the first use of the law in the Lutheran Confessions. He investigates the law in the Scriptures, particularly in the Old Testament. But his handling of the law is always subtle. It carries the richness and diversity, the multidimensionality of law as used in the Scripture and the Lutheran Confessions and also as used in government and society. In a time when law was used as a tool of repression and racism, and even of extermination of citizens, Bonhoeffer works to recast, rather than to abandon, those ethical structures stemming from the law. Central to that recasting is his christological focus, which allows him to affirm the congruence between the law of God and the laws of nations, but to refuse to absolutize any law, even the decalogue or the imperatives of Jesus in the Gospel narratives. Neither freedom from the law nor obedience to the law will suffice. If the law is to function properly in setting limits to human behavior, it must also be the law of life, living and not dead, assisting us to move in the direction of God's purpose for his world. That means, for Bonhoeffer, that the church must work at the recovery of the natural for the sake of the gospel.

The Recovery of the Natural

It is entirely understandable that the one who spoke of reality as the sacrament of the ethical would be offended by any conceptuality that would make "the natural" and "the sinful" somehow synonymous. Yet that has always been a logical counterpart of two-sphere thinking. When God and world are separated by definition, the natural is identified with the world, and the supernatural with God. In extreme forms of such conceptualities, nature and the natural are virtually equated with sin and the sinful.

In less extreme forms, the natural is negative only by implication, that is, it is looked upon as something "lower" than that which is supernatural; it must somehow be transcended and left behind if one is going to participate fully in the supernatural, whether God, or the true, the good, and the beautiful. This is often true even in Roman Catholic thought, where grace is supposed never to destroy but always to fulfill nature. In an essay on "Nature and Grace," Karl Rahner regretfully admits that in popular Roman Catholic piety, grace and nature are looked upon as two layers of reality, neither one having much or anything to do with the other.[142] It is perhaps most obviously and strikingly present in certain Christian circles, both Protestant and Roman Catholic, in which there is far greater excitement over an unexplained healing that can be called "divine healing" or "faith healing" or "supernatural healing" than there is over a healing that takes place by means of the body's own recuperative powers, or surgery, or through the use of medicine or physical therapy, or any other "natural" means.

Many observers have noted this phenomenon of the devaluation of the natural and have argued against it. No Christian who confesses faith in God the creator, in Jesus born of Mary, in the Holy Spirit who breathes into the church the hope of the resurrection of the body, can possibly be content for long with an entirely negative view of nature and the natural. Bonhoeffer differs from others in his passionate drive to recast, to restructure, this category in temporal terms in order to bring it into congruence with sin and grace. His question is how to recover the natural for the sake of the gospel.[143] It is parallel to his recasting of the orders of creation into the orders of preservation, which are "forms of working against sin in the direction of the Gospel."[144] The work he does on the natural is also parallel to that which he does on the law. The law cannot be totally negative even for Bonhoeffer the Lutheran. It must be essentially positive, because it is a way in which God orders his creation; it is a structure of the responsible life. The law must be seen, therefore, as the law of life, of nature. And nature also, then, must be seen as a structure of the responsible life.

When Bonhoeffer does get to the writing of a specific piece on "The Natural," he realizes that he is doing something unusual. He writes to Bethge from the Benedictine monastery at Ettal, where he is working on it, "You are right, it is dangerous material but all the more attractive for that very reason."[145]

Bonhoeffer's work to recover the natural for the sake of the gospel, however, was consistent with a lifetime of embracing and honoring nature and the natural. In his own family there was a strong dislike of anything artificial. Conversation was to be genuine and authentic. Children were discouraged from using clichés. Silence was respected; empty talk was not tolerated. A well-tailored article of wool clothing that would wear well was preferred to something in style that would soon be out of style. When Bonhoeffer later reflects on his childhood, the naturalness of it all is something he repeatedly mentions. He talks about the landscapes of the Kalkreuth paintings that hung on the walls of his home, and about the cabin with no electricity in the gentle Harz mountains where the family retreated for quiet times and to which he took his students during the Finkenwalde years. While in Barcelona he wrote about the naturalness of the simple people he met there. At Finkenwalde he recommended to his students Georges Bernanos's *Diary of a Country Priest* because these were real people, not counterfeit Christians, and the country priest was a genuine human being who participated in their sufferings and their joys. At Tegel prison he read again Stifter and other nineteenth-century novelists, and praised them for their simple, clear, direct grasp and portrayal of natural and authentic life. He wrote to Bethge while reading them that there must be something good about an era that could produce such genuine and natural literature. The dislike for pretension is evident in the autobiographical drama and novel fragments written at Tegel. Taking life in one's stride, *hilaritas*, the polyphony of life, distaste for scrupulosity, a calmness which was contagious, a feel for quality, a sense for priorities — all those characteristics and emphases so evident in Bonhoeffer and in his family — were consistent with his later formulations for the theological and ethical recovery of the natural.

In the section of the *Ethics* on "The Natural," Bonhoeffer says that the concept of the natural has fallen into discredit in Protestant ethics. The reason is that the emphasis on grace placed everything human and natural into "the night of sin, and now no one dared to consider the relative differences within the human and the natural, for fear that by their so doing grace as grace might be diminished."[146] Bonhoeffer sees this as a misguided attempt to underline grace, resulting in an obliteration of relative distinctions within the fallen creation and opening the way for every kind of arbitrariness and disorder. Years earlier he himself had been accused by Reinhold Niebuhr of "killing everything with Grace," and had been unable to understand Barth's insistence upon "lesser lights" consistent with the one great light. It is impossible to know how those conversations with Neibuhr and Barth would have gone a decade later. What is clear is that Bonhoeffer's lifelong essentially positive attitude toward the natural and his consistent rejection of two-sphere thinking flow together at Ettal as he works to recast the traditional spatial categories, in which natural is distinguished from supernatural, into a temporal framework in which natural is distinguished from unnatural.

> The concept of the natural must, therefore, be recovered on the basis of the gospel. We speak of the natural, as distinct from the creaturely, in order to take into account the fact of the Fall; and we speak of the natural rather than of the sinful so that we may include in it the creaturely. The natural is that which, after the Fall, is directed towards the coming of Christ. The unnatural is that which, after the Fall, closes its doors against the coming of Christ. There is indeed only a relative difference between that which is directed towards Christ and that which closes its doors to Christ; for the natural does not compel the coming of Christ, and the unnatural does not render it impossible. In both cases the real coming is an event of grace. And it is only through the coming of Christ that the natural is confirmed in its character as a penultimate, and that the unnatural is exposed once and for all as destruction of the penultimate. Thus, even in the sight of Christ, there is a distinction between the natural and the unnatural, a distinction which cannot be obliterated without doing grave harm.[147]

Two-sphere thinking leads to spatial theological and ethical categories that identify God with the timeless and the absolute, with the supernatural. Seeing that God and world have come together in the incarnate, crucified, and risen Christ leads to temporal categories for an ethical theology that knows that God is at work in the relativities of history, and that the structures of responsible life must reflect those relativities. Again, as is the case with all of Bonhoeffer's formulations, the recovery of the natural has to do specifically with Christology or, better, with Jesus Christ.

> The natural is the form of life preserved by God for the fallen world and directed towards justification, redemption and renewal through Christ. The natural is, therefore, determined according to its form and according to its contents. Formally the natural is determined through God's will to preserve it and through its being directed towards Christ. In its formal aspect, therefore, the natural can be discerned only in its relation to Jesus Christ Himself. As for its contents, the natural is the form of the preserved life itself, the form which embraces the entire human race.[148]

The cumulative and almost repetitive character of Bonhoeffer's constructive work in ethical theology is evident in these last two quotations. In the former he ties his work on the recovery of the natural to his categories of the penultimate and the ultimate, in the latter to his categories of form and formation, and to the notion of preservation. Former reflections about reason are also confirmed and expanded here. Reason is totally embedded in the natural and thus can also be part of the unnatural. Reason is now fallen reason, but it can be open to the coming of Christ. Bonhoeffer is specific about how his understanding of reason differs from both the Roman Catholic view and the Enlightenment view.

> This view differs from the Catholic theory in that (1) we regard reason as having been entirely involved in the Fall, while according to Catholic dogmatics reason still retained a certain essential integrity, and (2) according to the Catholic doctrine, reason may also grasp the formal determination of the natural, the second of these principles being connected with the first. Our view differs from the Enlightenment view in that it takes the natural to rest upon what is objectively given and not upon the subjective spontaneity of reason.[149]

The fact that Bonhoeffer refuses to equate the natural and the sinful does not mean that he is naively optimistic. Nor does the fact that he believes it necessary for Christians to exercise responsibility for the shaping of the future mean that he has a naive belief in inevitable progress, or in human ability to bring about unqualified development of potentialities. Yet he is always on the side of hope and believes that the natural is on the side of life. He would agree with Einstein that God does not play dice with the universe, and that God is not mean. He would agree with the Formula of Concord that the creation is "substantially good, accidentally evil," that nature, including human nature, is not "totally depraved." Life itself is on our side.

> It is in the last analysis life itself that tends towards the natural and keeps turning against the unnatural and bringing about its downfall. This, in the last analysis, is what underlies the maintenance and recovery of physical and mental health. Life is its own physician, whether it be the life of an individual or the life of a community.[150]

Yet that which is natural can always become unnatural. Life is never an absolute or an end in itself. If so, it becomes its own destroyer. In spite of his obvious fascination with and appreciation for Nietzsche, Bonhoeffer is consistently critical of Nietzschean vitalism because it absolutizes life and does not take seriously the possibility for self-destruction. He saw this vitalism running wild in the race, blood, and soil ideology of the Nazis. "Vitalism cannot but end in nihilism, in the destruction of all that is natural. Life in itself, in the strict sense of the word, is a void, a plunge into the abyss."[151] This is also true for both individual and social life. After saying that there is a way in which life tends toward the natural both in individual and social life, and that there is a solid basis for a hopeful view of human history, Bonhoeffer adds immediately that this legitimate vitalism, if absolutized, becomes unnatural and the destroyer of life.

This point of view, that it is "natural" to be open to Christ and to the will and purpose of God, and that it is "unnatural" to be closed to Christ and the will and purpose of God, is worked out by Bonhoeffer in a number of specific areas. Following the section in the *Ethics* on "The Natural" there are sections on "Natural Life," on the *suum cuique* (to each his own) of Roman law, on "The Right to Bodily Life," and on "The Natural Rights of the Life of the Mind." In these sections he deals with many traditional questions in ethics: rights and duties, conflict of duties, theodicy, recreation and play, war and the distinction between killing and murder, euthanasia and the distinction between allowing to die and killing, medical ethics and the management of serious incurable hereditary diseases, the giving up of one's life to save the life of another, abortion, sterilization, rape, slavery, torture, unlawful search and seizure. However tempting it is to do short summary statements on each of the topics, the temptation must be resisted. It would be misleading to ask and answer the question, "What is Bonhoeffer's position on abortion?" or, "What is his position on war?" unless one has the time and the space to analyze it in some detail. It should be abundantly clear at this point that what is important to Bonhoeffer and what should be important to those who study him is not so much the actual positions that he took on specific issues, which he himself would never agree to universalize, but rather the way in which he went about reaching these positions. It is possible that in a different time and a different place, a person following Bonhoeffer's ethical theology and working with his structures for responsible life could come to a position quite different from that to which Bonhoeffer came. So the reader is invited to go to these sections of the *Ethics*, to follow Bonhoeffer's argument on each of these topics, and to see whether what has been said here about his ethical theology is helpful. One caveat is that the word "principle" unfortunately occurs in the English text of these sections in quite a number of places where it does not occur in the German text. This is very misleading because the reader could be led by the translation to think that Bonhoeffer, having abandoned an ethic of principles, returns to such an ethic as soon as he gets to specific issues. However, this is not the case.

A final note on the recovery of the natural is that this emphasis places strength, power, and success into a new perspective. In two-sphere thinking such things almost always carry negative or at best neutral connotations. The natural is so antagonistic to, or at least less than, the supernatural that all human effort, progress, accomplishment is of little importance.

But if Christians are called to participate in the shaping of the future, to exercise moral decision making in the context of concern about how the next generation will live, then the results of one's action are extremely important. It is a gift to have the strength and to be able to exercise the power by which one registers some success at accomplishing what one sets out to do. The Christian who equates success and sin, or who thinks that strength and power are inevitably employed for evil purposes, is like that fanatic who Bonhoeffer says cannot forgive God his creation. If we embrace the natural, which is to be open to Christ, we ought not to be surprised if our actions are occasionally sufficiently congruent with God's purpose that good results follow. The section in the *Ethics* entitled "History and the Good" examines this notion at length.

The implications for witness and evangelism are significant. In traditional systems which see strength, power, and success as signs of human pride and therefore of sin, the point of contact for the gospel is to demonstrate to successful people that they are not successful, that their accomplishments are actually part of the evil of this world brought about precisely by pride in human strength and power. Bonhoeffer refuses this simplistic notion. Good should be recognized for what it is, as should success. We are all sinners, but that does not mean that people who do good have to be told that they are doing only evil. In the prison letters there is great struggle with this question, and the conclusion is that God is found not at the boundaries of life but in the center of life, not only in weakness but also in strength, not only in failure but also in success.

Strength, power, and success can be honored, but must be neither worshiped nor absolutized. Bonhoeffer also writes in the prison letters that a Christian is one who "shares the suffering of God in the life of the world," and that "only a suffering God can help." Larry Rasmussen suggests that traditional theology has had a strong God and a weak human being; Bonhoeffer has a weak God and a strong human being.[152] The result is the construction of an "ethics of the cross" which propels people with strength and power to use that strength and power in the service of the oppressed neighbor. The suggestion is extremely helpful as long as it does not become too rigid a scheme. For Bonhoeffer there is nothing in this whole fallen creation that cannot be "natural," open to Christ's coming, and nothing in this whole redeemed creation that cannot be "unnatural," opposed to Christ's coming. Finally, the question is again christological. It has to do with the one in whose name all things are judged and all distinctions made. It is because of him that the command of God is always permission to live.

The Command of God as
Permission to Live

We have seen that Bonhoeffer's attempt to formulate an ethical theology and to structure the responsible life results in an understanding of Christianity that is rooted in the Scriptures and the tradition, yet yields some surprising fruits. He is both conservative and radical, and to forget either of those notes would be to misunderstand him. His ethics is always theological because it is always focused in the question, "Who is Jesus Christ for us today?" And his theology is always ethical because it is focused in the statement, "What following Jesus means, that's what I want to know." Ethics cannot be cut off from theology if it is *Christian* ethics. Theology cannot ignore ethics if it is *Christian* theology. The centrality of Jesus Christ in Bonhoeffer's understanding of Christianity drives him to do ethical theology.

Everything follows from these basic commitments. Because God and world come together in Jesus Christ, every form of two-sphere thinking must be rejected. That means a turn to the real (rather than to the ideal) as the focus of Christian ethical theology. Reality is, in fact, the sacrament of the ethical. Ethical absolutism and ethical situationism tend to be individualistic. But the ethical theology that focuses in the reality of God and world together in Jesus Christ implies immediately and directly that we are both *with* one another and *for* one another, and that is not possible until time and history enter into the fabric of ethical theology as constitutive elements.

When time and history are taken seriously, then concrete times and places have to be taken seriously also. A changeless God who gives timeless ethical commands will no longer do. For the sake of Jesus Christ the whole conceptuality of Christianity must be recast. Ethical structures must embrace time and history, the here-and-now, and still provide for continuity and community. Thus we find Bonhoeffer struggling to find structures grounded in the whole creation "in and through and for" Jesus Christ. The same Jesus who called the disciples to follow him is the one "in whom and through whom and for whom all things exist," the one "through whose cross all things are reconciled to God" (Col. 1:15–16). The task of ethical theology is so to understand God and the world that one learns to embrace and get in on that reconciliation, to participate with God in the shaping of the future according to it. In order to facilitate that,

Bonhoeffer recasts much traditional language of theological ethics and comes up with categories such as the penultimate and the ultimate, the orders of preservation, the divine mandates, formation and conformation, the law of life, the recovery of the natural. "Command" and "commandment" as ethical categories are also recast by Bonhoeffer. They are recast to bring them into congruence with sin and grace. For Bonhoeffer that means, finally, that the command of God grants permission to live.

In much of traditional Christian ethics, commandment means a timeless and changeless imperative given directly by God. In Bonhoeffer's ethical theology the command of God is never separated from its focus in Jesus Christ. Command as permission may sound to some like a terrible confusion of law and gospel. Rather, according to Bonhoeffer, it is a correct understanding of both the *distinction and the connection* between law and gospel. The emphasis is present throughout his work. In a draft for a new catechism, he points to the fact that the commandments in Exodus are preceded by the word that God had brought his people out of Egypt. Seen in this context, the Ten Commandments are not harsh demands, but rather gracious signs of how to live now that God has acted so graciously on our behalf. The commands in the Sermon on the Mount are preceded by the gracious words of the Beatitudes. Even in *The Cost of Discipleship*, the book in which Bonhoeffer later recognized some legalistic tendencies, he is very clear that the command grows out of the gracious promise.[153] It is no doubt his deep attachment to the Old Testament and his appreciation for the richness of the Torah that also brings Bonhoeffer to see clearly that the command of God is always a gracious command. The following passage from his book on the Psalms is typical of his work on Old Testament texts.

> It is grace to know God's commands. They release us from self-made plans and conflicts. They make our steps certain and our way joyful. God gives his commands in order that we may fulfill them, and "his commandments are not burdensome" (1 John 5:3) for him who has found all salvation in Jesus Christ. Jesus has himself been under the law and has fulfilled it in total obedience to the Father. God's will becomes his joy, his nourishment. So he gives thanks in us for the grace of the law and grants to us joy in its fulfillment. Now we confess our love for the law, we affirm that we gladly keep it, and we ask that we may continue to be kept blameless in it. We do that not in our own power, but we pray it in the name of Jesus Christ who is for us and in us.[154]

Another Old Testament text, on the basis of which he comes to the same conclusion, is Genesis 1–3.

That which in us breaks hopelessly asunder is for God indissolubly one; the word of command and the event. With God the imperative is the indicative. The latter does not follow from the former, the indicative is not the effect of the imperative; it *is* the imperative. . . . The fact that it is absolutely impossible for us to think the indicative and the imperative at one and the same time indicates the fact that we no longer live in the unity of the active Word of God, that we are fallen.[155]

The one to whom Bonhoeffer is most obviously indebted for this emphasis on the command of God is Karl Barth. Barth's earliest lectures on ethics in 1928–29, which Bonhoeffer knew, have as a key word "the command of God." As they are now published, there are four chapters and each chapter contains in its title the word "command": "The Reality of the Divine Command," "The Command of God the Creator," "The Command of God the Reconciler," "The Command of God the Redeemer." In *Church Dogmatics* II/2, which Bonhoeffer also knew and about which he corresponded with Barth, chapter 8 is entitled "The Command of God." After a section on "Ethics as a Task of the Doctrine of God," the three remaining sections are entitled "The Command as the Claim of God," "The Command as the Decision of God," and "The Command as the Judgment of God." Again, in the final section of Barth's *Church Dogmatics*, the posthumously published lecture fragments of IV/4, the final chapter is entitled "The Command of God the Reconciler." Barth consistently talks about "the gracious God as the commanding God." Barth has throughout his entire theological work a stress upon the command of God, and he sees this command always in the context of grace. James Gustafson describes Barth's position accurately.

In his characteristic way of twisting and turning words to extract meanings and implications from them, he gives us the axis on which his discussion turns. "Obligation — the obligation of the real command — means permission. That was the first point. But the second is that permission — the permission which is the proper inmost form of the divine command — also means obligation." Right obligation is true permission, and right permission is true obligation. Such propositions make no sense when developed from the common usage of the key terms. They only make sense, Barth assures us, when seen in the faith of the church. "The propositions of Christian ethics are propositions of Christian dogmatics." The key presupposition is a tautology — grace is grace; or to make the first term synthetic, and thereby more meaningful: the sanctifying grace of the command of God is grace. "The fact that God gives us His command, that He puts us under His command, is grace." The immediate result of this statement is the double character of permission and obligation: the obligation of this command is at the bottom permission, and this permission is properly obligation.[156]

Another formula with which Barth expresses his position is: "The Law is a form of the Gospel, whose content is Grace."[157] One can see this Barthian note in Bonhoeffer's formula, "Only the one who believes obeys; only the one who obeys believes."[158] Many Lutherans do not like the second half of that formula. However, in his *Treatise on Christian Liberty*, Luther opens with a practically identical statement, "The Christian person is absolutely free, Lord of all; the Christian person is totally bound, servant of all."[159] When Gustafson used "command as permission" to sum up the fundamental style of the ethics of Bonhoeffer, Barth, and F. D. Maurice, he could have made a case for adding Luther to that list. It is, however, more obviously Bonhoeffer and Barth than it is Luther.

> One general inference drawn from fixing Christ's Lordship so centrally in Christian ethics is a qualification of an ethic of obligation to a commandment. Command becomes permission. At least it is qualified by the "permission" character of man's relationship in faith to what God has done for him. We can do, we are permitted to do, we are free to do freely what we must do, what we are commanded to do, what we are required to do. This is a consequence of the precedence of God's indicative over his imperative, of God's gracious action over evil and man's sin, and Christ's victory through resurrection over the power of death. Command does not become permissiveness; it becomes permission. God enables man to do freely and thankfully what he requires him to do. The subtlety of the relation of permission and command is seen in historical and personal terms more easily than in terms of formal logic.[160]

Permission does not mean permissiveness. The command of God grants permission to live, which means permission to act responsibly. The attack of Bonhoeffer's ethical theology is not only against legalism and antinomianism; it is also against the scrupulosity that freezes a person into inaction. Bonhoeffer says that the Christian does not forever stand like Hercules at the crossroads.[161] The Christian is able to make up his or her mind and come out into the tempest of living, because only in the responsible act is there freedom. The command of God as permission releases a person from the "crossroads character of life" and allows one to "take life in one's stride."[162] It allows one to see that discipleship requires discipline, but that this discipline is actually permission because one is a disciple of Jesus Christ who brings God's grace.

A sometimes confusing note is the connection between permission and necessity in Bonhoeffer. These two seem to be opposites. In Bonhoeffer's ethical theology they are coordinates. Permission has nothing to do with what is possible, with some long list of ethical options, but rather with that which is necessary. This is his way of saying that the command of God is always concrete, that it has to do with what is necessary in the here-and-now. We are not given permission to do anything that is possible, but rather only that which is "necessary," that is, the will of God.[163] The will of God is concrete because God Himself is concrete. Even in his second dissertation, Bonhoeffer says, "God is not free *of* man but *for* man. Christ is the Word of his freedom. God is *there*, which is to say: not in eternal non-objectivity, but [looking ahead for the moment] 'havable,' graspable in his Word within the Church."[164] If God were apart in some timeless realm, then the command could also be timeless. But since God is havable and graspable in the here-and-now, the command will always be concrete and therefore necessary rather than merely possible.

Command as permission is worked out by Bonhoeffer in many specific contexts. An illustration is his comment on the commandment "Thou shalt not commit adultery."

> It is only when the commandment no longer merely threatens me as a transgressor of the limits, it is only when it convinces and subdues me with its real contents, that it sets me free from the anxiety and the uncertainty of decision. If I love my wife, if I accept marriage as an institution of God, then there comes an inner freedom and certainty of life and action in marriage; I no longer watch with suspicion every step that I take; I no longer call in question every deed that I perform. The divine prohibition of adultery is then no longer the center around which all my thought and action in marriage revolves. (As though the meaning and purpose of marriage consisted of nothing except the avoidance of adultery!) But it is the honoring and the free acceptance of marriage, the leaving behind of the prohibition of adultery, which is now the precondition for the fulfillment of the divine commission of marriage. The divine commandment has here become the permission to live in marriage in freedom and certainty.[165]

One can find, of course, the same emphasis in Luther. In his Small Catechism, he turns the negative into a positive. Not to commit adultery means: "We should fear and love God, and so we should lead a chaste and pure life in word and deed, each one loving and honoring his wife or her husband." A similar comment is made by Luther in his commentary on the Sermon on the Mount.

> Therefore God has decreed that everybody should have his lawful wife or her lawful husband, in order that all lust and desire should be directed towards these alone. If you keep this order, He wishes you well and gives you His blessing, for it is pleasing unto Him since it is His ordinance and affair.[166]

Again, it is not that Bonhoeffer is here creating something entirely new. Augustine said against Pelagius that freedom consists not in choosing between right and wrong, but rather in choosing the right, in being in tune with the will of God. Freedom in marriage does not consist in the possibility of choosing between faithfulness and adultery. On the contrary, freedom in marriage consists in the permission granted by the command to be faithful to one's spouse.

Bonhoeffer's position on the command as permission to live is worked out by him in a similar manner in many other contexts. Our primary purpose is to attempt to understand as clearly as possible the ethical theology behind the formula. The striking thing about Bonhoeffer is the thoroughness with which he pursues the explications of a formula once he has put it together. His words in the *Ethics* are crisp and clear.

> The commandment of God permits man to be man before God. It allows the flood of life to flow freely. It lets man eat, drink, sleep, work, rest and play. It does not interrupt him. It does not continually ask him whether he ought to be sleeping, eating, working, or playing, or whether he has some more urgent duties. It does not make man a critic and judge of himself and of his deed, but it allows him to live and to act with certainty and with confidence in the guidance of the divine commandment. The self-tormenting and hopeless question regarding the purity of one's motives, the suspicious observation of oneself, the glaring and fatiguing light of incessant consciousness, all these have nothing to do with the commandment of God, who grants liberty to live and to act. The permission to live, which is granted in the commandment of God, takes account of the fact that the roots of human life and action lie in darkness and that activity and passivity, the conscious and the unconscious, are inextricably interwoven. Light comes into this life only through taking advantage of this divine permission; it comes only from above.
>
> Before the commandment of God man does not permanently stand like Hercules at the crossroads. He is not everlastingly striving for the right decision. He is not always wearing himself out in a conflict of duties. He is not continually failing and beginning again. Nor does the commandment of God itself make its appearance only in these great, agitated and intensely conscious moments of crisis in life. On the contrary, before the commandment of God man may at last really move forward along the road and no longer stand endlessly at the crossroads. He can now have the right decision really behind him, and not always before him. Entirely without inner conflict he can do one thing and leave undone another thing which, according to theoretical ethics, is perhaps equally urgent. He can already have made a beginning and he can allow himself to be guided, escorted and protected on his way by prayers as though by a good angel. And God's commandment itself can give life unity of direction and personal guidance only in the form of seemingly small and insignificant everyday words, sayings, hints and help.[167]

He would never think of them as autobiographical, but to a person acquainted with the blend of forceful decision and quiet confidence in Bonhoeffer's life, these paragraphs seem to be exactly that. It is to this fact that we now turn, to investigate the interplay of theory and practice, of ethical theology and moral decision, in Bonhoeffer's life.

NOTES

1. Cf. the notes of Wolf-Dieter Zimmermann on Bonhoeffer's seminar of the 1932 summer semester, on the theme "Is There a Christian Ethic?" in Eberhard Bethge, *Dietrich Bonhoeffer: Ein Biographie* (Munich: Chr. Kaiser, 1967), 1073ff. These notes are omitted from the English edition of the biography.

2. Rom. 14:23.

3. Cf. the readiness to change behavior patterns that Paul evidences in 1 Cor. 9:19–23. He says that he has "become all things to all people." It is important to note, however, that the aim of his behavior is that he "might win some."

4. The sentence has a slightly different tone with the inclusion of the "then." More subject to antinomian distortion is the simple reading "Love God and do as you please." Cf. Edward Long, Jr., *A Survey of Christian Ethics* (New York: Oxford Univ. Press, 1967), 131.

5. Martin Luther, "Treatise on Christian Liberty," in *Works of Martin Luther* (Philadelphia: Muhlenberg Press, 1943), 2:331.

6. Matt. 7:16–20.

7. Paul Lehmann, *Ethics in a Christian Context* (London: SCM Press, 1963), 14 and passim.

8. Anders Nygren, *Agape and Eros*, trans. Philip S. Watson (Philadelphia: Westminster Press, 1953), 75.

9. Joseph Fletcher, *Situation Ethics* (Philadelphia: Westminster Press, 1965), 87–102.

10. John Robinson, *Honest to God* (London: SCM Press, 1963), 105–21.

11. For a helpful discussion, cf. Thomas Oden, *Radical Obedience: The Ethics of Rudolf Bultmann* (Philadelphia: Westminster Press, 1964).

12. James Childress, for instance, evaluates these types of positions in this way in *Interpretation* (October 1980): 371–80. James Laney brings this criticism against not only Bonhoeffer, but against all christological ethics in "An Examination of Bonhoeffer's Ethical Contextualism," in *Bonhoeffer Legacy*, ed. A. J. Klassen (Grand Rapids: Wm. B. Eerdmans, 1981), 294–313. Larry Rasmussen in *Dietrich Bonhoeffer: Reality and Resistance* (Nashville: Abingdon Press, 1972) concludes that Bonhoeffer does not really ever come to the point of doing the work of ethics proper, 168ff.

13. Stanley Hauerwas, *Truthfulness and Tragedy* (Notre Dame, Ind.: Univ. of Notre Dame Press, 1977).

14. Ibid., 204–5.

15. Variations on this theme occur throughout the essay, "What Is Meant by 'Telling the Truth'?"

16. André Dumas, *Dietrich Bonhoeffer: Theologian of Reality*, trans. Robert McAfee Brown (New York: Macmillan Co., 1971), 215–32.

17. Ibid., 219. Although Dumas makes some references to "structuralism," it is my opinion that this is misleading. "Structuralism" is dependent precisely upon

that idealistic and Platonic metaphysic that Bonhoeffer thoroughly rejected as "two-sphere" thinking.

18. Ibid., 154.

19. Ibid., 147.

20. Heinrich Ott, *Reality and Faith*, trans. Alex. A. Morrison (Philadelphia: Fortress Press, 1972), 174.

21. Ibid., 177.

22. Ibid., 442ff. It would require an extensive digression from our argument to attempt to untangle and to weave together again the threads of Ott's indebtedness to Heidegger and Bultmann, and his peculiar uses of the words "ontological" and "existential." His point regarding Bonhoeffer's work at the intersection of situations and structures is clear and insightful, regardless of whether one knows the intricate movements of his own theological positon.

23. *E*, 8.

24. James Woelfel, *Bonhoeffer's Theology: Classical and Revolutionary* (Nashville: Abingdon Press, 1970).

25. Bonhoeffer's Lutheran commitments are everywhere present and often explicit. The most "Lutheran" interpretation of Bonhoeffer is probably that by his Finkenwalde student Gerhard Ebeling. Cf. "The Non-religious Interpretation of Biblical Concepts," in *Word and Faith* (London: SCM Press, 1963). Ebeling, however, misses the creative power of Bonhoeffer's formulations by reducing them to simple translations of Lutheran formulas. For a more balanced picture of this relationship, see Regin Prenter, "Bonhoeffer and the Young Luther," in *World Come of Age*, ed. R. Gregor Smith (Philadelphia: Fortress Press, 1967). For further essays, see *Bonhoeffer und Luther*, ed. Christian Gremmels (Munich: Chr. Kaiser, 1983).

26. *AB*, 172.

27. *GS* IV, 371.

28. *NRS*, 153–54. There is considerable scholarly debate about apparent shifts in his view of the relation of church and world, from insisting that the church have its own space in *The Cost of Discipleship*, for instance, to his talk in the *Ethics* about the church not having its own space. The point here is the continuity in Bonhoeffer's view that the church is always both under sin and under grace at the same time.

29. *GS* V, 452–57.

30. *NRS*, 203–4; *GS* II, 22–38.

31. *CD*, 56.

32. *E*, 120.

33. Ibid.

34. Ibid.

35. Ibid., 123.

36. Ibid., 124.

37. *CD*, 56.

38. *E*, 124–25.

39. Ibid., 126.

40. Ibid., 127. It is impossible not to wonder whether Bonhoeffer at this point recalled his own early conversations with Reinhold Niebuhr and Karl Barth, each

of whom thought he was "killing everything with grace." If Bonhoeffer was himself one-sided in his earlier days, it was certainly on the side of this "radical solution."

41. *E*, 130.

42. Ibid., 128–29.

43. Ibid., 136.

44. Ibid., 137.

45. Ernst Feil, "Dietrich Bonhoeffer's Understanding of the World," in *Bonhoeffer Legacy*, 250.

46. Ibid., 250–51.

47. Tiemo Peters, "Orders and Inventions: Political Ethics in the Theology of Dietrich Bonhoeffer," in *Bonhoeffer Legacy*, 314–15.

48. John Robinson, *Honest to God* (London: SCM Press, 1963), 105–21.

49. *E*, 261.

50. *DB*, 3–28.

51. *E*, 15.

52. Paul Lehmann, "Paradox of Discipleship," in *I Knew Dietrich Bonhoeffer*, ed. Wolf-Dieter Zimmermann and Ronald Gregor Smith (London: William Collins Sons, 1966), 45.

53. Otto Dudzus, "Arresting the Wheel," in *I Knew Dietrich Bonhoeffer*, 82.

54. *TP*, 73.

55. Reprinted in Appendix II in Arthur C. Cochrane, *The Church's Confession under Hitler* (Philadelphia: Westminster Press, 1962), 222–23.

56. *NRS*, 165–66.

57. Ibid., 167.

58. Ibid.

59. Ibid.

60. *CF/T*, 26.

61. Ibid., 88.

62. *E*, 278.

63. Ibid., 286–87. Cf. also "editor's note."

64. Ibid., 287.

65. Ibid., 288.

66. Ibid., 286.

67. Ibid., 288.

68. Ibid.

69. Ibid., 286.

70. *GS* III, 251; *NRS*, 144.

71. *E*, 255.

72. Ibid., 258.

73. Ibid., 196.

74. Ibid., 199.

75. *CC*, 63–64.

76. *NRS*, 108–9.

77. Rom. 12:2.

78. *E*, 84.

79. Dumas, *Dietrich Bonhoeffer*, 219.

80. Ibid., 217.
81. Ibid., 218.
82. Ibid., 219.
83. *E*, 64.
84. Ibid.
85. Ibid., 65.
86. Ibid., 67–68.
87. Dumas, *Dietrich Bonhoeffer*, 217.
88. *E*, 69.
89. Ibid., 80.
90. Ibid.
91. Ibid.
92. Ibid., 81.
93. Ott, *Reality and Faith*, 272.
94. Ibid., 272.
95. Ibid., 273.
96. Ibid., 274.
97. *E*, 87.
98. Ibid., 82.
99. Ibid., 81.
100. Ibid., 82.
101. *LT*, 30.
102. Ibid., 93.
103. *CS*, 71–72.
104. *AB*, 177.
105. *GS* III, 15.
106. *CF/T*, 81.
107. *E*, 66.
108. Ibid., 244.
109. Ibid., 243.
110. Ibid., 244.
111. Ibid., 247.
112. Ibid., 253.
113. Ibid., 252–53.
114. *CF/T*, 32.
115. Ibid., 33.
116. Ibid., 34.
117. Ibid.
118. William F. Connor, "The Laws of Life: A Bonhoeffer Theme with Variations," *Andover Newton Quarterly* (November 1977): 101–10.
119. *CS*, 41.
120. *NRS*, 39–48.
121. *GS* IV, 148.
122. John D. Godsey, *Preface to Bonhoeffer: The Man and Two of His Shorter Writings* (Philadelphia: Fortress Press, 1965), 27–47.
123. *GS* II, 91–119.

124. Connor, "Laws of Life," 103.

125. *GS* III, 340.

126. Connor, "Laws of Life," 103.

127. *E*, 328.

128. *GS* I, 358, as translated by Connor, "Laws of Life," 106.

129. Godsey, *Preface to Bonhoeffer*, 50–51.

130. Connor, "Laws of Life," 110.

131. *P*, 31.

132. Ibid.

133. Ibid., 32.

134. Ibid., 33.

135. *GS* IV, 509.

136. Werner Elert, *The Christian Ethos*, trans. Carl J. Schindler (Philadelphia: Muhlenberg Press, 1957), 49ff.

137. *E*, 306.

138. Ibid., 313.

139. Ibid., 317.

140. Hans Pfeifer, in *Bonhoeffer Legacy*, 33.

141. *E*, 318–19.

142. Karl Rahner, *Nature and Grace* (New York: Sheed & Ward, 1964), 117.

143. *E.*, 144.

144. *NRS*, 167.

145. *GS* II, 389; *TP*, 83.

146. *E*, 144.

147. Ibid., 144–45.

148. Ibid., 145–46.

149. Ibid., 146, n. 5.

150. Ibid., 147. One might compare Bonhoeffer's insights with those of modern developments in immunology, or with the experience of Norman Cousins, who literally laughed himself back to health (*Anatomy of an Illness* [New York: Bantam, 1981]). The entire current emphasis on "natural" foods is part of this move, so consistent with Bonhoeffer's attempt to "recover the natural." It is important, however, to note that what Bonhoeffer would *not* do is absolutize the goodness of, for instance, unprocessed foods and the harmfulness of processed foods. Working through his insights in this area would require a great deal more subtlety than is ordinarily present in current "natural food" faddists.

151. *E*, 149.

152. Larry Rasmussen, in *Bonhoeffer und Luther*, 129–66.

153. W. D. Davies uses as a preface to his extensive study of *The Setting of the Sermon on the Mount* (Cambridge: At the University Press, 1964) the passage in Matt. 11:28–30. "Come to me, all who labor and are heavy-laden, and I will give you rest. Take my yoke upon you, and learn from me; for I am gentle and lowly in heart, and you will find rest for your souls — For my yoke is easy, and my burden is light." Bonhoeffer also quotes this passage in his treatment of the Sermon on the Mount, *CD*, 48. C. H. Dodd and Barth both have pieces entitled *Gospel and Law*, indicating that one can make a case on either biblical or theological grounds for

setting the command of God in the context of his gracious act. Even the apostle Paul, on whose work the sharp Lutheran distinction between law and gospel, and the insistence upon that order, is based, can speak of "fulfilling the law of Christ" (Gal. 6:27).

154. *P*, 31–32.

155. *CF/T*, 23.

156. James Gustafson, *Christ and the Moral Life* (New York: Harper & Row, 1968), 37.

157. Karl Barth, "Gospel and Law," in *Community, State, and Church* (Garden City, N.Y.: Doubleday & Co., 1960), 80.

158. *CD*, 69.

159. Martin Luther, "Treatise on Christian Liberty," *Works of Martin Luther*, vol. 2 (Philadelphia: Muhlenberg Press, 1943), 312.

160. Gustafson, *Christ and the Moral Life*, 35.

161. *E*, 283.

162. *LPP*, letter of 21 July 1944, 370. The phrase is from the 1953 Reginald Fuller translation of *LPP*. It has a nice ring to it, and is implanted in the Bonhoeffer literature through its use as a title by Kenneth Hamilton for his Bonhoeffer study, *Life in One's Stride* (Grand Rapids: Wm. B. Eerdmans, 1968). The 1967 enlarged edition and new translation of *LPP*, which is used as a reference point throughout this book, reads "living unreservedly." Either translation is quite acceptable.

163. *E*, 285.

164. *AB*, 90–91.

165. *E*, 281.

166. Martin Luther, *WA*, 32,371,30 quoted in George Forell, *Faith Active in Love* (New York: American Press, 1954), 142.

167. *E*, 283–84.

3 | Engaging Concrete Places and Times

Acting in the Here and the Now

We have taken the position that in order to get at the ethics of Dietrich Bonhoeffer it is necessary to locate those ethics across the entire spectrum of his life and work, and that the materials when examined yield an essentially consistent point of view. We have attempted to gather those materials under the heading "Formulating an Ethical Theology" (chap. 1). Although it is obvious that this ethical theology runs risks of moral arbitrariness, of producing an ethic with no clear guidance for ethical decisions, we have argued that this is not in fact what results. We have attempted to show that Bonhoeffer works hard at structuring the responsible life, that he fights against moral arbitrariness as much as he does against moral absolutism. He seeks to articulate and insist upon structures (chap. 2) that provide both continuity and community for moral decision making and action. The position taken here is that Bonhoeffer is conservative in that he makes use of classic theological and ethical categories, but that he employs these categories in such a fashion that he recasts them to be congruent with sin and grace, and to express a firm commitment to time and history as ethical concomitants.

The argument is that the position, which pays considerable attention to consequences of action, can be grasped under the theme "Shaping the Future." The question is how all of this fits together, how it works, or whether it works at all. Is there here, granted, in unfinished form, the making of a position that can actually function in ethical decision making? It is abundantly clear that Bonhoeffer himself thought so, and that he was thoroughly convinced that the idealistic ethics against which he was fighting was deficient precisely because it did not work. He was ready to admit that people who build their ethics on universal principles might be "subjectively earnest," and was also ready to admit that his own dissatisfaction with that system might be "difficult to define." Yet he found those timeless principles without weight, unhelpful, and chaotic. He talked about that kind of ethics as being "conducted in a vacuum." According to Bonhoeffer, the only kind of ethics that makes any sense at all, that can actually be helpful, is "inseparably linked with particular times and places."

> Timeless and placeless ethical discourse lacks the concrete warrant which all authentic ethical discourse requires. It is an adolescent, presumptuous and illegitimate declamation of ethical principles, and however intense may be the subjective earnestness with which it is propounded, it is contrary to the essential character of ethical discourse in a way which is clearly felt, even though it may be difficult to define. In such cases it is often impossible to find fault with the process of abstraction and generalization or with the theories advanced and yet they do not possess the specific gravity of ethical propositions. The words are correct but they have no weight. In the end it must be felt that they are not helpful, but chaotic. . . . Ethical discourse cannot be conducted in a vacuum, in the abstract, but only in a concrete context. Ethical discourse, therefore, is not a system of propositions which are correct in themselves, a system which is available for anyone to apply at any time and in any place, but it is inseparably linked with particular persons, times and places.[1]

Bonhoeffer is relentless in his attack on idealistic ethical systems because he thinks they not only are unhelpful but are actually harmful. In a passage that parallels certain insights of the American psychoanalyst Karen Horney (who coined the phrase "the tyranny of the should"[2]), Bonhoeffer talks about idealistic ethics as a "pathological overburdening of life by the ethical." For Bonhoeffer the question is not only whether his own position works, but also whether proponents of idealistic ethics are able to see how miserably their own position fails.

> They seem to imagine that every human action has had a clearly-lettered notice attached to it by some divine police authority, a notice which reads either "permitted" or "forbidden." They assume that a man must continually be doing something decisive, fulfilling some higher purpose and discharging some ultimate duty. This represents a failure to understand that in historical human existence everything has its time (Ecclesiastes 3), eating, drinking, and sleeping as well as deliberate result and action, rest as well as work, purposelessness as well as the fulfillment of purpose, inclination as well as duty, play as well as earnest endeavor, joy as well as renunciation. Their presumptuous misjudgement of this creaturely existence leads either to the most mendacious hypocrisy or else to madness. It turns the moralist into a dangerous tormentor, tyrant and clown, a figure of tragi-comedy.[3]

The rejection of timeless and placeless ethics and the insistence upon responsible action in concrete times and concrete places grow directly out of Bonhoeffer's strong christological commitments. To move away from the once-for-all there-and-then event to the universalizability of timeless and placeless principles is, according to Bonhoeffer, to reject God and God's world, both of which are known in Jesus Christ. The only way for the Christian to move is from that there-and-then to this here-and-now. Bonhoeffer is very clear about it.

This leads us away from any kind of abstract ethic and towards an ethic which is entirely concrete. What can and must be said is not what is good once and for all, but the way in which Christ takes form among us here and now. The attempt to define that which is good once and for all has, in the nature of the case, always ended in failure. Either the proposition was asserted in such general and formal terms that it retained no significance as regards its contents, or else one tried to include in it and elaborate the whole immense range of conceivable contents, and thus to say in advance what would be good in every single conceivable case; this led to a casuistic system so unmanageable that it could satisfy the demands neither of general validity nor of concreteness. The concretely Christian ethic is beyond formalism and casuistry. Formalism and casuistry set out from the conflict between the good and the real, but the Christian ethic can take for its point of departure the reconciliation, already accomplished, of the world with God and the man Jesus Christ and the acceptance of the real man by God.

But the question of how Christ takes form among us here and now, or how we are conformed with His form, contains within itself still further difficult questions. What do we mean by "among us", "now" and "here"? If it is impossible to establish for all times and places what is good, then the question still arises for what times and places can any answer at all be given to our enquiry. It must not remain in doubt for a single moment that any one section to which we may now turn our attention is to be regarded precisely as a section, as a part of the whole of humanity. In every section of his history man is simply and entirely the man taken upon Himself by Christ. And for this reason whatever may have to be said about this section will always refer not only to this part but also to the whole. However, we must now answer the question regarding the times and places of which we are thinking when we set out to speak of formation through the form of Christ. These are in the first place quite generally the times and places which in some way concern us, those of which we have experience and which are reality for us. They are the times and places which confront us with concrete problems, set us tasks and charge us with responsibility. The "among us," the "now" and "here" is therefore the region of our decisions and encounters. This region undoubtedly varies very greatly in extent according to the individual, and it might consequently be supposed that these definitions could in the end be interpreted so widely and vaguely as to make room for unrestrained individualism. What prevents this is the fact that by our history we are set objectively in a definite nexus of experiences, responsibilities and decisions from which we cannot free ourselves again except by an abstraction. We live, in fact, within this nexus, whether or not we are in every respect aware of it.[4]

Essential to note is the fact that Bonhoeffer's ethical theology calls upon the reality of God and world together in Jesus Christ to provide continuity and community, and thus to avoid the arbitrary situationism that might otherwise be implied by his stress upon the here and the now. In his 1933 Christology lectures he had made very clear his commitment to the Lutheran doctrine of the ubiquity of the incarnate Christ. "Even as the risen one, Jesus Christ remains in the man Jesus in time and space. Because Jesus Christ is man, he is present in time and place; because Jesus Christ is God, he is eternally present."[5] The same Luther who insisted that if anyone wants to see God that person must point to the man Jesus and say, "This man is God" also insisted that this Jesus, now risen, but still incarnate, is ubiquitous, everywhere present. It is not as pure spirit or as timeless principle or as universalizable ethical rule that Christ comes to us. He comes to us as the risen Lord who is the incarnate and crucified Jesus. The ethical concomitant of the doctrine of the ubiquity of the incarnate Christ, as interpreted by Bonhoeffer, is an ethic of the here-and-now which is an ethic for every here-and-now. Every here-and-now does not mean timeless, but rather always timely, always in concrete times and concrete places. Bonhoeffer is as much against "partiality" and for "wholeness" in his talk about decision making in the *Ethics* as he is in his talk about nonreligious Christianity in the prison letters.[6] In both cases his position is grounded in the everywhere-present incarnate, crucified, and risen Christ. The wholeness of the counterpoint which makes possible the polyphony of life is dependent upon a clear and steady *cantus firmus*.[7]

It is this uncompromising concentration on the once-for-all Christ event in Jesus of Nazareth, coupled with the claim of his presence and power for every new time and every new place, that is so strange and even shocking to people who have different understandings of Christianity from that of Bonhoeffer. But it is that without which Bonhoeffer's ethical theology is unintelligible, and his ethical decisions ungraspable. To attempt to escape from one's own particular time and one's own particular place is to attempt to escape from responsibility for the present but also from responsibility for the future.

The fact that Bonhoeffer talks at such length in the *Ethics* about the history of the West and about Western civilization,[8] and also spells out his notions about nonreligious Christianity in the context of a certain reading of recent centuries in Western history,[9] must be understood in the light of his commitment to moral decision and ethical reflection as historical acts in specific times and places. It does not grow out of any idea that the West is superior to the East. In fact, his repeatedly frustrated plans to visit Gandhi are indicative of his conviction that there was a great deal to learn from the East. Nor is it a matter of thinking that the present is necessarily superior to the past. It is, rather, simply a matter of acting responsibly in one's own time and one's own place. But because that time and place are always stretched out, moving backward and forward into continuity and community with all other times and all other places, the limits of one's responsibility are set in the context of the limitlessness of the effects of one's actions for the future of the world.

One way to try to determine whether and how this position works is to see whether theory and practice intersect, whether Bonhoeffer's talk about decision making is congruent with the actual decisions that he made. The task is extremely precarious and probably presumptuous. It is not possible to understand thoroughly the mind of any person with regard to decisions that person makes, but it is notoriously difficult to get inside the mind of Bonhoeffer. He was very reluctant to share his inner struggles. He was not inclined to give moral advice to other people and he lacked the naiveté to let others make decisions for him.[10] There was a "distance" about him, an aristocratic reserve which kept him from opening his inner life to anyone other than the most intimate of friends. He even expressed disdain for those who presume to dig around in another person's internal passions and reflections.[11]

Yet we do know a great deal about Bonhoeffer through the biography by Eberhard Bethge, and also through remembrances from a great number of family members, friends, and acquaintances. He struggled with important decisions but seldom looked back once the decision was made. This was not always the case nor was it true that he was unable to change his mind, as is evident in his return to Germany after coming to the United States in 1939. But he was very much against scrupulosity. He was able to live calmly in the midst of great distress and crisis. He regarded indecision as particularly unproductive, and thought that often it is better to make a wrong decision than to make no decision at all.

There is no nice pattern left by Bonhoeffer about how to make decisions by the numbers. It could be that the model for decision making that fits with Bonhoeffer's ethical theology is not so much that of the logician as that of the artist. Theodore Gill has written about "Bonhoeffer as Aesthete."[12] The suggestion has even been made that Bonhoeffer reverses Kierkegaard in that his movement is from transcendence to immanence to ethics to aesthetics rather than the other way around. It is a refreshing and fascinating suggestion. It would be a mistake to forget that Bonhoeffer was an accomplished pianist and that all of the arts played an important role in his life. His interest in good taste marked him as a person who took life in his stride and did it with a flair. Life was utterly serious for him but never without strong doses of *hilaritas*. To some ethicists all of this may seem chaotic. Someone who, like James Gustafson, talks about "moral discernment" and the moral agent as "virtuoso" is apt to enter into it more sympathetically.

What we have at hand is considerable material from Bonhoeffer about his attempt to formulate an ethical theology and to structure the responsible life, together with a very detailed biography in which we know with some precision about decisions he actually made. The question we are addressing in this section is whether we can see in the Bonhoeffer who engaged concrete times and places the same Bonhoeffer who reflected about how this should be done. There are many cases on which to focus. Sermons — for instance, the one on church election day when the takeover of the church by the Nazis was at stake — fit his concept of preaching as presentation. Or one could ask about whether his response to the "Aryan clause" and to "Crystal Night" fits with the things that he said about the Jews. One could investigate his decision to return to Germany in 1939, or his setting up the curriculum at Finkenwalde to include meditation and study of the Sermon on the Mount. Or one could examine his decision to support tyrannicide in the light of his distinction in the *Ethics* between murder and killing. In each case the problem would be to see how the action and the reflection in a particular situation fit with his overall ethical theology.

It is not possible to look at more than one case with any thoroughness. So a selection has been made. Truth telling is a classic issue for ethical reflection. It is also something about which Bonhoeffer wrote specifically, and something in which he was engaged while being interrogated at Tegel prison. While struggling under interrogation with what is meant by telling the truth, he was engaged in writing an essay about the same issue. Although there are many cases on which to focus, this seems to be the most promising.

Telling the Truth: A Case Study

In Benjamin Reist's splendid volume *The Promise of Bonhoeffer*,[13] the chapter on ethics is divided into two parts. The first is an exposition of Bonhoeffer's piece "Thinking in Terms of Two-spheres." The second is an exposition of his essay "What Is Meant by 'Telling the Truth'?" Both of these are in the *Ethics* volume. If one is going to write only a few pages on Bonhoeffer's ethics, it is difficult to imagine a better choice of focus than that selected by Reist. He moves directly from the most central statement of Bonhoeffer's ethical theology to his most thorough and explicit treatment of a traditional ethical issue. The interpretation of the Bonhoeffer material as well as the selection of it by Reist is in close agreement with the position taken in this book. Reist makes a bold claim in introducing the essay on truth telling. He says:

> The test question for any worthy attempt at an ethic of any sort is always the question of truth. Bonhoeffer wrestled with this question in an absolutely unprecedented way. . . . The importance of the fragment simply cannot be over-stated. One could almost divide those who respond to Bonhoeffer's efforts into two camps—those who see this section as decisive, and those, who, for any reason, do not.[14]

Bethge talks about the "confusing content" of Bonhoeffer's essay on truth telling and says that it can be understood only against the background of the conspiracy and its consequences.[15] The biographical material he then sketches as background for the essay is extremely valuable, but there is no attempt in the biography to deal with the essay in a systematic way. Renate Bethge is of the opinion that the essay reflects the very matter-of-fact way in which the family understood truth telling and practiced it.[16] To my knowledge there is no extended treatment of this essay anywhere in the Bonhoeffer literature. It is therefore all the more surprising that some people who are doing ethics quite apart from any special interest in Bonhoeffer have found the essay to be worth studying. Gustafson and James Laney include it as one of the source documents in their ethics textbook *On Being Responsible*.[17] They choose four essays for the section "On Being Responsible in Speech." The four authors are Immanuel Kant, Bonhoeffer, Paul Lehmann, and Bernhard Häring. In *Lying: Moral Choice in Public and Private Life* by Sissela Bok,[18] this essay is printed in the appendix along with essays on truth telling by Augustine, Aquinas, Francis Bacon, Hugo Grotius, Kant, Sidgewick, Harrod, and Warnock. Bok's book is an extensive treatment of truth telling without any particular Christian or religious bias; it is thus doubly significant that she includes the Bonhoeffer essay. There are those who consider this essay important without any biographical context whatsoever.

However, since the issue of truth telling is here a way at getting at the ethics of Bonhoeffer, this essay is taken as a "test case." The question is whether this essay fits into the life and literature as a whole, and what light it sheds on Bonhoeffer's ethical theology. It is a way of getting at the question of whether his ethical theology works, and if so, how. While under interrogation at Tegel prison, Bonhoeffer sought to tell the truth, but he struggled with the question of what, in that time and place, it meant to do so. He struggled with the question in his own actions and words as he was interrogated, but also in his reflection, during the same period, on the classic ethical issue of truth telling. What we have is a rare interpenetration of moral action and ethical reflection focused in a single time and place, a perfect window through which to examine Bonhoeffer's ethical theology at work.

The Time and the Place

Bonhoeffer is constantly striving for concreteness in ethics, for free and responsible action in concrete times and concrete places. This is the case also for truth telling, and Bonhoeffer is very specific about it. In the essay "What Is Meant by 'Telling the Truth'?" he says that "it is only the cynic who claims to 'speak the truth' at all times and in all places to all people in the same way."[19] The reason that one cannot claim to speak the truth at all times and in all places is that "speech does not accompany the natural course of life in a continual stream, but it has its place, its time and its task, and consequently also its limits."[20] Although, then, there are those who think it possible to study this essay without any biographical context whatsoever, it would, finally, be a violation of the text and of the position it states to attempt to do that.

The essay was written at Tegel prison during the period of Bonhoeffer's interrogation. If discovered, it would have had a devastating effect on his case. He did, however, manage to work on it without detection, and to smuggle it out to his father after the failure of the 20 July plot, when prison security measures became much tighter.[21]

His problem was complicated by the fact that two other conspirators, Josef Müller and Bonhoeffer's brother-in-law Hans von Dohnanyi, were being interrogated at the same time. The three had to see to it that their stories did not conflict and that the Gestapo got no information about the conspiracy from them. They had agreed prior to their arrest on a unified strategy of assigning responsibility for all details to those who gave the orders in the Abwehr (the military intelligence unit for which they worked), namely Canaris, Oster, and von Dohnanyi. They were also able to communicate through family members by placing a faint pencil mark under a letter on every tenth page, starting from the back, in books that were brought to Bonhoeffer for recreational reading. With the help of these messages, and by sticking to the agreed-upon strategy, Bonhoeffer was able to avoid contradictions during the interrogation sessions as well as to avoid disclosing information about the conspiracy.[22]

Von Dohnanyi was relieved of some of the pressure he would otherwise have had to endure because he was ill during the time of his interrogation. He used that illness, however, as a weapon against his interrogators, claiming to be more ill than he actually was and artfully displaying symptoms in order to prolong the appearance of illness as much as possible.[23]

There is no question but that Bonhoeffer was constantly at work to deceive the Gestapo. He "played dumb," presenting himself as a pastor unfamiliar with military and intelligence matters. In a note to himself, made in preparation for an interrogation session, he wrote:

> I am the last person to deny that I might have made mistakes in work so strange, so new and so complicated as that of the *Abwehr*. I often find it hard to follow the speed of your questions, probably because I am not used to them.[24]

It is clear that everything was designed in awareness of the fact that the lives of others depended upon his skill in deceiving the Gestapo, and that the conspiracy itself could collapse if he became careless even for a moment.

Although the pressures on Bonhoeffer during the interrogation were extreme, and the essay was written in this particular time and place, the content of the essay is such that it is consistent with other things that he wrote and with other actions that he took. The essay is reproduced here in toto so that the reader can have a ready reference to the text as further exposition unfolds. The first number is the last digit of the page number of the English edition of the *Ethics* (3 = p. 363, 0 = p. 370, 1 = p. 371, etc.). The second number is the line.[25]

The Essay: "What Is Meant by 'Telling the Truth'?"

3/1   From the moment in our lives at which we learn to speak
3/2   we are taught that what we say must be true. What does
3/3   this mean? What is meant by "telling the truth"? What
3/4   does it demand of us?
3/5   It is clear that in the first place it is our parents who
3/6   regulate our relation to themselves by this demand for
3/7   truthfulness; consequently, in the sense in which our

3/8   parents intend it, this demand applies strictly only within
3/9   the family circle. It is also to be noted that the relation
3/10   which is expressed in this demand cannot simply be
3/11   reversed. The truthfulness of a child towards his parents is
3/12   essentially different from that of the parents towards their
3/13   child. The life of the small child lies open before the
3/14   parents, and what the child says should reveal to them
3/15   everything that is hidden and secret, but in the converse
3/16   relationship this cannot possibly be the case. Consequently,
3/17   in the matter of truthfulness, the parents' claim on the child
3/18   is different from the child's claim on the parents.
3/19   From this it emerges already that "telling the truth"
3/20   means something different according to the particular
3/21   situation in which one stands. Account must be taken of
3/22   one's relationships at each particular time. The question
3/23   must be asked whether and in what way a man is entitled
3/24   to demand truthful speech of others. Speech between
3/25   parents and children is, in the nature of the case, different
3/26   from speech between man and wife, between friends,
3/27   between teacher and pupil, government and subject, friend and
3/28   foe, and in each case the truth which this speech
3/29   conveys is also different.
4/1   It will at once be objected that one does not owe truthful
4/2   speech to this or that individual man, but solely to God.
4/3   This objection is correct so long as it is not forgotten that
4/4   God is not a general principle, but the living God who has
4/5   set me in a living life and who demands service of me
4/6   within this living life. If one speaks of God one must not
4/7   simply disregard the actual given world in which one lives;
4/8   for if one does that one is not speaking of the God who
4/9   entered into the world in Jesus Christ, but rather of some
4/10   metaphysical idol. And it is precisely this which is deter-
4/11   mined by the way in which, in my actual concrete life
4/12   with all its manifold relationships, I give effect to the truth-
4/13   fulness which I owe to God. The truthfulness which we
4/14   owe to God must assume a concrete form in the world.
4/15   Our speech must be truthful, not in principle but con-
4/16   cretely. A truthfulness which is not concrete is not truthful
4/17   before God.
4/18   "Telling the truth," therefore, is not solely a matter of

4/19 moral character; it is also a matter of correct appreciation
4/20 of real situations and of serious reflection upon them. The
4/21 more complex the actual situations of a man's life, the
4/22 more responsible and the more difficult will be his task of
4/23 "telling the truth." The child stands in only one vital
4/24 relationship, his relationship to his parents, and he, there-
4/25 fore, still has nothing to consider and weigh up. The next
4/26 environment in which he is placed, his school, already
4/27 brings with it the first difficulty. From the educational
4/28 point of view it is, therefore, of the very greatest importance
4/29 that parents, in some way which we cannot discuss here,
4/30 should make their children understand the differences
4/31 between these various circles in which they are to live and
4/32 the differences in their responsibilities.
4/33   Telling the truth is, therefore, something which must be
4/34 learnt. This will sound very shocking to anyone who thinks
4/35 that it must all depend on moral character and that if this
4/36 is blameless the rest is child's play. But the simple fact is
5/1 that the ethical cannot be detached from reality, and con-
5/2 sequently continual progress in learning to appreciate
5/3 reality is a necessary ingredient in ethical action. In the
5/4 question with which we are now concerned, action consists
5/5 of speaking. The real is to be expressed in words. That is
5/6 what constitutes truthful speech. And this inevitably raises
5/7 the question of the "how?" of these words. It is a question
5/8 of knowing the right word on each occasion. Finding this
5/9 word is a matter of long, earnest and ever more advanced
5/10 effort on the basis of experience and knowledge of the real.
5/11 If one is to say how a thing really is, i.e., if one is to speak
5/12 truthfully, one's gaze and one's thought must be directed
5/13 towards the way in which the real exists in God and
5/14 through God and for God.
5/15   To restrict this problem of truthful speech to certain
5/16 particular cases of conflict is superficial. Every word I utter
5/17 is subject to the requirement that it shall be true. Quite
5/18 apart from the veracity of its contents, the relation between
5/19 myself and another man which is expressed in it is in itself
5/20 either true or untrue. I speak flatteringly or presump-
5/21 tuously or hypocritically without uttering a material un-
5/22 truth; yet my words are nevertheless untrue, because I am

5/23 disrupting and destroying the reality of the relationship
5/24 between man and wife, superior and subordinate, etc. An
5/25 individual utterance is always part of a total reality which
5/26 seeks expression in this utterance. If my utterance is to be
5/27 truthful it must in each case be different according to whom
5/28 I am addressing, who is questioning me, and what I am
5/29 speaking about. The truthful word is not in itself constant;
5/30 it is as much alive as life itself. If it is detached from life
5/31 and from its reference to the concrete other man, if "the
5/32 truth is told" without taking into account to whom it is
5/33 addressed, then this truth has only the appearance of truth,
5/34 but it lacks its essential character.
5/35   It is only the cynic who claims "to speak the truth" at all
5/36 times and in all places to all men in the same way, but who,
6/1 in fact, displays nothing but a lifeless image of the truth.
6/2 He dons the halo of the fanatical devotee of truth who can
6/3 make no allowance for human weaknesses; but, in fact, he
6/4 is destroying the living truth between men. He wounds
6/5 shame, desecrates mystery, breaks confidence, betrays the
6/6 community in which he lives, and laughs arrogantly at the
6/7 devastation he has wrought and at the human weakness
6/8 which "cannot bear the truth." He says truth is destructive
6/9 and demands its victims, and he feels like a god above these
6/10 feeble creatures and does not know that he is serving
6/11 Satan.
6/12   There is a truth which is of Satan. Its essence is that
6/13 under the semblance of truth it denies everything that is
6/14 real. It lives upon hatred of the real and of the world
6/15 which is created and loved by God. It pretends to be
6/16 executing the judgment of God upon the fall of the real.
6/17 God's truth judges created things out of love, and Satan's
6/18 truth judges them out of envy and hatred. God's truth has
6/19 become flesh in the world and is alive in the real, but
6/20 Satan's truth is the death of all reality.
6/21   The concept of living truth is dangerous, and it gives rise
6/22 to the suspicion that the truth can and may be adapted to
6/23 each particular situation in a way which completely
6/24 destroys the idea of truth and narrows the gap between
6/25 truth and falsehood, so that the two become indistinguish-
6/26 able. Moreover, what we are saying about the necessity

6/27 for discerning the real may be mistakenly understood as
6/28 meaning that it is by adopting a calculating or school-
6/29 masterly attitude towards the other man that I shall decide
6/30 what proportion of the truth I am prepared to tell him. It
6/31 is important that this danger should be kept in view. Yet
6/32 the only possible way of countering it is by means of
6/33 attentive discernment of the particular contents and limits
6/34 which the real itself imposes on one's utterance in order to
6/35 make it a truthful one. The dangers which are involved in
6/36 the concept of living truth must never impel one to abandon
7/1 this concept in favour of the formal and cynical concept of
7/2 truth. We must try to make this clear. Every utterance or
7/3 word lives and has its home in a particular environment.
7/4 The word in the family is different from the word in
7/5 business or in public. The word which has come to life in
7/6 the warmth of personal relationship is frozen to death in
7/7 the cold air of public existence. The word of command,
7/8 which has its habitat in public service, would sever the
7/9 bonds of mutual confidence if it were spoken in the family.
7/10 Each word must have its own place and keep to it. It is a
7/11 consequence of the wide diffusion of the public word
7/12 through the newspapers and the wireless that the essential
7/13 character and the limits of the various different words are
7/14 no longer clearly felt and that, for example, the special
7/15 quality of the personal word is almost entirely destroyed.
7/16 Genuine words are replaced by idle chatter. Words no
7/17 longer possess any weight. There is too much talk. And
7/18 when the limits of the various words are obliterated, when
7/19 words become rootless and homeless, then the word loses
7/20 truth, and then indeed there must almost inevitably be
7/21 lying. When the various orders of life no longer respect
7/22 one another, words become untrue. For example, a teacher
7/23 asks a child in front of the class whether it is true that his
7/24 father often comes home drunk. It is true, but the child
7/25 denies it. The teacher's question has placed him in a
7/26 situation for which he is not yet prepared. He feels only
7/27 that what is taking place is an unjustified interference in
7/28 the order of the family and that he must oppose it. What
7/29 goes on in the family is not for the ears of the class in
7/30 school. The family has its own secret and must preserve it.

7/31 The teacher has failed to respect the reality of this institu-
7/32 tion. The child ought now to find a way of answering
7/33 which would comply with both the rule of the family and
7/34 the rule of the school. But he is not yet able to do this. He
7/35 lacks experience, knowledge, and the ability to express
7/36 himself in the right way. As a simple no to the teacher's
8/1 question the child's answer is certainly untrue; yet at the
8/2 same time it nevertheless gives expression to the truth that
8/3 the family is an institution *sui generis* and that the teacher
8/4 had no right to interfere in it. The child's answer can
8/5 indeed be called a lie; yet this lie contains more truth,
8/6 that is to say, it is more in accordance with reality than
8/7 would have been the case if the child had betrayed his
8/8 father's weakness in front of the class. According to the
8/9 measure of his knowledge, the child acted correctly. The
8/10 blame for the lie falls back entirely upon the teacher. An
8/11 experienced man in the same position as the child would
8/12 have been able to correct his questioner's error while at the
8/13 same time avoiding a formal untruth in his answer, and he
8/14 would thus have found the "right word." The lies of
8/15 children, and of inexperienced people in general, are often
8/16 to be ascribed to the fact that these people are faced with
8/17 situations which they do not fully understand. Conse-
8/18 quently, since the term lie is quite properly understood as
8/19 meaning something which is quite simply and utterly
8/20 wrong, it is perhaps unwise to generalize and extend the use
8/21 of this term so that it can be applied to every statement
8/22 which is formally untrue. Indeed here already it becomes
8/23 apparent how very difficult it is to say what actually
8/24 constitutes a lie.
8/25   The usual definition of the lie as a conscious discrepancy
8/26 between thought and speech is completely inadequate. This
8/27 would include, for example, even the most harmless April
8/28 fool joke. The concept of the "jocular lie," which is
8/29 maintained in Catholic moral theology, takes away from
8/30 the lie its characteristic features of seriousness and malice
8/31 (and, conversely, takes away from the joke its characteristic
8/32 features of harmless playfulness and freedom); no more
8/33 unfortunate concept could have been thought of. Joking
8/34 has nothing whatever to do with lying, and the two must

8/35 not be reduced to a common denominator. If it is now
8/36 asserted that a lie is a deliberate deception of another man
8/37 to his detriment, then this would also include, for example,
9/1 the necessary deception of the enemy in war or in similar
9/2 situations.* If this sort of conduct is called lying, the lie
9/3 thereby acquires a moral sanction and justification which
9/4 conflicts in every possible way with the accepted meaning of
9/5 the term. The first conclusion to be drawn from this is that
9/6 the lie cannot be defined in formal terms as a discrepancy
9/7 between thought and speech. This discrepancy is not even
9/8 a necessary ingredient of the lie. There is a way of speaking
9/9 which is in this respect entirely correct and unexception-
9/10 able, but which is, nevertheless, a lie. This is exemplified
9/11 when a notorious liar for once tells "the truth" in order to
9/12 mislead, and when an apparently correct statement contains
9/13 some deliberate ambiguity or deliberately omits the essential
9/14 part of the truth. Even a deliberate silence may constitute
9/15 a lie, although this is not by any means necessarily the
9/16 case.
9/17   From these considerations it becomes evident that the
9/18 essential character of the lie is to be found at a far deeper
9/19 level than in the discrepancy between thought and speech.
9/20 One might say that the man who stands behind the word
9/21 makes his word a lie or a truth. But even this is not enough;
9/22 for the lie is something objective and must be defined
9/23 accordingly. Jesus calls Satan "the father of the lie" (John
9/24 8:44). The lie is primarily the denial of God as He has
9/25 evidenced Himself to the world. "Who is a liar but he that
9/26 denieth that Jesus is the Christ?" (1 John 2:22). The lie is
9/27 a contradiction of the word of God, which God has spoken
9/28 in Christ, and upon which creation is founded. Conse-
9/29 quently the lie is the denial, the negation and the conscious
9/30 and deliberate destruction of the reality which is created
9/31 by God and which consists in God, no matter whether this
9/32 purpose is achieved by speech or by silence. The assigned
0/1 purpose of our words, in unity with the word of God, is to

---

*Kant, of course, declared that he was too proud ever to utter a falsehood; indeed he unin-
tentionally carried this principle *ad absurdum* by saying that he would feel himself obliged
to give truthful information even to a criminal looking for a friend of his who had concealed
himself in his house.

0/2   express the real, as it exists in God; and the assigned
0/3   purpose of our silence is to signify the limit which is
0/4   imposed upon our words by the real as it exists in God.
0/5   In our endeavours to express the real we do not encounter
0/6   this as a consistent whole, but in a condition of disruption
0/7   and inner contradiction which has need of reconciliation
0/8   and healing. We find ourselves simultaneously embedded
0/9   in various different orders of the real, and our words, which
0/10 strive towards the reconciliation and healing of the real, are
0/11 nevertheless repeatedly drawn in into the prevalent dis-
0/12 union and conflict. They can indeed fulfil their assigned
0/13 purpose of expressing the real, as it is in God, only by taking
0/14 up into themselves both the inner contradiction and the
0/15 inner consistency of the real. If the words of men are to be
0/16 true they must deny neither the Fall nor God's word of
0/17 creation and reconciliation, the word in which all disunion
0/18 is overcome. For the cynic the truthfulness of his words will
0/19 consist in his giving expression on each separate occasion to
0/20 the particular reality as he thinks he perceives it, without
0/21 reference to the totality of the real; and precisely through
0/22 this he completely destroys the real. Even if his words have
0/23 the superficial appearance of correctness, they are untrue.
0/24 "That which is far off, and exceeding deep; who can find
0/25 it out?" (Eccl. 7:24).
0/26   How can I speak the truth?
0/27   a By perceiving who causes me to speak and what
0/28 entitles me to speak.
0/29   b By perceiving the place at which I stand.
0/30   c By relating to this context the object about which I
0/31 am making some assertion.
0/32   It is tacitly assumed in these rules that all speech is
0/33 subject to certain conditions; speech does not accompany
0/34 the natural course of life in a continual stream, but it has
0/35 its place, its time and its task, and consequently also its
0/36 limits.
0/37   a Who or what entitles or causes me to speak? Anyone
1/1   who speaks without a right and a cause to do so is an idle
1/2   chatterer. Every utterance is involved in a relation both
1/3   with the other man and with a thing, and in every utter-
1/4   ance, therefore, this twofold reference must be apparent.

1/5   An utterance without reference is empty. It contains no
1/6   truth. In this there is an essential difference between
1/7   thought and speech. Thought does not in itself necessarily
1/8   refer to the other man, but only to a thing. The claim that
1/9   one is entitled to say what one thinks is in itself completely
1/10 unfounded. Speech must be justified and occasioned by the
1/11 other man. For example, I may in my thoughts consider
1/12 another man to be stupid, ugly, incapable or lacking in
1/13 character, or I may think him wise and reliable. But it is
1/14 quite a different question whether I have the right to
1/15 express this opinion, what occasion I have for expressing it,
1/16 and to whom I express it. There can be no doubt that a
1/17 right to speak is conferred upon me by an office which is
1/18 committed to me. Parents can blame or praise their child,
1/19 but the child is not entitled to do either of these things with
1/20 regard to his parents. There is a similar relation between
1/21 teacher and pupil, although the rights of the teacher with
1/22 regard to the children are more restricted than those of the
1/23 father. Thus in criticizing or praising his pupil the teacher
1/24 will have to confine himself to single particular faults or
1/25 achievements, while, for example, general judgments of
1/26 character are the business not of the teacher but of the
1/27 parents. The right to speak always lies within the confines
1/28 of the particular office which I discharge. If I overstep
1/29 these limits my speech becomes importunate, presumptuous,
1/30 and, whether it be blame or praise, offensive. There are
1/31 people who feel themselves called upon to "tell the truth,"
1/32 as they put it, to everyone who crosses their path.*

Some Observations on the Essay

The entire essay is marked by a grasp of totality, of wholeness. Bon-hoeffer begins by saying that we are taught that what we say must be true. The question that he then addresses to that fact is not whether we agree that what we say must be true. He assumes that it is the case that what we say must be true. Everything that we say must be true. He does not ask the when question as though there are times when what we say need not be true. Everything we say must always be true. He does not ask the to whom question as though there are some people to whom we need not tell

*Editor's note. Unfinished. . . .

the truth. Everything we say to everyone must always be true. Bonhoeffer refuses all partiality questions. He begins by assuming that the question of truth is a totality question. What we say must be true. It is unthinkable that the Bonhoeffer who fought partiality and stressed wholeness throughout his life would attempt to solve his problem in Tegel prison by deciding that it is proper to lie under some circumstances.

What he does ask is the meaning question, the hermeneutical question: What is meant by "telling the truth"? This is a sharp departure from those people who assume that we know what it is to tell the truth and that all that we need is the moral courage to do it. Bonhoeffer is very clear that telling the truth is something that does not come easily. It is something that must be learned (4/34, 5/2). He is aware that he is going directly contrary to those who think that knowing what telling the truth means is no problem at all ("child's play") and that everything simply depends upon "moral character" (German *Gesinnung*, better translated "intention") (4/35, 36).

The fact that he is working for a "totality" understanding of truth telling is also clear in that he specifically in this prison interrogation context says that "to restrict this problem of truthful speech to certain particular cases of conflict is superficial. Every word I utter is subject to the requirement that it shall be true" (5/16, 17). There are those who understand this essay to be a borderline or boundary kind of solution for a difficult situation, and thus not applicable to truth telling in general. It is clear that Bonhoeffer himself did not consider it so. What he is saying has to do, in his own opinion, with all our speech in all situations. So he talks about silence and gestures and chattering and newspapers and radio. He is not just talking about particular situations, and he is certainly not saying that it is appropriate to lie from time to time in a desperate case. He is talking about the necessity of always telling the truth.

Yet this "always" and "everywhere," this totality, is not a matter of universal ethical rule because it is never abstract. The always and the everywhere are concrete in specific times and places. He says that it is only the cynic who claims "to speak the truth" at all times and in all places to all people in the same way (5/35, 36). He puts "to speak the truth" in quotation marks, because he is not disagreeing only on some detail with those people whom he calls cynics. He is in fundamental disagreement about what it *means* to tell the truth, which is why he entitles the essay as he does.

Bonhoeffer recognizes the very great complexity of telling the truth. He realizes that knowing the meaning of telling the truth is not "child's play" (4/36). One gets a hint of this even from the various expressions that Bonhoeffer uses. He does not simply talk about "the truth." He talks a great deal about "truthfulness," a quality that can be ascribed to a wide network of words and gestures. He says that a word "loses truth" when it becomes "rootless and homeless" (7/19, 20). Misplaced truth is not truthful. There is talk about "truthful speech." On the other hand, it is possible for a word to "contain no truth," or to be "empty" (1/5). He asks how a word can "become true." The force is lost in the English translation "How can I speak the truth?" (0/26). The notion of a word *becoming* true is another sign of the complexity of truth telling for Bonhoeffer. He deals with silence as well as speech. There are times when in order to speak the truth one must be silent (7/30). On the other hand, silence can sometimes be a lie (9/14). We have seen already that there is the truth of the cynic. There is also a truth of Satan (6/12). The many ways in which Bonhoeffer talks about truth signal the fact that he is seeking a total grasp of truth telling in the context of the wholeness of life.

A similar thing happens when he talks about the opposite of truth, the lie. He speaks about the lie, but also the untruth. Words actually can "become" untrue (7/22). There is falsehood. There is "formal untruth" (8/13, 21). There is error (8/12). Speech can become "importunate" or "presumptuous" (1/29). Knowing what telling the truth means is very difficult. It is also extremely difficult to say what a lie is (8/23).

As soon as he begins to give positive content to the answer to his question, he begins talking about parents and children, and thus about relationships. This is no surprise to anyone who has a grasp of Bonhoeffer's ethics. It would be very strange, in fact, if the sociality of Christ, first formulated in *The Communion of Saints*, did not play a role in his struggle to tell the truth in Tegel prison. We have seen that relationality and responsibility are tied together in Bonhoeffer's ethical theology, and that the family is an order of preservation or a divine mandate. So here there is immediate talk about parents and children in relationship with one another (3/5–18). Relationality and responsibility in concrete times and places mean that different relationships require different forms of speech if one is going to speak responsibly. "Speech between parents and children is, in the nature of the case, different from speech between man and wife, between friends, between teacher and pupil, government and subject, friend and foe, and in each case the truth which this speech conveys is also different"(3/24–29). Actual life has "manifold relationships" (4/12). These relationships get to be complex and the "more complex" the relationship, the "more difficult" is the task of truth telling (4/21–23). The relationships in which truth must be told include not only relationships between people but also relationships between people and things (1/3). Since God is the creator of all things, and God and the world come together in the flesh of Jesus of Nazareth, "God is in the facts" and truth telling for the Christian can never be a purely personal matter. We must deal truthfully with things as well as with people.

It is astonishing that Bonhoeffer is able to use the word "order" to express the presence of these relationships. We have seen how he struggled against the misuses of the orders of creation doctrine by the National Socialists and the German Christians, and how he recast this whole doctrine in the new language of the mandates. Yet he uses the word "order" here a number of times. The word occurs in the phrases "various orders of life" (7/21) and "order of the family" (7/28). But the word *Ordnung* occurs in the German text more often, and is translated in the English edition in other ways, for instance, "institution" (7/31) or "rule" (7/33). Bonhoeffer says that the family is an order *sui generis* (8/3). In this context Bonhoeffer also uses the word "office" (1/17, 28). It is a word (*Amt*) also much misused in Nazi Germany. Yet he uses it positively in this prison essay. Truth-in-relationship does not mean the absence of structures, but the presence of structures.

But the structures vary. It is the cynic who claims to speak the truth at all times and in all places to all people in the same way (5/35–36). Different relationships make different demands for truth on us. "The truthfulness of a child towards his parents is essentially different from that of the parents towards their child" (3/11–13). Almost immediately, specific place and time enter the discussion. "From this it emerges already that 'telling the truth' means something different according to the particular place [translated "situation"] in which one stands. Account must be taken of one's relationships at each particular time" (3/19–22). The emphasis upon place occurs frequently (5/36; 7/10; 0/29). Sometimes he talks about not the place of the word but the "home" of the word (7/3, 8, 19). The important thing about stressing the "place" and "time" of the word is that these times and places vary. One is different from another, and Bonhoeffer stresses this repeatedly (3/12, 18, 20, 25, 29; 4/30, 32; 5/27; 7/13).

To the obvious objection of the absolutist who is nervous about all of these differences in various relationships demanding different kinds of truthful speech, who says that we owe truth not to people but to God, the assumption being that God is timeless and placeless, Bonhoeffer responds that God is not a general principle but the "living God who has set me in a living life and who demands service of me within this living life" (4/4–6). The God of the Bible is not a "general principle" (4/4) or a "metaphysical idol" (4/10), but the "God who entered into the world in Jesus Christ"

(4/8–9). So Bonhoeffer concludes that truthful speech must certainly be truthful before God, but that means specifically that it must be truth that takes "concrete form in the world" (4/14) and therefore that it is "living truth" (6/4, 21, 36).

Bonhoeffer's celebration of life comes into play in his struggle to tell the truth in Tegel prison and to reflect on what it means to tell the truth. So the cynic who claims to speak the truth at all times and in all places to all people in the same way (5/35–36) does in fact display "nothing but a lifeless image of the truth" (6/1). It is not insignificant that the word "image" here is *Gotzenbild*, a word that means idol and is a direct reference back to the passage (4/10) where he connects "metaphysical idol" with "God as a general principle" and thus with truth as lifeless rather than as living.

If we worship "the living God," then we must practice "living truth" (6/4, 21, 36). "The truthful word is not in itself constant; it is as much alive as life itself" (5/29–30). "The word which has come to life in the warmth of personal relationship is frozen to death in the cold air of public existence" (7/5–7).

Of course, for Bonhoeffer God is living and the living God implies living truth because of Jesus Christ. He believes that it is for the sake of Christ that he deals with his interrogators as he does. Thus, although the name Jesus does not occur often in this essay, it does occur at very decisive places. As soon as he begins to address those who say that one owes truth only to God and not to individual people, Bonhoeffer says that God is living and refers immediately to God entering the world in Jesus Christ (4/8–10). Again, he says that "God's truth has become flesh in the world and is alive in the real, but Satan's truth is the death of all reality" (6/18–20). We know that God is alive because he has come to us in the flesh of Jesus of Nazareth. In John's Gospel Jesus calls Satan the father of the lie (9/23–24). In John's First Epistle the liar is specifically that one who denies that Jesus is the Christ (9/26). Although Bonhoeffer does not make specific reference to his favorite passage in Colossians (1:15–20), he does refer to the connection between Christ and creation when he defines the lie as a "contradiction of the word of God, which God has spoken in Christ, and upon which creation is founded" (9/26–28). His christocentric understanding of reality pervades and informs his understanding of the common human problem of truth telling. It is exactly what one would expect. The one who decided that "reality is the sacrament of the ethical" returns to the theme of reality repeatedly in this essay. Truth is for Bonhoeffer not an idea toward which to strive, but a reality in which to participate.

If there is a short key definition in this essay for what is meant by telling the truth, it is probably the following: "The real is to be expressed in words. That is what constitutes truthful speech" (5/5–6). Bonhoeffer's ethical theology has to do with reality and realization. Truthful speech is, then, expressing the real in words.

It is because "the ethical cannot be detached from reality" (5/1) that speaking truthfully means saying "how a thing really is" (5/11). It is not just a matter of "the brute facts." It has to do with "the way in which the real exists in God and through God and for God" (5/13–14). It is a matter of "the reality of the relationship" (5/23). The truth that is of Satan has the semblance of truth, but it denies everything that is real (6/12–14). In the *Ethics* Bonhoeffer talks about the fanatic who hates the world that God created. Here he talks about the truth of Satan which hates the real and hates the world which is created and loved by God (6/15). For Bonhoeffer the "lie is the denial, the negation and the conscious and deliberate destruction of the reality which is created by God and which consists in God, no matter whether this purpose is achieved by speech or by silence" (9/29–32). Therefore, expressing the real (0/1–4) is telling the truth, and denying the real is telling a lie.

The problem, then, in telling the truth is to find "the right word" (5/7–9), expressing oneself in "the right way" (7/36; 8/14). Years earlier Bonhoeffer had struggled with the question of how the church can find the right word at the right time. In prison he struggles for the right word and reflects in this essay on the struggle. It is not child's play (4/36). It is not something that depends just on courage or "moral character" (4/35). Telling the truth is something that must be learned. It is entirely appropriate and consistent that Bonhoeffer says this, shocking as it may sound to some people (4/33–34). It is not something for which we can rely on conscience. He has been very clear about that from the beginning of his theological work in *The Communion of Saints*. There is no way to rely on intuition, or on reason alone, or on a flash of divine guidance. There is no automatic or easy way to do it. One must *learn* how to tell the truth, just as one must learn how to pray.[26]

One of the reasons that truth telling must be learned is that sin has distorted the whole created order. In perfect step with his talk about the recovery of the natural, Bonhoeffer says that if the words of people are to be true "they must deny neither the fall nor God's word of creation and reconciliation, the word in which all disunion is overcome" (0/16–18). There is, after the fall, both an "inner contradiction" and an "inner consistency" of the real (0/14–15). This insistence is a corollary of the *simul iustus et peccator* (at the same time justified and sinner) of Lutheran theology, or of the "substantially good, accidentally evil" formula of the Lutheran doctrine of sin as described in the *Formula of Concord*, Article I. Expressing the real in words might be "child's play" if we were in a condition without sin. The fact, however, is that "in our endeavors to express the real we do not encounter this as a consistent whole, but in a condition of disruption and inner contradiction which has need of reconciliation and healing" (0/5–8). The fundamental disunity that makes one's conscience less than a perfect guide for behavior also makes truth telling something that requires more than moral courage.

It requires also knowledge and awareness and reflection. Ethics is a matter of history and of the earth. Bonhoeffer said it repeatedly since the Barcelona lectures. If truth is going to be living truth that expresses the truth of the living God in the incarnate, crucified, and risen Christ, whom to deny is a lie, then one must have some information, one must know something, and one must think about it. Finding the right word "is a matter of long, earnest and ever more advanced effort on the basis of experience and knowledge of the real" (5/9–10). Telling the truth is a matter of "correct appreciation of real situations and of serious reflection upon them" (4/19–20). One must consider and weigh up things (4/25). It means "continual progress in learning to recognize [English translation, appreciate] reality" (5/2–3). Recognizing the real is not a mechanical accumulation of data. "Discerning the real may be mistakenly understood as meaning that it is by adopting a calculating or school-masterly attitude towards the other man that I shall decide what proportion of the truth I am prepared to tell him" (6/27–30). In his discussion of the child in the schoolroom, Bonhoeffer refers a number of times to the factor of experience or the lack of it (8/11, 15). Perceiving the real does not mean an atomistic time-to-time expression of what one perceives on each separate occasion. There must be recognition of the totality of the real, lest the real be destroyed (0/19–23).

An obvious fear is that such talk could lead to an elitist ethic, a system in which only the most sensitive and intelligent and experienced could even be expected to tell the truth, so complicated is the process. Yet Bonhoeffer is able to make a positive judgment upon the child's comment to the teacher and says, "According to the measure of his knowledge, the child acted correctly" (8/8–9).

Although the word "responsibility" does not occur often in this essay, it is used. Bonhoeffer says the more complex the relationships of a person's life, the more responsible and the more difficult will be the task of telling the truth (4/21–23). He also says that differences in various relationships also mean differences in responsibility (4/31–32). This understanding of the responsibility goes along with his understanding of the limits within which that responsibility is exercised. The notion of limits receives no systematic treatment in this essay. It does, however, occur in two very important sentences. "Speech does not accompany the natural course of life in a continual stream, but it has its place, its time and its task, and consequently also its limits" (0/33–36). "The right to speak always lies within the confines of the particular office which I discharge. If I overstep these limits my speech becomes importunate, presumptuous, and, whether it be blame or praise, offensive" (1/27–30).

Under interrogation in Berlin's Tegel prison, Bonhoeffer was keenly aware of both the importance and the difficulty of his task. It was not the first time he had faced such a problem, nor was it the first time he had subjected the problem to careful scrutiny. What he did and what he wrote fit together in a remarkable way. The coherence of deed and word is also consistent with his handling of the truth telling question throughout his adult life.

Bonhoeffer on Truth Prior to the Tegel Essay

It has been stated that what Bonhoeffer did during his interrogation and what he wrote at that time about truth telling are consistent with actions previously taken and themes previously developed. Exercising responsibility in concrete times and places does not mean arbitrary or irrational decision making. There are structures for responsible living, even though those structures do not yield timeless norms or universalizable rules.

Truth was a fundamental theme for Bonhoeffer from the beginning. When Adolf Harnack died on 10 June 1930, Bonhoeffer spoke on behalf of Harnack's students at the memorial service. He said of Harnack, "He made it plain to us that truth is born only of freedom. We saw in him a champion of the free expression of truth when it has been recognized, who continually revised his free judgment and always plainly expressed it, notwithstanding the anxious restraint of the many."[27] Ernst Wolf, in his introduction to *Act and Being*, correctly describes the whole book as developed around the theme of "being in the truth." He sees that "the dialectic of *simul iustus et peccator* is here met with as the dialectic of 'being in Adam,' that is, 'in untruth' and 'being in Christ,' that is, 'in truth.' "[28] A study of the meaning of truth throughout the Bonhoeffer life and literature would require a monograph. What can be done here is to show briefly that in the *Ethics*, and then also in other actions and reflections, Bonhoeffer does and says things regarding truth telling that fit with his actions under interrogation at Tegel and with his prison essay on that topic.

In the *Ethics*

In his discussion of "The Theoretical Ethicist and Reality," Bonhoeffer says that our rusty swords must be replaced by sharp ones and that a person can "hold his own" only if he combines simplicity with wisdom.[29] To be simple is to be single-hearted (James 1:8). It is to be unfettered by principles. It is to cling to the commandments and judgments and mercies which come from God's mouth every day afresh. Then simplicity becomes wisdom, and the wise man is the one who sees reality as it is. Wisdom is recognizing the significant in the factual. It recognizes the "limited receptiveness of reality for principles." Reality "rests upon the living and creating God." So that "to look in freedom at God and at reality, which rests solely upon him, this is to combine simplicity with wisdom. There is no true simplicity without wisdom and there is no wisdom without simplicity."[30] There is an obvious relation between Bonhoeffer's exposition of simplicity and wisdom and his talk in the essay about truth as the expression in words of reality.

His comments on the French Revolution, though qualified, are essentially positive. He sees technology as having arisen in the West, in a world shaped by Christianity and specifically by the Reformation. There can be no return to a pretechnical era. It is something essentially new in the history of the world that reason is a working hypothesis, a heuristic principle, and we can never again be exempt from the inner obligation to make clean and honest use of reason.[31] This "free exercise of reason created an atmosphere of truthfulness, light and clarity," so that "contempt for the age of rationalism is a suspicious sign of failure to feel the need for truthfulness."[32] The passage is a clear basis for struggling with the requirements of truth telling in a world-coming-of-age.

Bonhoeffer's sensitivity to silence as well as to speech, to the gesture as well as to the word, to the requirement for truthfulness in the here and the now, is evident in his comments regarding pastoral care for the bereaved.

> So that this may become quite clear, let us ask why it is that precisely in thoroughly grave situations, for instance when I am with someone who has suffered a bereavement, I often decide to adopt a "penultimate" attitude, particularly when I am dealing with Christians, remaining silent as a sign that I share in the bereaved man's helplessness in the face of such a grievous event, and not speaking the biblical words of comfort which are, in fact, known to me and available to me. Why am I often unable to open my mouth, when I ought to give expression to the ultimate? And why, instead, do I decide on an expression of thoroughly penultimate human solidarity? . . . Does one not in some cases, by remaining deliberately in the penultimate, perhaps point

all the more genuinely to the ultimate, which God will speak in His own time (though indeed even then through a human mouth)?[33]

It is instructive to notice how Bonhoeffer weaves his structural formulations in and out of one another, in this case making use of the categories of penultimate and ultimate. And when he talks about correspondence with reality, the fit with the essay on truth telling is perfect.

> This concept of correspondence to reality certainly needs to be defined more exactly. It would be a complete and a dangerous misunderstanding if it were to be taken in the sense of that "servile conviction in the face of the fact" that Nietzsche speaks of, a conviction which yields to every powerful pressure, which on principle justifies success, and which on every occasion chooses what is opportune as "corresponding to reality." "Correspondence with reality" in this sense would be the contrary of responsibility; it would be irresponsibility. But the true meaning of correspondence with reality lies neither in this servility towards the factual nor yet in a principle of opposition to the factual, a principle of revolt against the factual in the name of some higher reality. Both extremes alike are very far removed from the essence of the matter. In action which is genuinely in accordance with reality there is an indissoluble link between the acknowledgment and the contradiction of the factual. The reason for this is that reality is first and last not lifeless; but it is the real man, the incarnate God. It is from the real man, whose name is Jesus Christ, that all factual reality derives its ultimate foundation and its ultimate annulment, its justification and its ultimate contradiction, its ultimate affirmation and its ultimate negation. To attempt to understand reality without the real man is to live in an abstraction to which the responsible man must never fall victim; it is to fail to make contact with reality in life; it is to vacillate endlessly between the extremes of servility and revolt in relation to the factual.[34]

The penetration of sin in the created order, the new reality in Christ, the necessity to weigh circumstances,[35] the themes of relationality and responsibility, the structured orders within which one makes concrete decisions, the importance of recognizing the significant in the factual — all the elements and all the themes of the Tegel essay are there in the *Ethics* documents written prior to his arrest. He had thought the whole thing through thoroughly. He was well prepared for what was required of him in the time and place of the Tegel interrogation.

Prior to the *Ethics*

The preparation did not start, however, with the writing of the *Ethics* documents. Truth telling, as has been said, was a theme from the beginning. In *Act and Being* he insists on understanding truth relationally and christologically.

Consequently, only the person already placed in truth can understand himself as in truth. For from within truth he can, in his potential reproduction of his "being known" by God . . . understand or recognize that he is situated in truth, i.e., re-created from untruth into truth. But only from within truth, i.e., in revelation, which is to say, whether judged or pardoned, in Christ.[36]

In the Christology lectures Bonhoeffer says that a person acts as a brother toward his fellow only if he does not withhold the truth from him, and that truth is Jesus Christ.[37] "Christ the Word is the truth. There is no truth apart from the Word and by the Word. . . . God's Word carries the destroying lightning and the life-giving rain. As Word, it destroys and it creates the truth."[38] Also in the Christology lectures, he is clear that since Jesus Christ is not timeless truth, the truth also is not timeless but is an address that demands a community and thus can happen only in history.

Christ as idea is timeless truth, the idea of God embodied in Jesus, available to anyone at any time.

The Word as address stands in contrast to all this. While it is possible for the Word as idea to remain by itself, as address it is only possible between two. Address requires response and responsibility. It is not timeless but happens in history. It does not rest and is not accessible to anyone at any time. It happens only when the address is made. The word lies wholly and freely at the disposal of the one who speaks. Thus it is unique and every time new. Its character as address requires the community. The character of truth in this addressing word is such that it seeks community, in order to face it with the truth. Truth is not something in itself, which rests for itself, but something that happens between two. Truth happens only in community. It is here for the first time that the concept of the Word acquires its full significance.

Christ as Word in the sense of address is thus not timeless truth. It is truth spoken into the concrete moment; it is address which places a man in the truth before God.[39]

Creation and Fall sounds many of the same notes. Speaking of the poetic language of the creation story, Bonhoeffer says,

Pictures are not lies: they denote things, they let the things that are meant shine through. But pictures change, of course; the pictures of a child are different from those of an adult, those of the man of the desert are different from those of the man of the city.[40]

In *The Cost of Discipleship* the connection between action and knowledge is clear. It is only through obedience that one comes to learn the truth.

Every moment and every situation challenges us to action and to obedience. We have literally no time to sit down and ask ourselves whether so-and-so is our neighbor or not. We must get into action and obey — we must behave like a neighbor to him. But perhaps this shocks you. Perhaps you still think you ought to think out beforehand and know what you ought to do. To that there is only one answer. You can only know and think about it by actually doing it. You can only learn what obedience is by obeying. It is no use asking questions; for it is only through obedience that you come to learn the truth.[41]

The section in *The Cost of Discipleship* which is an exposition of Matt. 5:33–37 is headed "Truthfulness" by Bonhoeffer. The entire discussion of oaths is instructive and the themes that occur in his discussion of truth are familiar.

> The oath which the Old Testament set against the lie is seized by the lie itself and pressed into service. It is thus able through the oath to establish itself and to take the law into its own hands. So the lie must be seized by Jesus in the very place to which it flees, in the oath. Therefore the oath must go, since it is a protection for the lie. . . . *Every* word they (the disciples) utter is spoken in his presence, and not only those words which are accompanied by an oath. . . . Since they always speak the whole truth and nothing but the truth, there is no need for an oath, which would only throw doubt on the veracity of all their other statements. . . . The commandment of complete truthfulness is really only another name for the totality of discipleship. Only those who follow Jesus and cleave to him are living in complete truthfulness. . . . There is no truth towards Jesus without truth towards man. Untruthfulness destroys fellowship, but truth cuts false fellowship to pieces and establishes genuine brotherhood. We cannot follow Christ unless we live in revealed truth before God and man.[42]

It is not only in books that Bonhoeffer discusses truth. He makes similar comments in sermons and lectures. In July 1932, he preached on John 8:32, "The truth will make you free."[43] He begins by saying that this is perhaps the most revolutionary word of the New Testament. Truth is unexpected, a surprise. With great homiletical skill he describes a child among adults who naively blurts out the truth, and the jester in the king's court who says the truth that no one else can say. Finally Bonhoeffer points to the Truth, the crucified Christ. Truth happens. It happens unexpectedly, on a cross. The essence of the lie is hate. The essence of truth is love.

In 1933 Bonhoeffer says that the student of theology must bring his passions with him to his calling, that ministry involves the total person and the total passion of Christ.[44] It is necessary to learn to call the truth truth and error error. That learning process may lead to a point of declaring the church *in statu confessionis*, because there is always a close link between truth and confession. The task at Barmen and at Dahlem was not fighting for "the Christian life" or for "Quaker meetings." The spirit works through word and confession, and therefore to be in a state of confession means that the church must now fight for the truth.[45] But "proving"[46] the truth, recognizing it, knowing it, comes only in the doing, in following the one who is the Truth. There is no other way.[47]

In a sermon from 1934 on Prov. 16:9, Bonhoeffer consistently connects the truth with the word of God and says, "There is no word of God for the whole of our life. God's word is new and free today and tomorrow, it is only applicable to the very moment in which we hear it."[48]

In a Finkenwalde homiletics lecture from 1935–36, Bonhoeffer says that truth is not the result of deduction. Truth happens. The form of happening truth is discipleship. Happening truth is living truth.[49]

What seems to be a repetitious and circular, at times even confused, attempt to say something meaningful about truth is in fact the careful and systematic reflection of one who knows that following Jesus Christ in a complex sin-penetrated world inevitably means doing things differently from the way one would do them in a perfect society. There is only one world in which to act, the world which is "in Adam" and "in Christ" at the same time. The recognition of this fact, that sin and grace affect also our truth telling, sets Bonhoeffer apart from the classic handling of truth telling by Immanuel Kant and his followers.

Immanuel Kant as Bonhoeffer's Foil

When Sissela Bok describes the ethical aspects of truth telling, she writes, "The major dividing line separates those who believe with Kant that there can be no sufficient justification for lying and those who believe that there are times when deception can be justifiably undertaken."[50] Kant is taken to be the central figure in the debate on truth telling because he holds a position that can be clearly described and understood, a position probably held in theory by the majority of people and thought by most people to be the "Christian" position. Although Bonhoeffer agrees with Kant that the truth must always be told, his departure is obvious as soon as he begins to ask what telling the truth means. This is clear not only in the truth telling essay, but in Bonhoeffer's lifelong understanding of truth. From the time of his first careful reflection on ethics at Barcelona, he self-consciously and explicitly sets himself in opposition to Kant. It is no surprise when he makes direct reference to Kant in the Tegel essay and even includes him in the notes sketched for the completion of the piece.[51]

That Bonhoeffer is not only one who in general opposes Kant on truth telling, but who deals with the truth telling question in an ingeniously non-Kantian manner, is attested to by the fact that Bonhoeffer's essay is included in a number of collections along with Kant's essay entitled "On a Supposed Right to Lie from Altruistic Motives." The presence of these essays in books by Gustafson and Laney, and by Bok, has already been mentioned. Lehmann also, in his *Ethics in a Christian Context*, deals extensively with Kant on truth telling, after which he deals with Bonhoeffer.[52] There is good reason to look at Kant as a paradigm of truth telling in a two-sphere thinking mode, both because Bonhoeffer himself is consciously combating Kant and also because others have seen these two in sharp contrast.

Bonhoeffer knew Kant very well and referred to him often. Even when not naming Kant specifically, he made use of him and his ideas. His essentially positive attitude toward the Enlightenment necessarily brings with it many specific aspects of appreciation for the work of Kant. He says, for instance, that it is impossible to think of going behind Lessing and that means also of going behind Kant. The phrase "world coming of age" is derived from Kant, although Bonhoeffer adapts it to his own use. There is appreciation for Kant, but on ethics, and thus on ethical theology, the opposition is persistent and sharp.

In *The Communion of Saints*, Bonhoeffer sees in stoicism that notion of the universally valid obligation, later explicated by Kant, which in Bonhoeffer's opinion is so destructive of personhood.

> It was Stoicism with its concept of *hagemonikon* which for the first time in the history of philosophy formed the concept of the ethical person. A man becomes a person by submitting to a higher obligation. This obligation is universally valid, and by obedience to it persons form a realm of reason, in which each soul, submissive to the obligation, is at one with eternal reason and thus also with the soul of other persons.
>
> But here too, in spite of the emphasis upon the ethical and "personal," that which really makes a person goes beyond the individual. It is the ethical and reasoning life of the person which is his essence, and it is so in abolishing him as an individual person.[53]

Although Bonhoeffer sketches four basic approaches, one of which he calls "the Stoic and the Christian" and another which he calls the view of German idealism,[54] associated with Kant, it is clear that the problem in stoicism is similar to the problem in Kant. Kant's "ethical formalism" is a correlate of his epistemology. The purely transcendental category of the universal can never reach the real existence of alien subjects.[55] Kant's emphasis on the "perceiving eye" keeps him from arriving at any adequate understanding of sociality. "So long as my mind is dominant, and claims universal validity, so long as all contradictions that may arise with the perception of a subject as an object of knowledge are thought of as immanent in my mind, I am not in the social sphere."[56] The move into talk about the ethical and the real is logical and quick, and Bonhoeffer, as can be expected in this context, criticizes Kant for attempting to deal with ethics as timeless.

> Kant taught that the uninterrupted flow of time should be understood as a purely intuitive form of our mind. As a result his thinking, and that of the whole of idealism, is in principle timeless. In Kant's epistemology this is obvious; but in ethics, too, he did not consciously get beyond this view.[57]

Bonhoeffer insists that both Kant and Fichte talked a great deal about ethics, but neither accomplished much because of their faulty epistemology. A corollary, according to Bonhoeffer, is that idealism, Kant in particular, has no profound concept of sin and thus no conception of movement.

> [The responsible] person is not the idealist's reasoning person or personified mind, but a particular living person. He is not divided in himself, but it is the entire person who is addressed. He is not present in timeless fullness of value and spirituality, but he is responsible within time, not in time's uninterrupted flow, but in the value-related — not value-filled — moment. In the concept of the moment the concept of time and its relations of value are included. The moment is not the briefest part of time, as it were a mechanically conceived atom, but the time of responsibility, of relations of value — let us say, of relations with God — and essentially it is concrete time, where alone the real moral claim is realized. And only in responsibility am I fully aware of being bound to time. It is not by my having a reasoning mind that I make universally valid decisions, but I enter into the reality of time by relating my concrete person in time in all its particularities to this obligation, by making myself morally responsible.[58]

In his first book, *The Communion of Saints*, Bonhoeffer realizes that he is making "a fundamental separation from idealism"[59] and he does this self-consciously and consistently throughout his life and throughout his writings.

Act and Being begins with descriptions of what Bonhoeffer considers to be mutually exclusive philosophical positions, the transcendentalism of Kant and the ontology of Heidegger. A footnote at the bottom of the first page is extremely important.

> All that follows below by way of representing Kantian or idealist philosophy is stylised (and therefore dispenses with quotations). Kant is represented as a pure transcendental philosopher, which he never was entirely, though we believe he intended to be one. It is the system we debate, not matters of historical fact.[60]

The point is not that Bonhoeffer is uninterested in historical accuracy and detail. He is simply eager to let his readers know exactly what he is doing.

It demonstrates that Bonhoeffer is carving out a position that is contrary to a widely held point of view which he calls "Kantian." What is important is the confessing and following of Jesus Christ, and in order to make that clear, "Kantianism" must be combated. Direct references and indirect allusions to Kant can be found from these first dissertations and on throughout the entire corpus of Bonhoeffer's writings. But it is in his *Ethics*, as one would expect, that he repeatedly clarifies his own position by contrasting it with that of Kant. He seems to do it effortlessly and sometimes casually. He says, for instance, that "the fact that he was ashamed when he was discovered praying was for Kant an argument against prayer."[61] The point could have easily been made without reference to Kant. The fact that he uses him as a foil shows that Kant was frequently there in the background of his thinking. When he discusses ethics as formation, Bonhoeffer even contrasts Christ with Kant![62] He says that the form of Christ is one and the same in all times and in all places. And yet Christ is not a principle. He is not the proclaimer of a system of what would be good today and at all times. He teaches no abstract ethics. He did not, like a moralist, love a theory of the good. He was not, like a philosopher, interested in the "universally valid," but rather in that which was of help to the real and concrete human being. What worried him was not, like Kant, whether the maxim of an action can be a principle of general legislation, but whether my action is at this moment helping my neighbor to become a person before God. It seems audacious to contrast Christ with Kant, but this is precisely what Bonhoeffer does.

When Bonhoeffer lays out his thinking about the penultimate and the ultimate, he contrasts Kant and the Bible which is certainly equally audacious! "To idealistic thinkers it may seem out of place for a Christian ethic to speak first of rights and only later of duties. But our authority is not Kant; it is the Holy Scripture."[63]

> From the principle of truthfulness Kant draws the grotesque conclusion that I must even return an honest "yes" to the enquiry of the murderer who breaks into my house and asks whether my friend whom he is pursuing has taken refuge there; in such a case self-righteousness of conscience has become outrageous presumption and blocks the path of responsible action. Responsibility is the total and realistic response of man to the claim of God and of our neighbour; but this example shows in its true light how the response of a conscience which is bound by principles is only a partial one. If I refuse to incur guilt against the principle of truthfulness for the sake of my friend, if I refuse to tell a robust lie for the sake of my friend (for it is only the self-righteously law-abiding conscience which will pretend that, in fact, no lie is involved), if, in other words, I refuse to bear guilt for charity's sake, then my action is

in contradiction to my responsibility which has its foundation in reality. Here again it is precisely in the responsible acceptance of guilt that a conscience which is bound solely to Christ will best prove its innocence.[64]

A contrast between this passage and the Tegel essay is that here Bonhoeffer talks about incurring guilt through the telling of a "robust lie," and even chastises the one who pretends that it is not a lie. The Tegel essay on the meaning of truth telling says, to the contrary, that the truth must always be told, but one must pay attention to the meaning of truth. The statements do differ from one another in this respect. At the moment, however, the point is Bonhoeffer's disagreement with Kant.

When Bonhoeffer discusses responsibility as containing both obedience and freedom, he again takes sharp issue with Kant. "To make obedience independent of freedom leads only to the Kantian ethic of duty, and to make freedom independent of obedience leads only to the ethic of irresponsible genius."[65] This is, in very clear and simple terms, a rejection of both deontology and situationism.

It is clear that Kant represents for Bonhoeffer an understanding of religion and morality that he sees as directly opposed to the reality he confesses in Jesus Christ. His attack is frontal. The contrast he sees to his own position is diametric. In order to understand better Bonhoeffer's position, it is helpful to understand something of what Kant represents to him.

The position can be called idealistic ethics. It can also be called the chief paradigm of deontological ethics, that is, the ethics of obligation and duty.[66] Stanley Hauerwas calls it the "standard account," to which he is at work finding an alternative.[67] Hauerwas says, in somewhat the same way that Bonhoeffer does, that what is important is the position that has come to be known as Kantian. He is opposing a position in order to clarify his own. He is not primarily concerned with the intricacies of historical and critical Kant studies.

> We have not based our criticism of the standard account on the debates between those who share its presuppositions. It is, of course, true that as yet no single theory of the standard account has proved to be persuasive to those who share in its presuppositions. We still find Kant the single most satisfying statement of the program implied by the standard account.[68]

When Hauerwas discusses the basic content of Kant's position under the heading "the standard account," he sees its basic flaw as detachment from actual persons in historical contexts. For Bonhoeffer and for Hauerwas (and for many others) the point is not to enter into intramural debates among Kant scholars. The point is to oppose a position in ethics which is widely held and also widely assumed to be the only or the only "right" position to take in ethics. Whether it is finally necessary to argue nuances in understandings of Kant, there is little question but that Bonhoeffer and Hauerwas have grasped an essential note in Kant's position.

In *The Fundamental Principles of the Metaphysics of Ethics*[69] Kant begins by separating morality proper from practical anthropology. Practical anthropology has an empirical base; it says what actually happens. Morality proper is purely rational. It has to do with what ought to happen. The first sentence in the book states that it is impossible to conceive of anything anywhere in the world or even anywhere out of the world that can without qualification be called good, except a good will. The goodness of the good will has been arrived at through reason, and Kant distinguishes his position sharply from that of Aristotle by saying that the good is not happiness or moderation or usefulness or inclination. Furthermore, it has to do not with an indicative, but with an imperative. And that imperative is not "hypothetical," leading to some good result with some degree of probability, as Aristotle and the utilitarians would say. It is "categorical," without any exception, universal. Therefore Kant's ethic of duty is also talked about as an ethic of the categorical imperative. The categorical imperative is an ethical absolute; it applies to all people in all places and in all times. Further, the imperative implies a possibility. Kant says, "I ought, therefore I can." Thus the categorical imperative is not simply an ideal to strive after; it is an ideal that can actually be done because it ought to be done. Kant illustrates each point he makes with four classic cases, one of which is truth telling. His examples are extremely practical, as down to earth as is Bonhoeffer's child in the classroom.

> Another person is in need and finds it necessary to borrow money. He knows very well that he will not be able to repay it, but he also realizes that he will not receive a loan unless he promises solemnly to pay at a definite time. He has a desire to make this promise, but he still has enough conscience to ask himself whether it is not improper and contrary to duty to relieve distress in this manner. If he should nevertheless decide to do so, then the maxim of his action would read thus: When I think that I am in need of money I will borrow and promise to repay, even though I know that I will never do so. Now this principle of my love of self or advantage may perhaps well agree with my whole future well-being; the next question, however, is, whether it is right. Thereby I change the interpretation of self-love into a universal law and arrange my question thus: How would things be if my maxim were a universal law? Then I see at once that it could never count as a universal law of nature and still agree with itself, but must necessarily contradict itself. For the universality of a law, according to which anyone who believed himself in distress could promise anything he pleased with no intention of keeping it, would make promises themselves and any purpose they may have impossible;

since nobody would believe that a promise had been made, but everybody would ridicule such statements as vain pretenses.[70]

There can be no question about the compelling force of Kant's argument. Any rational person can follow his logic. Promise keeping is not identical to truth telling, but it is close enough so that it serves well to describe Kant's principle of universalizability.

Kant's position on truth telling is laid out in classic form in his essay "On a Supposed Right to Lie from Altruistic Motives."[71] Kant begins his argument against a certain French philosopher, Benjamin Constant, who limits the duty to tell the truth by saying that it is a duty only toward one who has a right to the truth, not, for instance, to a murderer who asks if one's friend is at home. Kant argues that the problem with this position of Mr. Constant is that the real question is not about committing a wrong against a particular person but a wrong against duty itself. A wrong done to duty itself is a move toward violating all rights based on contracts and thus is a wrong done to humankind generally. Kant then argues from a matter of law and claims that a person could be punished under civil law if he, thinking his friend was in the house, told a murderer at the door that his friend was not in the house, and his friend, having left the house, was found along the way by the murderer and was killed. Lehmann argues, on the basis of conversation with Harold Berman of Harvard Law School, that Kant was incorrect in this legal judgment, although Kant's position does not hang on that illustration.[72] Kant says, "To be truthful (honest) in all declarations, therefore, is a sacred and absolutely commanding decree of reason, limited by no expediency."[73] That position is held consistently by him regardless of any examples that might be brought forward.

The position depends on and grows out of Kant's metaphysics. The principle of universalizability finally requires a changeless God to attach to moral decision. The entire system is based on a "metaphysical dualism, a noumenal world and a phenomenal world."[74] It is entirely consistent with this, then, that when Kant talks about the kingdom of ends, which ought to have some connection with sociality as a moral nexus, the system remains individualistic because for Kant the democratic principle is always a "pure democracy" where the good of the individual is simply within the individual. "This permits each to go his own way unhampered, and each member of Kant's kingdom of ends is a rugged individualist, except that his ruggedness is rational and not the more familiar animal type prevalent in ordinary *laissez-faire* democracy."[75]

Kant's ethics is consistent with his metaphysics. Bonhoeffer's ethical theology is a single piece of cloth. The two positions are diametrically opposed. Kant seeks to rise above time and history through the principle of universalizability. Bonhoeffer seeks to embrace time and history by insisting on responsible action in concrete times and concrete places. In place of Kant's metaphysical dualism, Bonhoeffer positions the name of Jesus Christ, who brings God and world together. In place of timeless truths, Bonhoeffer posits living truth. In place of the assumption that truth and falsehood are relatively simple to define, Bonhoeffer says that they are extremely difficult to get at. In place of rugged individualism, Bonhoeffer works with a complex nexus of relational responsibilities. In place of a purely rational ethic, Bonhoeffer talks about something that involves the total person.

While being interrogated in Tegel prison, Bonhoeffer knows that everything that he says should be the truth. He also knows very clearly how Kant would understand that, and he knows that he disagrees. So he tries to understand what he does, what he says and does not say, in that time and place, and begins an essay on truth telling that puts together his clearest reflection on the subject at that time. There are surely dangers in what he says. There are also new possibilities.

Truth Telling as Verbal Expression of the Real

About midway through the truth telling essay Bonhoeffer notes that "the concept of living truth is dangerous."[76] He is quite aware of the fact that the line he is taking

> gives rise to the suspicion that the truth can and may be adapted to each particular situation in a way which completely destroys the idea of truth and narrows the gap between truth and falsehood, so that the two become indistinguishable.[77]

That is of course the problem. Any reflective person is immediately aware of it. Yet Bonhoeffer says the dangers which are certainly there must never impel one to abandon the concept of living truth in favor of the "formal and cynical concept of the truth," which is Bonhoeffer's code phrase for the traditional view exemplified by Kant.

There are those who are not impressed by Bonhoeffer's attempt to guard against these very obvious dangers. One such is James Laney. He discusses Bonhoeffer's "ethical contextualism" under three rubrics: the context of interpretation, the context of decision, and the context of the action.[78] He talks about the "great and continuing influence of Bonhoeffer's ethics on recent developments in Christian ethics" and finishes his discussion by saying that Bonhoeffer's ethics are so close to the major questions of Christian ethics today that this is "a remarkable tribute to the suggestiveness of his thought and a continuing testimony to the vitality of his legacy."[79] Laney understands the basic drive of Bonhoeffer's ethics very well:

> The starting point of ethical understanding for Bonhoeffer lies not in an ideal to be realized, a norm to be approximated, or even essentially in a command to be obeyed, but in a reality to be expressed. This reality consists of the "recovered unity" and reconciliation established in Christ and in which the Christian is called to participate. Because the actions of a Christian do not reflect the "irreconcilable cleavage between vitality and self-denial, between 'secular' and 'Christian' or between 'autonomous ethics' and the 'ethics of Jesus,'" but rather spring from joy in the accomplishment of the reconciliation of the world with God, they already move in a sphere which lies beyond the fatal antinomies in which traditional ethics is embroiled.[80]

Laney does, however, distinguish between the sphere of the pre-ethical and the ethical properly speaking, and says that "by its very nature, this approach does not provide criteria for evaluating or testing Christian action. The ethical question is ruled out a priori as an expression of — if not outright identification with — mankind's 'defection from Christ.' "[81]

When discussing "the context of decision" Laney points to Bonhoeffer's talk about "proving" the will of God. He refers to Bonhoeffer's talk about "intelligence, discernment, attentive observation of the facts" coming into live operation. He points to Bonhoeffer's comment about the fact that there should be "extremely serious consideration" of any action that would violate the will of God. Yet he concludes:

> Thus, aside from counseling self-examination to insure against the intrusion of subjectivity, Bonhoeffer offers no criteria by which even the exceptional case may be tested either for its consequences or for the validity of the command which is presumed to be the basis of that decision.[82]

Laney does, then, discuss the truth telling essay. He comments on the fact that "instead of using the negative criterion that defines lie as a conscious discrepancy between thought and speech, Bonhoeffer introduces the idea of truth as a correspondence with reality."[83] Although Laney considers Bonhoeffer's essay to be both "cogent and compelling" and full of "sensitivity and responsibility," his major objection is that the degree of ethical sensitivity and self-awareness that Bonhoeffer requires for truth telling indicates a subjective reliance that makes the possibilities of self-deception very great. Laney asks whether there is not some principled approach, some objective criteria to which both the speaker and the addressee are related. His argument, then, goes directly back to Kant.

> However wooden seems Kant's logical conclusion that the truth must be told under all circumstances, nonetheless that position points to the existence of the total human community, which also lays a claim on all people at all times to tell the truth. Finally, Bonhoeffer's refusal to term even a deception a "lie" if it is justified by the situation reveals a basic problem in his entire ethical position, namely, the refusal to admit the tragic antinomies of existence without attempting premature resolution. In any case of war, the fact that lying is necessary points to one of war's morally debilitating aspects; to deny that results in more confusion than clarity because it blunts the meaning of truth itself. There is, in other words, an objective dimension of ethical reality that stands in tension with the concrete situation and cannot be abstracted from it or collapsed into it. In this case, it results in a prima facie claim for truth regardless of the relationships involved, with the burden of any exception falling to the agent.[84]

Finally, Laney says:

> In discussing specific cases Bonhoeffer implies that this ethical perception is very much akin to artistic sensitivity. One is left wondering about those who fail to develop such sensitivity or lack the capacity to begin with. Does this tend to become an insider's ethic after all?[85]

The dangers of Bonhoeffer's thoughts on truth telling are obvious to him as he writes, as they are to any reflective person. They are acute to many professional ethicists, including some who are essentially sympathetic to Bonhoeffer, such as Laney. The worry is that the distinction between truth and falsehood could become blurred. If that were to happen, it would constitute not only an immediate moral tragedy for the individual, but finally also a breakdown of society which depends on basic reliability of speech in truth telling and promise keeping. Are there no relatively objective criteria by which truth and falsehood can be sorted out, no reasonably public methods of deliberation and adjudication by which an individual can justify to others, or even to himself or herself, the words that have been spoken? There are ways to qualify Kant's absolutism by allowing for exceptions but placing the burden of responsibility for those exceptions on the one who takes them. Laney's use of a "*prima facie* claim for truth"[86] is such a qualified Kantian position.

Further, the question is raised whether the kind of reflection demanded here does not require such sensitivity to people and to issues, such breadth of information and depth of insight, that only a few mature moral virtuosi could be equipped to handle it. Is it not, at best, only for an elite? Does it raise fears of setting a few Nietszchean "supermen" above the law of the masses, subject only to their own will and power?

And does not the intensely christological base on which the whole thing is built make it virtually inaccessible to those who do not confess that name? Yet truth telling is a public necessity, a societal obligation to which Christian and non-Christian must bring some common commitment.

In spite of these dangers of which he is aware, Bonhoeffer does not abandon his attempt to deal with the "living truth" which gives verbal expression to that which is real. Even though the Tegel essay is unfinished, there is no indication that a finished essay would bring any surprises. Laney is representative of those ethicists who, although appreciative of Bonhoeffer's concerns, come down finally on the side of Kant. Lehmann is representative of those who, although appreciative of Kant's concerns, come down finally on the side of Bonhoeffer.

Lehmann was one of Bonhoeffer's good friends, in close touch with him from the time they were fellow students at Union Seminary in New York in 1930. He has written relatively little Bonhoeffer interpretation, although the congeniality of their positions is obvious to anyone who reads them both. In the preface to *Ethics in a Christian Context*, Lehmann sketches out his indebtedness to the Protestant Reformation.

> The Protestant Reformation introduced into the Western cultural tradition a liberating grasp of the ways of God with men and thus also the possibility of ever fresh and experimental responses to the dynamics and the humanizing character of the divine activity in the world. This meant for ethics the displacement of the prescriptive and absolute formulation of its claims by the contextual understanding of what God is doing in the world to make and to keep human life human. It also meant for ethics an open door for the discovery of its genuinely descriptive character. Ethics could now be a *descriptive* discipline, not in contrast to a normative discipline (a distinction which presupposes another context), but in the sense of providing an account of the transformation of the concrete stuff of behavior, i.e., the circumstances, the motivations, and the structures of action, owing to the concrete, personal, and purposeful activity of God.[87]

He has the same emphasis on community that Bonhoeffer has and adopts *koinonia*, the Greek word for communal fellowship, as one of his key terms. A *koinonia* ethic, says Lehmann, acquires a concrete and contextual character. It is concerned with relations and functions, not with principles and precepts. He moves specifically, as does Bonhoeffer, against Kant.

It will help us to see what is involved in this contrast if we take up a distinction which is not always made, a failure which makes for confusion in Christian ethical analysis. The distinction is between *contextual ethics* and what might be called *absolutist ethics*.[88]

When Lehmann discusses truth telling, he not only distinguishes sharply between contextualist and absolutist ethics, but also recognizes that truth telling is a test case for ethical systems. He defines an ethical absolute as a standard of conduct that can be and must be applied to all people in all situations in exactly the same way, and says that absolutist ethics pays a very high price for its claims. "The price is abstraction from the complexity of the actual situation out of which the ethical problem arises."[89] In addition, Lehmann levels the charge that the absolutist position is "based upon a conception or standard of truth which is foreign to the focus and foundations of a Christian ethic."[90]

Lehmann then moves into a discussion of Kant's treatise "On a Supposed Right to Tell a Lie from Altruistic Motives" as a *locus classicus* for the absolutist position on truth telling, and into a discussion of Bonhoeffer's essay "What Is Meant by 'Telling the Truth'?" as an example of a contextualist ethic. His opinion is that "a contextualist ethic begins at the opposite point from the one at which Immanuel Kant begins."[91]

Lehmann's stress on *koinonia* is very similar to Bonhoeffer's stress on the sociality of Christ. In both cases, the context of concrete place and concrete time is the actual, empirical church rather than an ideal society. Lehmann makes the point eloquently.

Nevertheless, the empirical church points, despite its ambiguity, to the fact that there is in the world a *laboratory of the living word*, or, to change the metaphor, a *bridgehead of maturity*, namely, the Christian *koinonia*. In the *koinonia* a continuing experiment is going on in the concrete reality and possibility of man's interrelatedness and openness for man. In the *koinonia* ethical theory and practice acquire a framework of meaning and a pattern of action which undergird the diversity and the complexity of the concrete ethical situation with vitality and purpose.[92]

As does Bonhoeffer, Lehmann says that ethics in a Christian context has always primarily to do with an indicative rather than an imperative. "The 'ought' factor cannot be ignored in ethical theory. But the 'ought' factor is not the primary ethical reality."[93] Lehmann realizes, as does Bonhoeffer, that what he is saying has obvious dangers and that the charge of ethical anarchy or ethical expediency is going to come quickly to the mind of the reader. He also knows that there is the possibility of self-deception due to the lack of objective criteria. He responds to potential critics, reminding them of the fact that the position is structured by Christian commitments to God's action in the world.

> This is why a contextual ethic does not lead to ethical anarchy or ethical expediency. If what God is doing in the world is to relate men to each other in and through an enterprise of the new humanity, if God is setting the conditions for and bestowing the enabling power of maturity — if this is what God is doing, then it is meaningless to say that if one doesn't tell the truth unconditionally the fabric of society will be shredded by mistrust; it is meaningless to say that if one can claim that whatever occurs to him at the moment to say is the truth, the whole field of truth and falsehood is reduced to anarchy and confusion. Such concerns may have standing in some other kind of ethical climate, but for a Christian ethic they are false concerns.[94]

Lehmann's final example in this discussion of absolutist and contextualist ethics, of Kant and Bonhoeffer, with truth telling as the test case, is an example from his own experience.

> Almost the first more than casual impact of death upon me occurred in the passing of a lady in early middle life who had come to be virtually a second mother to me. She was stricken, as it seemed, quite suddenly, with a particularly virulent form of carcinoma and died under this ghastly, body-wasting disease. When I saw her for the last time, as she lay upon her hospital bed, she said to me, "What do the doctors say? Is there anything that can be done?" At this moment there came to mind the profound and humiliating observation of Dostoevsky which, it has always seemed to me, ought to serve as the rubric under which the healthy relate themselves to the ill, and in particular as the rubric under which pastoral calls upon the sick are made. "In every misfortune of one's neighbor," says Dostoevsky, "there is always something cheering for an onlooker — whoever he may be." I knew that this lady would never leave her bed of pain alive. I knew, too, that I was leaving the hospital to take a train for my own work and that I was not in the slightest inclined to exchange places. What should I have replied to her question? How white is a lie? And how black can the truth, the whole truth, and nothing but the truth be? What in such a situation *is* the truth?
>
> Is it telling the truth to say in as sympathetic and tactful a way as possible, "There is no hope!"? Or should one say, "Don't worry! Everything will come out all right!"?
>
> The point at issue here is not the celebrated ethical question of the right of the patient to the truth. The point at issue is, granted that the patient has a right to the truth, what is the truth to which the patient has a right, and how would a *Christian* ethic deal with this right? My own attempt ran something like this: "The doctors are doing all that they can. But you and I have always been Christians. Part of what that has meant has been that we have said in our prayers and confessed in our faith that Jesus Christ is Savior and Lord. I do not claim to understand all that this involves. But if it means anything at all, it seems to me to mean at least this — when in the next days and

weeks the going gets hard, remember you are not alone! Jesus Christ has been there before!"[95]

Bonhoeffer assumes that we are to tell the truth, but asks what is meant by telling the truth. Lehmann grants that this patient has a right to the truth, but asks what the truth is to which the patient has a right. The risks that go with asking such questions are very high. What Bonhoeffer and Lehmann claim is that the risks that go with not asking such questions are far higher. The absolutist position assumes that the meaning of truth telling is clear, and that what is required is the moral courage to do it or, if a lie is required, the courage to take responsibility for justifying in the public arena the telling of that lie. Within certain circumstances, under certain conditions, the absolutist program works fairly well. It did not work well for life under Hitler, in Bonhoeffer's opinion, and specifically not for his time of interrogation at Tegel prison. A system that works well only when life is proceeding smoothly is not very promising, because life seldom does so proceed, especially for those who engage concrete times and concrete places for the sake of the future of God's world.

It is therefore curious that one of Laney's criticisms is that Bonhoeffer refuses "to admit the tragic antinomies of existence without attempting premature resolution."[96] Except for use of the "antinomy" language, which is itself Kantian, Bonhoeffer's criticism of Kantian notions about truth telling are exactly the same, that they refuse to admit not only how complex real-life situations are, but how penetrated they are both by sin and by grace. It simply will not do to bracket off most of life as a neutral zone where truth can be simply known and simply told, leaving the anguish of decision to border areas where one is caught in some tragic situation such as war which then allows for exceptions to the rules. The result of this procedure is an unrealistic carving up of life and a relegating of both sin and grace to the private, rather than the public, arena. In this case, one seeks to live with a "good conscience," telling acceptable lies only when there are secondary rules under which such lies can be justified. Bonhoeffer calls it a "cynical" idea of truth because his reading of reality is marked by wholeness, God and world together at the same time in Jesus Christ. The whole is in motion, moving from the penultimate to the ultimate, from the unnatural to the natural, from that which is false to that which is true. It is not just a "Christian perspective." It is the way things really are. Dostoevsky said, "If someone proved to me that Christ is outside the truth, and that *in reality* the truth were outside of Christ, then I should prefer to remain with Christ rather than with the truth."[97] One can find no statement even somewhat similar to this in Bonhoeffer, because for him truth, reality, and Jesus Christ are indivisibly together. When the Christian describes truth telling as verbal expression of reality, that truth and that reality are "here and now" for the unbeliever as well as the believer, even though the unbeliever does not know that the name of it is Jesus Christ. Jesus Christ does not separate the Christian from the non-Christian, but rather ties together in the real world those who believe and those who do not in the freedom and the obligation to do the truth by putting into words that which is really the case. It may mean living with an uneasy conscience. It certainly does mean "the acceptance of guilt." But it also means grace, forgiveness, freedom, permission.

Whatever else might be said about Bonhoeffer's theory and practice of truth telling, it is clear that his work in this area is remarkably consistent throughout his career and in almost every detail a piece of the whole of his attempt to formulate an ethical theology. Truth telling is indeed a test case. It would be strange to take a position on this aspect of his life and thought that would be different from that position one takes on the whole of his life and thought. The position taken in this study is clearly positive. Bonhoeffer's ethical theology was never finished. The truth telling essay itself was never finished. What he has done is to leave for us work worth doing, together with sufficient substance to get us well on our way. It is a great legacy. From one who did his writing on the run, and was executed at age thirty-nine, we ought not to ask more.

NOTES

1. *E*, 270–71.
2. Cf. Karen Horney, *The Neurotic Personality of Our Time* (New York: W. W. Norton, 1937).
3. *E*, 264–65. Perhaps the quintessential portrayal in literature of the moralist is Javert in Victor Hugo's *Les Miserables*. His long search for Jean Valjean in order to bring him to "justice" demonstrates not only the madness of the moralist but also the danger of such people to others over whom they exercise authority.
4. *E*, 85ff.
5. *CC*, 45.
6. Cf. Bethge's analysis in *DB*, 778–79.
7. *LPP*, letter of 20 May 1944, 303.
8. *E*, 88ff.
9. *LPP*, letter of 30 April 1944, 280.
10. One illustration is Bonhoeffer's decision to go to London in 1933. He wrote Barth only after the decision had been made. Barth disagreed with him, but Bonhoeffer still decided to stay in London. Cf. *DB*, 254–55.

11. *LPP,* letter of 8 June 1944, 326–27. *LPP,* letter of 8 July 1944, 344–45.

12. Theodore Gill, "Bonhoeffer as Aesthete" (paper read to the Bonhoeffer Society at the 1975 Annual Meeting of the American Academy of Religion).

13. Benjamin Reist, *The Promise of Bonhoeffer* (Philadelphia: J. B. Lippincott, 1969).

14. Ibid., 90.

15. *DB,* 717, 733.

16. From a conversation with Renate Bethge in Villiprott, Germany, 14 January 1982.

17. James Gustafson and James Laney, eds., *On Being Responsible* (New York: Harper & Row, 1968).

18. Sissela Bok, *Lying: Moral Choice in Public and Private Life* (New York: Pantheon Books, 1978).

19. *E,* 365.

20. Ibid., 370.

21. *DB,* 717–18.

22. Ibid., 716.

23. Ibid., 714.

24. Ibid., 717.

25. This essay was not intended by Bonhoeffer to be part of his ethics book, but is included in *Ethics* because of its obviously appropriate content. It is the last item in the book, listed as Section V in Part 2, 363–71.

26. The parallel is striking. In his exposition of the Psalms, he writes: "Lord, Teach Us to Pray!" So spoke the disciples to Jesus. In making this request, they confessed that they were not able to pray on their own, that they had to learn to pray. The phrase "learning to pray" sounds strange to us. If the heart does not overflow and begin to pray by itself, we say, it will never "learn" to pray. But it is a dangerous error, surely very widespread among Christians, to think that the heart can pray by itself. For then we confuse wishes, hopes, sighs, laments, rejoicings — all of which the heart can do by itself — with prayer. And we confuse earth and heaven, man and God. Prayer does not mean simply to pour out one's heart. It means rather to find the way to God and to speak with him, whether the heart is full or empty. No man can do that by himself. For that he needs Jesus Christ. (*Psalms: The Prayerbook of the Bible,* 9–10)
Learning how to tell the truth is not a notion incompatible with the New Testament. When John speaks of "doing the truth" (John 3:21), and when the writer to the church at Ephesus tells them to "speak the truth in love" (Eph. 4:15), the implication is that truth telling is not something that happens automatically. Quite apart from Christian commitments, a similar point is made about love by Rollo May in *Love and Will* (New York: W. W. Norton, 1969) and by Erich Fromm in *The Art of Loving* (New York: Harper & Brothers, 1956).
The rejection by Bonhoeffer of the common idea that good (justified) people spontaneously do good (true and loving) works is obvious. His relation to his Lutheran background and commitments is never a simple one.

27. *DB,* 102.

28. *AB,* 5–6.

29. *E*, 64ff.
30. Ibid., 68–69.
31. Ibid., 97ff.
32. Ibid., 97.
33. Ibid., 126.
34. Ibid., 228.
35. Ibid., 234.
36. *AB*, 79.
37. *CC*, 76.
38. Ibid., 49.
39. Ibid., 50.
40. *CF/T*, 49.
41. *CD*, 86.
42. Ibid., 152–55.
43. *GS* IV, 79–87.
44. *GS* III, 243.
45. *GS* II, 214.
46. *E*, 37ff.
47. *GS* II, 323ff.
48. *GS* IV, 177.
49. Ibid., 250ff.
50. Sissela Bok, "Truth-telling: Ethical Aspects," in *The Encyclopedia of Bioethics* (New York: Free Press, 1978), 4:1685.
51. *E*, 371–72.
52. Paul Lehmann, *Ethics in a Christian Context* (London: SCM Press, 1963).
53. *CS*, 23.
54. Ibid., 25.
55. Ibid., 28.
56. Ibid., 28–29.
57. Ibid., 29–30.
58. Ibid., 30.
59. Ibid., 40.
60. *AB*, 19.
61. *E*, 21.
62. Ibid., 84–85.
63. Ibid., 151.
64. Ibid., 245.
65. Ibid., 253.
66. The word comes from the Greek impersonal verb, meaning "it is necessary." Discussion of deontology can be found in any of the standard ethics texts, e.g., William Frankena, *Ethics* (Englewood Cliffs, N.J.: Prentice-Hall, 1973).
67. Stanley Hauerwas, *Truthfulness and Tragedy* (Notre Dame, Ind.: Univ. of Notre Dame Press, 1977).
68. Ibid., 208.
69. Immanuel Kant, *The Fundamental Principles of the Metaphysics of Ethics*, trans. Otto Manthey-Zorn (New York: Appleton-Century, 1938).
70. Ibid., 39–40.

71. Printed in Bok, *Lying*, 267ff.

72. Lehmann, *Ethics*, 127.

73. Bok, *Lying*, 269.

74. D. W. Gotshalk, "The Central Doctrine of the Kantian Ethics," in *The Heritage of Kant*, ed. G. T. Whitney and D. F. Bowers (New York: Russell & Russell, 1962), 191.

75. Ibid., 190.

76. *E*, 366.

77. Ibid.

78. James T. Laney, "An Examination of Bonhoeffer's Ethical Contextualism," in *Bonhoeffer Legacy*, ed. A. J. Klassen (Grand Rapids: Wm. B. Eerdmans, 1981), 294–313.

79. Ibid., 312.

80. Ibid., 294–95.

81. Ibid., 299.

82. Ibid., 303.

83. Ibid.

84. Ibid., 304–5.

85. Ibid., 311.

86. The phrase is used by W. D. Ross in an impressive elaboration of a qualified deontological position. Cf. W. D. Ross, *The Right and the Good* (Oxford: Oxford Univ. Press, 1930).

87. Lehmann, *Ethics*, 14.

88. Ibid., 124.

89. Ibid., 125. No ethicist, of course, wants to be read as avoiding the complexities of life, and it is common to accuse one's opponents of doing exactly that.

90. Ibid.

91. Ibid., 129.

92. Ibid., 131.

93. Ibid.

94. Ibid., 131–32.

95. Ibid., 132–33.

96. Laney, "Examination of Bonhoeffer's Legacy," 304.

97. Quoted in *Context*, 1 June 1984, ed. Martin E. Marty, 6.

Afterword

This has not been a conversation with Bonhoeffer as much as it has been the presentation of the result of a conversation, specifically a conversation about ethics. Little has been said about his position on ethical issues. The emphasis has been upon method. There has been no attempt to go "beyond Bonhoeffer," to suggest trajectories along which his thought might lead us in questions of peace and justice, or of the liberation of the oppressed, or of attitudes and actions regarding nuclear energy, or abortion, or care for the terminally ill. This book has been, rather, an attempt to present as clearly as possible the task to which Bonhoeffer set himself in the field of ethics, and the lines along which he proceeded to address that task. It has been a modest attempt, and yet a presumptuous one, because in order so to present Bonhoeffer it has been necessary to claim to take into account the entirety of his life and work, as well as to take seriously the ways in which other interpreters have dealt with him. His work was unfinished. But his agenda was clear. He wanted to work at the structuring of responsible life in the context of the demise of metaphysical and moral absolutes, a demise which he welcomed as the result of the proclamation of the word about Jesus Christ.

And that is the last word as it is the first word with Bonhoeffer — the name of Jesus. For Bonhoeffer Jesus is *the* question. All other questions follow from that one question. The question is not "how" but "who." "Who is Jesus Christ for us today?" "What following Jesus means, that is what I want to know." Not even Christology, but Jesus, the babe in the manger and the man on the cross, is the question.

It is a totally different conceptuality from that indicated by the phrase "Christ is the answer." Bonhoeffer consistently regards ebionitism as a less dangerous heresy than docetism. He has a Colossians-style full-blown Chalcedonian Christology, but it is always and at every point tied to the *hapax*, the once-for-all event of God-with-us in Jesus of Nazareth. Providing "answers" to "problems" is the function of "religion," of the "god-of-the-gaps," of the "*deus ex machina.*" Jesus makes it clear that God does not meet us on the borders of life, but in the midst of life; not at the edges, but at the center. The only kind of Christianity which can be true to Jesus is "nonreligious Christianity," God and world together in Jesus, which demands in our actions and in our speech the total rejection of two-sphere thinking.

So Christians are people who keep asking the Jesus question. And as they do so they find themselves released from duplicity and embraced by totality, a totality that is always in motion, pressing toward the future. Ethics has to do with being concerned with "how the coming generation will live," and that means with taking responsibility for the shaping of the future. This passion and this joy marked his life and his work in every area, including the area of ethical action and reflection.

On 28 December 1944, he sent birthday greetings to his mother from the Gestapo prison at Prinz-Albrecht-Strasse in Berlin, to which he had been transferred following the failure of the 20 July plot on Hitler's life. He took the occasion to send New Year's greetings to his family.

> My wish for you and father and Maria and for us all is that the New Year may bring us at least an occasional glimmer of light, and that we may once more have the joy of being together. May God keep you both well![1]

With the letter he sent a poem.

Powers of Good

With every power for good to stay and guide me,
comforted and inspired beyond all fear,
I'll live these days with you in thought beside me,
and pass, with you, into the coming year.

The old year still torments our hearts, unhastening;
the long days of our sorrow still endure;
Father, grant to the souls thou hast been chastening
that thou hast promised, the healing and the cure.

Should it be ours to drain the cup of grieving
even to the dregs of pain, at thy command,
we will not falter, thankfully receiving
all that is given by thy loving hand.

But should it be thy will once more to release us
to life's enjoyment and its good sunshine,
that which we've learned from sorrow shall increase us,
and all our life be dedicate as thine.

Today, let candles shed their radiant greeting;
lo, on our darkness are they not thy light
leading us, haply, to our longed-for meeting?—
Thou canst illumine even our darkest night.

When now the silence deepens for our hearkening,
grant we may hear thy children's voices raise
from all the unseen world around us darkening
their universal paean, in thy praise.

While all the powers of good aid and attend us,
boldly we'll face the future, come what may.
At even and at morn God will befriend us,
and oh, most surely on each newborn day!

It was almost the last message received from him prior to his death.

NOTES

1. *LPP*, Letter of 28 December 1944, 399–401.

Reading Bonhoeffer: A Map to the Literature

This map is designed to guide those interested in Bonhoeffer through the literature. The place to begin is *Costly Grace: An Illustrated Introduction to Dietrich Bonhoeffer* by Eberhard Bethge (New York: Harper & Row, 1979). This short paperback contains, in addition to the tightly-packed text, numerous illustrations and a chronological table aligning events of Bonhoeffer's life with important political and ecclesiastical events. It is all here, clear and crisp, by the one who knew and knows Bonhoeffer best. With this material in hand, the reader will be prepared to sample some of the primary literature. Historical contexts should be kept clearly in mind as one proceeds through the following: the first ("Community") and the last ("Confession") chapters of *Life Together*; the introductory essays prior to the exposition of Matthew 5 – 7 in *The Cost of Discipleship*; the section in the *Ethics* labeled "Christ, Reality and Good"; the material in the *Letters and Papers from Prison* beginning with the letter of 30 April 1944. How then, assuming this, should one proceed?

Bibliography

Bibliography is the first place to go because there is no better way to get the lay of the land, some notion of well-traveled roads, detours, blind alleys, express routes, than to unfold the whole map for at least a quick overview. There is fortunately a single best way to do that. It is to acquire a duplicated copy from a theological library of the thirty-three-page bibliography by Clifford J. Green in the *Union Seminary Quarterly Review* (hereafter *USQR*) 31 (1976): 227–60. Green's opening paragraphs should be read carefully. The piece was a kind of interim report on the English-language materials for the International Bonhoeffer Bibliography, a project that has been underway since 1969 and is currently a high priority item for the International Bonhoeffer Society. Regular supplements to the

Green bibliography have been and continue to be published in the *Newsletter* of the English Language Section of the society. Information about the *Newsletter* can be obtained from Dr. Geffrey Kelly, La Salle College, Philadelphia, PA 19141. Readers can thus be relatively certain that they have all the English-language materials if they have checked the Green article and back copies (to 1976) of the *Newsletter*.

Biography

It is usually helpful in understanding a person's work to know something about that person's life. In the case of Bonhoeffer that connection is absolutely essential and for at least four reasons. First, there is the shortness of Bonhoeffer's life (thirty-nine years) and the fragmentary character of much of his writing. Second, there is the coincidence of Bonhoeffer's career with the Nazi dictatorship. He began teaching at the University of Berlin in 1933, the year that Hitler came to power, and was executed in 1945, the year that Germany was defeated and Hitler committed suicide. To abstract Bonhoeffer's "ideas" from that context is to risk gross misunderstanding. Third, he was one of those people who said what he did and did what he said, so that his life is a commentary on his writings, and his writings on his life. Fourth, the question of sharp changes (turns, shifts) or continual development (growth, maturation) arises as soon as one begins to read him. It is one of the major points of controversy among Bonhoeffer interpreters, and it is only by working through the connections between biography and theology that some independent (even if tentative) judgment on this important matter can be made.

It has already been stated that the short illustrated introduction by Eberhard Bethge is the first book that a newcomer to Bonhoeffer should read. It can be added that the large biography by Bethge, *Dietrich Bonhoeffer: Man of Vision, Man of Courage*, is essential for serious Bonhoeffer study. It can be skimmed, read in sections according to one's interests and needs, or enjoyed as a single extended delight. It is, one does not hesitate saying, a masterpiece. The 867 pages are carefully designed, well organized, and clearly written to lead the reader through the intricacies not only of Bonhoeffer's life and work, but also of the times in which he struggled. It is available in paperback. It should be purchased and used as a basic reference point, a place to which to return whenever the way gets a bit confusing.

There are, of course, other places to go, and time and interest will determine the frequency and extent of such explorations. Two biographies that served to introduce the Bonhoeffer story prior to the translation of the

Bethge volume into English are *In Pursuit of Dietrich Bonhoeffer* by William Kuhns (Dayton: Pflaum, 1967) and *The Life and Death of Dietrich Bonhoeffer* by Mary Bosanquet (New York: Harper & Row, 1969). Since there is no possibility of reporting without interpreting, each of these authors (as well as all others mentioned here, including Eberhard Bethge) has a point of view which shows up in the handling of the data. The point of reading these two now might only be that independent critical judgment on the part of the reader develops as different points of view are carefully examined.

Not to be missed is *I Knew Dietrich Bonhoeffer: Reminiscences by His Friends*, edited by Wolf-Dieter Zimmermann and Ronald Gregor Smith (New York: Harper & Row, 1966). The book contains thirty-nine slice-of-life sketches in six chronological sections. Also of interest is a volume by one of Bonhoeffer's sisters, Sabine Liebholz-Bonhoeffer, *The Bonhoeffers: A Portrait of a Family* (New York: St. Martin's Press, 1971). Friendship and family are major themes in Bonhoeffer's writings. These two volumes help those themes come alive.

The life is so powerful as story that it should be no surprise that creative artists have been attracted to it. The first of this genre was Elizabeth Berryhill's *The Cup of Trembling: A Play in Two Acts* (New York: Seabury Press, 1958). A study guide to the play, by Donald Stauffer, is available from the same publisher. Another play entitled *Coming of Age* by Wilfrid Harrison (Trotten, England: Fernhurst, 1973) has been produced in England for a decade. A third play, *Testament—The Life and Death of Dietrich Bonhoeffer*, by Steve Pederson of Northwestern College in Orange City, Iowa, was produced for the first time in April 1985. All three pieces are suitable for chancel dramas and can be performed with a minimum of stage properties. Trinity Films of Minneapolis has been engaged for several years in a major "Bonhoeffer Project" which will finally include a documentary film suitable for TV or classroom use, a stage play, and a major feature-length film. The documentary film, *Dietrich Bonhoeffer: Memories and Perspectives* had its premiere in May 1982. Readers should be on the lookout for the appearance of a novel currently being written by Mary Glasner after several years of research.

Two fictional treatments for skimming only are *Memo for a Movie: A Short Life of Dietrich Bonhoeffer* by Theodore A. Gill (New York: Macmillan Co., 1971) and *The Last Days of Dietrich Bonhoeffer* by Donald Goddard (New York: Harper & Row, 1976).

A relatively new experiment in theology that seems to be growing into a movement attempts to be historically accurate and hermeneutically clear about the interpenetration of biography and theology. Various phrases ("psychohistory," "theology as biography," "theology as autobiography," "faith development theory") are used to signal this approach, which has roots in Erik Erikson and others who have stressed the factor of development in psychoanalytic theory. Bonhoeffer is an obvious candidate for such treatment and important questions about continuity and change in his life are now being sorted out through these new grids. Three examples of this approach are "Dietrich Bonhoeffer: Religionless Christianity — Maturity, Transcendence, and Freedom" by Roger A. Johnson, in *Critical Issues in Modern Religion* edited by Roger A. Johnson (Englewood Cliffs, N.J.: Prentice-Hall, 1973); "Dietrich Bonhoeffer: Witness in an Ambiguous World" by Robin Lovin and Jonathan P. Gosser, in *Trajectories in Faith* by James W. Fowler, Robin W. Lovin et al. (Nashville: Abingdon Press, 1980); and "Bonhoeffer in the Context of Erikson's Luther Study" by Clifford Green, in *Psychohistory and Religion: The Case of 'Young Man Luther,'* edited by Roger A. Johnson (Philadelphia: Fortress Press, 1977). Every interpreter must somehow face the issue of the relationship of biography and theology. The very great dangers of universalizing a particular theory of psychosocial development and then pressing the data into the categories of that theory, however, should be kept in mind as one reads the results of this kind of research.

Primary Literature

Readers should be aware that various editions and translations of Bonhoeffer's writings do differ from one another in significant and sometimes aggravating ways. There is a complicated story behind the publishing of almost every document. Some sensitivity to those stories can be developed by careful attention to prefaces and forewords, particularly those by Eberhard Bethge. Further insights into publishing and translating difficulties can be gained from Bethge's article, "The Editing and Publishing of the Bonhoeffer Papers," *The Andover Newton Bulletin* 52 (December 1959): 1-24; from John Godsey's "Reading Bonhoeffer in English Translation: Some Difficulties," *USQR* 23 (1967): 79-90, reprinted in *Bonhoeffer in a World Come of Age*, edited by Peter Vorkink II (Philadelphia: Fortress Press, 1968); and from John Deschner's "Bonhoeffer Studies in English," *Perkins School of Theology Journal* 22 (Spring 1969): 60-68. Corrections and improvements have been in general cumulative, so that as a rule later editions are to be preferred to earlier ones.

Bonhoeffer's first two books, *The Communion of Saints* and *Act and Being* were university dissertations. These most academic of his writings detail philosophical and theological (as well as sociological and psychological!) foundations for his later reflections.

Christ the Center is a reconstruction from student notes of Bonhoeffer's 1933 university lectures on Christology. Since Jesus Christ is indeed at the center of Bonhoeffer's life and work (so much so that some accuse him of "Christomonism"), the importance of these lectures cannot be overemphasized. Earlier and later writings come into sharper focus as one pursues his argument that the real christological questions are who and where, rather than how.

Bonhoeffer was a systematic theologian who knew very well, as did Barth (and Luther and Calvin), that if theology is going to be *Christian* theology, it must be done in constant conversation with biblical texts. When one examines the entire corpus of Bonhoeffer's writings, the amount of straightforward biblical exposition is astonishing. Even the number of books devoted to specific biblical texts may be surprising. *Creation and Fall*, based on his 1933 university lectures, and *Temptation*, a series of Bible studies given to Finkenwalde alumni in June 1938, are now published in a single paperback. The first is an exposition of Genesis 1–3, the second a comparison of the biblical stories of the temptation of Adam and the temptation of Christ. Both presuppose careful exegetical work (and there is evidence that it was in fact done), but the result of that work comes to the reader in theological, sometimes homiletical, lyrical, even rhapsodic, form. Another treatment of Old Testament texts is *Psalms: The Prayerbook of the Bible* in which it is argued that Christians can pray the Psalms because Jesus prayed them. It is said, in fact, that the Psalms are a way in which Jesus *teaches* his disciples, and us, to pray. The christological exposition of Old Testament texts may seem a bit heavy-handed until one becomes aware of what some "German Christians" were doing to separate the New Testament from what some of them referred to as "the Old Testament with its Jewish money morality, livestock handlers, and pimps." Even Bonhoeffer's neighbor and family friend Adolf von Harnack regarded the twentieth-century retention of the Old Testament as Christian Scripture as highly questionable. The best treatment of Bonhoeffer's interpretation of the Old Testament is *The Old Testament as the Book of Christ: An Appraisal of Bonhoeffer's Interpretation* by Martin Kuske (Philadelphia: Westminster Press, 1976).

The two most widely read and best known books by Bonhoeffer, *The Cost of Discipleship* and *Life Together*, come from the period of his work with the Confessing Church seminary at Finkenwalde. He was convinced that the Sermon on the Mount should be a regular part of the theological curriculum, and the first volume is a result of his work on this text with his students. He was also convinced that theological education should foster Christian community, and the second book is a result of his efforts toward that end. Later he wrote about the "dangers" of the first book, but indicated he would still "stand by" it (letter of 21 July 1944). Readers of the second book should bear in mind that in his foreword (unfortunately omitted from the English edition) Bonhoeffer says that the study "should not be considered as more than just one contribution" to the question. Both books are widely and effectively used for group study in congregations.

The two books of the "last period" of his life are books only because Eberhard Bethge brought the materials together and published them. *Ethics* was originally published in Germany in 1949 and *Letters and Papers from Prison* in 1951 (hereafter *LPP*). The *Ethics* is a compilation of four attempts by Bonhoeffer to begin to draft such a book. *LPP* is exactly what that title describes. One need only read the essay entitled "What Is Meant by 'Telling the Truth'?" in the *Ethics*, or to read the letter of 30 April 1944 in the *LPP*, to realize that there are some very unusual things going on here. When one keeps in mind that the radicality of Bonhoeffer's reflection arises directly from the radical claim that God and world come together in Jesus Christ, it all takes on greater clarity and greater significance.

Three volumes of additional Bonhoeffer materials have been edited by Edwin H. Robertson under the titles *No Rusty Swords, The Way to Freedom,* and *True Patriotism.* These materials have been selected from the six-volume *Gesammelte Schriften* edited by Eberhard Bethge (hereafter *GS*). In addition to many translation and editing flaws, a major problem with the Robertson volumes is that it is virtually impossible to locate documents in them. A lecture or letter from the *GS* referred to in the biography, for instance, may or may not be translated and included in one of the Robertson volumes, but there is no proper index enabling one to locate it quickly or even to determine whether it is there at all. Fortunately, there is a "Correlation Table" constructed by Clifford Green and included in the *USQR* bibliography which does solve the problem. Only a few of the sermons (located primarily in *GS* IV and V) are now translated. His homiletics lectures from Finkenwalde, however, are included in *Bonhoeffer: Worldly Preaching* by Clyde E. Fant (New York: Thomas Nelson, 1975). They can be read with profit even apart from any specific interest in Bonhoeffer.

A new translation of prison attempts (1943) to draft a play and a novel has been published under the title *Fiction from Prison.* Bonhoeffer had no interest in excessive introspection and deplored the public exhibition of personal feelings. Through this device, however, without violating the sense for "distance" that was so much a part of his aristocratic reserve, Bonhoeffer allows the reader some intimate insights. The decoding of the frequently autobiographical references in these sketches is facilitated by the introductions by Renate and Eberhard Bethge and by Clifford Green, along with the commentary by Ruth Zerner.

Other primary materials in English are scattered about here and there. "Thy Kingdom Come: The Prayer of the Church for God's Kingdom on Earth" is included in *Preface to Bonhoeffer* by John D. Godsey (Philadelphia: Fortress Press, 1965). In 1967 Maria von Wedemeyer-Weller, Bonhoeffer's fiancée, published a few excerpts from his letters to her in an article "The Other Letters from Prison" which appeared first in *USQR* 23 (1967): 23–29. The article is now included in the enlarged (fourth) edition of *LPP*. The excerpts serve to underline Bonhoeffer's massive affirmation of the earth and of physical life in the context of confidence about the future. The actual letters to Maria are not available at the present time.

Secondary Literature

The best short statement on the entire complex unity of the Bonhoeffer legacy is still Eberhard Bethge's 1961 Alden-Tuthill Lectures delivered at Chicago Theological Seminary, entitled "The Challenge of Dietrich Bonhoeffer's Life and Theology," and published in *World Come of Age*, edited by Ronald Gregor Smith (Philadelphia: Fortress Press, 1967). That volume also contains articles on Bonhoeffer by Karl Barth, Rudolf Bultmann, Regin Prenter, and others. A second very useful short statement is *The Promise of Bonhoeffer* by Benjamin A. Reist (Philadelphia: J. B. Lippincott, 1969). Either one of these is an excellent place to begin exploring secondary literature. After that, where does one go?

There are about a dozen one-author, single-volume major treatments in English of Bonhoeffer's theology. At or near the top of everyone's list is *The Theology of Dietrich Bonhoeffer* (Philadelphia: Fortress Press, 1985), H. Martin Rumscheidt's translation of *Die Theologie Dietrich Bonhoeffers* by Ernst Feil (Munich: Chr. Kaiser, 1971). It is an extremely careful and thorough presentation of the unity of Bonhoeffer's theology seen as an interplay of hermeneutics and Christology and understanding of the world. Feil will be the most recent volume in English. The earliest was John Godsey's *The Theology of Dietrich Bonhoeffer* (Philadelphia: Westminster Press, 1960). In *Christ for Us in the Theology of Dietrich Bonhoeffer* (New York: Harper & Row, 1967) John Phillips attempts to show that Christology is the key to both unity and development in Bonhoeffer, a "secular Christ" receiving more attention than an "ecclesiastical Christ" as Bonhoeffer moves toward the "Christology of the prison letters." André Dumas, in *Dietrich Bonhoeffer: Theologian of Reality* (New York: Macmillan Co., 1971), emphasizes the unity and continuity of Bonhoeffer's life and work around the theme of reality. It is a solid statement that reads very smoothly. The theme of James Woelfel's interpretation is clear in his title *Bonhoeffer's Theology, Classical and Revolutionary* (Nashville: Abingdon Press, 1970). One of its continuing values is a series of sketches of relationships between Bonhoeffer and others, for example, Nietzsche, Kierkegaard, Barth, and Bultmann. One of the most careful statements, surely the best available on the "early" Bonhoeffer, is Clifford Green's *Bonhoeffer: The Sociality of Christ and Humanity* (Missoula, Mont., Scholars Press, 1972). Two more volumes emphasizing the "reality" theme appeared in 1972, *Dietrich Bonhoeffer: Reality and Resistance* by Larry L. Rasmussen (Nashville: Abingdon Press, 1972), and *Reality and Faith: The Theological Legacy of Dietrich Bonhoeffer* by Heinrich Ott (Philadelphia: Fortress Press, 1972). Rasmussen's is a treatment of Bonhoeffer's ethics; Ott's is a "dialogue" rather than a comprehensive interpretation. He says that the book is not primarily "about" Bonhoeffer, but "*with* him about his *subject*." David H. Hopper, in *A Dissent on Bonhoeffer* (Philadelphia: Westminster Press, 1975), argues that personal and existential concerns probably outweigh those that are primarily systematic in Bonhoeffer's writings, but that it may be his final statement of rather traditional Christian faith that is the most significant and most lasting. In *Liberating Faith: Bonhoeffer's Message for Today* (Minneapolis: Augsburg Pub. House, 1984), Geffrey B. Kelly presents the life and writings of Bonhoeffer as significant both for the development of a christocentric spirituality and for the liberation of peoples.

Some of the valuable material on Bonhoeffer is located in journal articles and in shorter pieces in book-length collections. One such collection is *A Bonhoeffer Legacy: Essays in Understanding*, edited by A. J. Klassen (Grand Rapids: Wm. B. Eerdmans, 1981). Following the introduction by Eberhard Bethge there are nineteen essays, all by people who have done doctoral dissertations on Bonhoeffer. Papers are read and discussed at annual meetings of the English Language Section of the International Bonhoeffer Society, as they are at occasional international gatherings of the society, and many of these find their way into book-length collections. A recent agreement between the society and the Edwin Mellen Press of Lewiston, New York, will facilitate publication of such research. Several volumes are already projected. The first in the series has been released under the title *Ethical Responsibility*. Those interested in archival materials will find them in the Bonhoeffer Archives at Union Theological Seminary, New York, and in West Germany.

Any selection of tertiary literature would include items dealing with the Church Struggle under Hitler, with the Holocaust, with the liberation of oppressed peoples. A starting point in each case could be *The Nazi Persecution of the Churches* 1935–45 by J. S. Conway (New York: Basic Books, 1968); *The German Church Struggle and the Holocaust*, edited by Franklin H. Littell and Hubert G. Locke (Detroit: Wayne State Univ. Press, 1974); and Eberhard Bethge, *Bonhoeffer: Exile and Martyr* (New York: Seabury Press, 1975). The last volume is a series of lectures delivered by Bethge in South Africa at the invitation of the South African Council of Churches. It also contains a piece entitled "Bonhoeffer in South Africa: An Exploratory Essay" by John de Gruchy of the University of Capetown.

The journey continues. It is clear that the importance of Bonhoeffer for the faith and life of the church cannot be reduced to the hagiography of martyrdom or to the novelty of clever phrases. There are many who think that the exploration of Bonhoeffer's contribution has just begun. When one looks at the many routes by which one can travel with him, one is inclined to agree.

Index

Important names and subjects which occur in the table of contents or with great frequency throughout the book are not included in the index.